TRACING THE thread

**A 52-WEEK JOURNEY THROUGH
THE STORY OF THE BIBLE**

Tracing The Thread: A 52-Week Journey Through The Story of The Bible

ISBN 13: 9781935832461
ISBN 10: 1935832468

Lot: [AUG19]

TRACING

THE

thread

A 52-WEEK JOURNEY THROUGH
THE STORY OF THE BIBLE

Published by: YM360

TABLE OF CONTENTS

WHAT IS
THIS BOOK
ALL ABOUT?

Put simply, this book is a story. Or better yet, it's a guide to the story.

Do you know the story of the Bible? Maybe the better question is whether or not you even realized the Bible *was* a story. The Bible is the story of God's mission to rescue us, His children, from the separation and death caused by our sin. It's a powerful story that covers thousands of years and thousands of characters. Maybe you knew that already.

BUT MAYBE YOU DIDN'T.

The truth is that many teenagers think the Bible is a collection of verses and lists, mixed in with a bunch of rules and stories. Most of these stories are awesome. Some seem kind of weird. Most people are familiar with the psalms and the few books about Jesus. And they may know that Paul wrote a bunch of letters. Oh, and there's Genesis and Revelation. But other than that, they don't grasp the connective threads that hold the story together.

Does this describe your understanding of the Bible?

If it does, it's OK. You're not alone. A lot of teenagers (and adults) don't get the big-picture story of the Bible. And maybe it's because you've never been told any differently. Maybe you don't understand the story because it's never been shown to you. Well, don't worry. Because that's what this book is all about.

The book you hold in your hands will guide you through the story of the Bible. Not only that, it will help you pull out some very valuable truths from the stories you'll be reading. You'll be reading the big-picture story of the Bible and applying it to your life. In the process, you'll learn more about God and about yourself. You and your world will be changed as a result.

The Bible's story is amazing. It's God's story, recorded so that we would know God and His ways. Get ready for an awesome journey.

HOW DOES THIS BOOK WORK?  FOR TEENAGERS

5 DAYS A WEEK, 52 WEEKS
The goal of this journal is to teach you the story of the Bible and how it relates to your life. It accomplishes this by providing five devotions for each week of the year. That gives you a couple days a week to catch up, if need be.

GO AT YOUR OWN SPEED
You may be reading this as part of a group with other teenagers in your church, and an adult leader. If so, you'll want to stay on track as best as possible. But if you're doing it on your own, feel free to go at your own speed. It may take more than a year to get through the book. There's nothing wrong with that.

HAVE A BIBLE AND A PEN HANDY
Borrow a real Bible, use one Online, or download a Bible app on your phone or tablet . . . whatever you do, it's important that you have one for this journey you're on. This book uses the English Standard Version (ESV) of the Bible. You can use the ESV, or another translation if you want. And make sure you have a pen or pencil. You'll need it!

HOW DOES THIS BOOK WORK?  FOR ADULTS

The teenagers who will be working through this book are taking on a big task, one that many adults have never even attempted. They will be more successful at sticking with this journal if you are there to offer encouragement and support. Don't be afraid to take this journey with the teenagers in your life, whether you're a youth worker or a parent. You'll both benefit greatly from it.

This book was produced in conjunction with the one-year Bible study curriculum, *The Thread*. This book is meant to provide a parallel, more in-depth journey through the big-picture story of the Bible. If you're a youth worker teaching a youth group *The Thread* curriculum, in every lesson you'll notice reminders at the end to tell students which weeks to read. However, this book was also designed as a stand-alone piece, completely independent of *The Thread* Bible study curriculum. It's a great resource whether you're using the curriculum or not.

DISCOVERING GOD
AS YOU GO

The cool thing about God is that He makes Himself known to us through the Bible. In the Bible, we see that God has various characteristics. Just like you have different characteristics that make you who you are, so does God. The difference? God is perfect in all His ways. He is perfectly loving, perfectly just, and so on.

We want you to know more about God and His character. As you read this journal, these icons will let you know that the story you're reading is a great example of one of God's characteristics. (This isn't a complete list of God's characteristics, but it's a good start.) When you see an icon in one of your devotions, flip back over to this page and read the paragraph that corresponds with the icon.

GOD IS LOVING
God's love is awesome. The Bible says that God very literally IS love (1 John 4:8)! God sent His Son to save us from our sins all because He loves us (John 3:16). God's love is unconditional and unfailing. His love is the foundation of our relationship with Him.

GOD IS HOLY
There is no one like God. He is holy. To be holy is to be perfect. It is to be set apart as different from everything else. God and His ways are far beyond anything we can imagine (Is. 55:9). And yet, He still loves us and wants a relationship.

GOD IS ALL-POWERFUL
There is nothing God can't do. He created all things out of nothing simply by speaking (Gen. 1), and the world around you is evidence of His awesome power (Ps. 19:1). No one is His equal (Jer. 10:6).

GOD IS SOVEREIGN
This means God is King. He rules over all people everywhere (Ps. 22:28). Nothing can keep His desires from being accomplished (Ps. 115:3). His rule also covers events and circumstances. In other words, nothing happens without God's will allowing it (Pr. 16:33).

GOD IS FAITHFUL
God never gives up on us. He is always true to His promises (Ps. 33:4). He will never leave us alone (Ps. 9:10). His faithfulness doesn't depend on our actions.

GOD IS ALL-KNOWING
There is nothing that's beyond God's knowledge. God knows everything that's being done, and everything that has been done, by all people, everywhere, throughout all time (Prov. 15:3). But God knows us as individuals, too. God knows all His children (1 Cor. 8:3) and cares about the details of our lives (Matt. 6:32).

GOD IS RIGHTEOUS
To be righteous is to be good. Perfectly good (Ps. 25:8). And God is righteous! All His actions are born out of His goodness (Jer. 9:24). There is no wrongdoing in Him. And God is incapable of leading us to wrongdoing, as well (James 1:13).

GOD IS JUST
God is a god of justice (Ps. 33:5). All sin is rebellion against God, and His punishment is perfect (Ps. 51:1-4). God's holiness means that He must punish our sin with death. Thankfully, in His grace, God allowed Jesus to pay the penalty our sin earned for us.

GOD IS FORGIVING
God doesn't have to forgive our sins. He would be within His rights to punish us any way He saw fit. But in His great love, God chose to provide a way to satisfy His judgment while providing life for us (Eph. 2:1-10). Through faith in Christ, God offers forgiveness from sin.

GOD IS COMPASSIONATE
Scripture is clear: God is compassionate (Ps. 103:8-14). He hears the cries of the sad, the poor, and the needy. His heart breaks for the lost (Mt. 9:36). And He loves to see us, His children, show compassion to others (Mt. 25:31-46).

LEARNING
THE GOSPEL
AS YOU GO

In this journal, you'll be learning the big-picture story of the Bible. But you also have the chance to learn the Gospel as you go. Do you know what the Gospel is? Could you define it?

The term gospel comes from the Greek phrase that means "good news." So, the Gospel is essentially the good news of Jesus' sacrificial death on the cross for the payment of our sins. That is, after all, really good news. But what does it have to do with the big-picture story of the Bible? Great question . . .

The Gospel is the fullest expression of God's grace, mercy, love, and forgiveness. And if you begin to look for it, you see signs of the heart behind the Gospel all throughout the Bible. See, the Bible really is the story of God's desire to rescue us from the penalty of our sins, and to restore us to a perfect relationship with Him. As we read the Bible, we can see the thread of the Gospel weaving itself through the entire story of Scripture. It's pretty cool, actually.

One of the goals of this journal is to highlight where we see evidence of the Gospel as you read the Bible's story. You'll do this in the form of weekly memory verses.

On the first day of each week, you'll be challenged to memorize a verse or two of Scripture. Take this chance seriously. Being able to meditate on God's Word as you go through your day is a vital aspect of growing in your faith. And the best way to think about the Bible is to "hide it in your heart," as the psalmist says.

So, embrace the idea of learning the Bible more. You're about to get your first chance to do so.

WEEK 1

WEEK 1, DAY 1

**"IN THE BEGINNING WAS THE WORD,
AND THE WORD WAS WITH GOD, AND
THE WORD WAS GOD." – JOHN 1:1**

So, this is your first chance in this book to memorize a verse of Scripture. If you read page 5, this is not a surprise. (If you didn't read page 5, go read it now. It will make more sense if you do.) This is your first chance to trace the Gospel thread through a specific part of Scripture.

This week you'll be looking at parts of the creation account. The cool thing about John 1:1 is that it puts Jesus present when God spoke the world into being. Our understanding of the trinity teaches us that Jesus is literally God. Jesus was with God the Father and the Holy Spirit at creation (more on the Holy Spirit on Day 3). Jesus loved you enough to create you, and then later, loved you enough to die for you. That's a lot of love!

So, let's memorize John 1:1. You can do this! One of the best ways to memorize a verse is the 5-5-5 method. Read the verse five times slowly and, if you can, out loud. Listen to yourself read it. Now, write the verse five times. See if you can do parts of it from memory. Then, finally, see if you can say it five times out loud without looking. You'll be surprised how easy it is to learn a verse this way.

Hiding God's Word in your heart is an awesome way to draw closer to God. Give it your best effort today. You won't be sorry!

WEEK 1, DAY 2

**"IN THE BEGINNING, GOD CREATED
THE HEAVENS AND THE EARTH."
- GENESIS 1:1**

Is it possible to pack more wonder into fewer words?

Read Genesis 1:1 again. With these verses, the Bible comes to life, starting its long, winding journey from Genesis to Revelation. However, these words also speak to another beginning. These words speak to the beginning of all things. And look who we see in the middle of the action . . .

God.

Look at the first four words of the Bible. "In the beginning God . . ." In the beginning, God. In the beginning, God was. And there was only God. Before anything else existed, God did. Nothing created Him. He wasn't born. He just was. And He just is.

The same God that pre-existed time and creation exists today. But He doesn't merely exist. He is active. He is active in world affairs, in natural events, and in all circumstances. Most importantly for you, He is active in your life. The God who spoke everything into being knows you and loves you. He wants you to know and love Him more, too.

So, today, just sit back and reflect on the awesomeness of God. Look around you. Those trees? That sunset? Your life? His handiwork. Today, think about what it means that God created all things and that He chose to include you in His creation.

 **THIS DEVOTION SPEAKS TO GOD'S POWER. GO TO
PAGE 4 FOR A DESCRIPTION OF THIS ATTRIBUTE.**

WEEK 1, DAY 3

"THE EARTH WAS WITHOUT FORM AND VOID, AND DARKNESS WAS OVER THE FACE OF THE DEEP. AND THE SPIRIT OF GOD WAS HOVERING OVER THE FACE OF THE WATERS. AND GOD SAID, 'LET THERE BE LIGHT,' AND THERE WAS LIGHT. " - GENESIS 1:2-3

There are times that we read the Bible and we struggle to wrap our brains around what we've read. Sometimes this is due to the fact that the Bible was written thousands of years ago in a cultural context different from ours. We have to work to find the central truth of what we're reading and apply it to our lives. But sometimes, we can be blown away by what we read simply because God is overwhelmingly awesome to our human brains. Genesis 1:2-3 is one of those times.

Read Genesis 1:2-3. Can you imagine what this is describing? A time before light? What do you think the "surface of the deep" means? Sounds a little scary. The Bible describes the Holy Spirit as alive and active, in motion, hovering, existing, being . . . Hovering over the waters? What waters? And then BOOM! God says, "let there be light," and there was light. Amazing.

It's human nature to want to understand things. We aren't comfortable with the unknown. We also like to be in charge. But God doesn't work that way. While we can know a ton about God, we'll never understand all of Him. He's too awesome for that. And we'll never be in charge of Him. He'll always be above us. And that's OK.

When we read verses like these, it's perfectly OK to be blown away by them. We don't have to have all the answers. It's part of what makes God majestic and wonderful. In these moments, it's OK to sit back and just marvel at who God is and how amazing His ways are. It's actually a healthy part of knowing and loving God. So today, do that. Just be amazed by God. Go to Him in prayer and tell Him how awesome He is.

WEEK 1, DAY 4

"GOD CALLED THE DRY LAND EARTH, AND THE WATERS THAT WERE GATHERED TOGETHER HE CALLED SEAS. AND GOD SAW THAT IT WAS GOOD." - GENESIS 1:10

If someone lets you borrow or use something they value, what is your attitude toward it? You're pretty careful with it, right? For instance, if your friend lets you see her new phone, you're not likely to toss it back to her in the air, are you? No. Because she values it, you value it. You respect the fact that this is a new, good thing.

Read Genesis 1:6, 9-10. This is a bit of a combination of what God did on days two and three of creation. The creation account pictures God crafting and shaping the universe. The cool thing about the account is how often God steps back at the end of a day's work and summarizes the work He just did.

Throughout the creation account, God looks at His handiwork and proclaims it "good." God was pleased with the work He did. God looked at the order of things created and said, "Nice work." Here's a random question you might not have ever considered: how do you view God's handiwork? What is your attitude toward the world God has made? Interesting question, isn't it?

God values His creation. That includes the earth, the animals, and other people. As we said at the beginning of this devotion, you most likely try to value the things that people you care about value. The way you treat God's creation says a lot about how you feel about Him.

SOMETHING TO THINK ABOUT . . .

· Do you see yourself as someone who tries to take care of the environment? If it's God's creation, shouldn't this be something you are intentional about?
· Do you look at other people and see the goodness that God sees in them? If not, what keeps you from doing so?

WEEK 1, DAY 5

**"SO GOD CREATED MAN IN HIS OWN IMAGE, IN THE IMAGE OF
GOD HE CREATED HIM; MALE AND FEMALE HE CREATED THEM."
- GENESIS 1:27**

What's your most valuable possession? Is it a piece of technology, such as a phone or a gaming system? Is it your car? Or is it something more sentimental? Maybe it's a gift given to you by someone you love. Whatever it is, visualize it. Think about it. What feelings does it evoke in you? Why is it so valued? What would you feel like if you were suddenly without it?

Now read Genesis 1:26-27. We're nearing the end of the creation account in Genesis 1. And before He was finished, God made Adam and Eve. There are a couple of things to note here. First, as verse 27 states, we were made in God's image. No other part of God's creation was described this way. We are unique in this aspect. And it hints at our extreme value to God. While all of God's creation is beautiful, humans are the crowning achievement of God's creative work. Also, if you were to look down a little further in the passage, you'd see that when God looked back over all creation, with humans in the mix, He pronounced it very good. God was pleased.

We can be guilty of having a low opinion of ourselves. When we make mistakes, do dumb things, blow opportunities, or just act like dorks, we can be our own worst critics. We don't like the way we look, or feel, and we get down on ourselves. The fact of the matter is this: God loves you immensely. You were made in His image. He created you with Himself in mind. That should make you smile.

SOMETHING TO THINK ABOUT . . .
· What causes you to feel down, or to have a low opinion of yourself?
· What does it do to your self-worth knowing that God created you and loves you with an unending love?

WEEK 2

WEEK 2, DAY 1

**"IN THE BEGINNING WAS THE WORD, AND
THE WORD WAS WITH GOD, AND THE WORD
WAS GOD. HE WAS IN THE BEGINNING WITH
GOD. ALL THINGS WERE MADE THROUGH HIM,
AND WITHOUT HIM WAS NOT ANY THING MADE
THAT WAS MADE." - JOHN 1:1-3**

This week is your second chance at learning a memory verse on the first day of your week of devotions. The cool thing is that this week's verse builds off last week's verse.

Last week you learned John 1:1. This week you'll have the chance to add John 1:2-3 to it. These three verses form a powerful reminder of Jesus as both the messenger of God's love, and the embodiment of the message itself.

If you've never attempted to memorize a verse, there are a lot of ways to do it. One of the most effective is the 5 – 5 – 5 method. Try it and see if it works for you.

FIRST, read the verses five times. On the last couple of times, read it slowly and out loud, if possible. Focus on the words.

NEXT, write the verses five times. Some people find it helpful to say the words out loud as you write them. On the last few times, see if you can write the verses without looking at them.

FINALLY, see if you can say the verses out loud five times without looking at your Bible or the page you've written the verses on. (Even if it takes more than five times, stick with it until you can.)

Knowing God's Word is a powerful tool in your relationship with Him. Give this a try today.

WEEK 2, DAY 2

"SO GOD BLESSED THE SEVENTH DAY AND MADE IT HOLY, BECAUSE ON IT GOD RESTED FROM ALL HIS WORK THAT HE HAD DONE IN CREATION." - GENESIS 2:3

Would you say that your life is characterized by a lot of down-time? Do you often find yourself with nothing to do? Do you constantly wonder what to do with all the free time you have? If you're like most teenagers, this does not describe you. Most teenagers are over-committed, stressed out, and worn out. School, sports, family, friends, church, maybe even a job . . . All that you are committed to takes a big toll on your life.

Take a moment and read Genesis 2:3. It's a short verse. Simple, actually. But it communicates so much. First, it signifies that God was done with creating the world. He had acted powerfully to craft all things as He saw fit. He was done. Second, out of reverence for the work He had done, God made the day holy. That means it was special. Different. Set apart. What made it different? That's the third point. It was different because it was a day of rest. God didn't make anything. He stopped creating. A day where no work was done honored the previous days of vigorous work.

By making the seventh day different, God honored the idea of rest. He made rest something to be valued. Do you need rest in your life? Do you ever make time to just stop? God made you in His image, remember? That means you need rest, too. What can you do this week to carve out moments of peace? How can you use those moments to reflect on God and on the many blessings He's given you? Don't overlook it. It's important. What will you do to make this change?

THIS DEVOTION SPEAKS TO GOD'S HOLINESS. GO TO PAGE 4 FOR A DESCRIPTION OF THIS ATTRIBUTE.

"NOW THE SERPENT WAS MORE CRAFTY THAN
ANY OTHER BEAST OF THE FIELD THAT THE
LORD GOD HAD MADE. HE SAID TO THE WOM-
AN, 'DID GOD ACTUALLY SAY, 'YOU SHALL NOT
EAT OF ANY TREE IN THE GARDEN'?"
- GENESIS 3:1

Is there anything worse than being lied to? Few things hurt as badly as finding out someone has twisted the truth. Especially if it's someone you know. When you find out, you go through a range of emotions. You feel angry. You feel embarrassed. You feel sad. You feel dumb. And maybe you feel angry all over again. Lies can destroy relationships, sometimes permanently.

READ GENESIS 3:1-5. This passage represents the beginning of the end of the perfect harmony that existed in the Garden of Eden. God had made Adam and Eve, and gave them every-thing they needed to live a perfect, happy life. The only thing they were not allowed to do was eat from this one specific tree, the tree of the "knowledge of good and evil" (Gen. 2:17). That's it. And yet, what we see here is the serpent, who rep-resents Satan, twisting God's words. He is planting the seed of doubt in Eve's mind. And he's doing so by lying. He knew what God had actually said. He was laying a trap to try and get Eve to go against God. And it ultimately worked.

In John 8:44, Satan is called the father of lies. He still lies to us today. That voice that tells you you're not good enough? It's a lie. That voice that says you're not pretty enough? Lie. That no one cares about you? Lie. That you're all alone? Lie. That you have to give in in order to fit in? Lie. The world is full of lies. And they all stand to come in between God and you. Never forget how much God loves you, how badly He wants to know you, and that you're a vital part of His plan to bring peace to the world. Pray to God today and ask Him to remind you how much He cares for you. And stop listening to the lies.

WEEK 2, DAY 4

"SO WHEN THE WOMAN SAW THAT THE TREE WAS GOOD FOR FOOD, AND THAT IT WAS A DELIGHT TO THE EYES, AND THAT THE TREE WAS TO BE DESIRED TO MAKE ONE WISE, SHE TOOK OF ITS FRUIT AND ATE, AND SHE ALSO GAVE SOME TO HER HUSBAND WHO WAS WITH HER, AND HE ATE." - GENESIS 3:6

READ GENESIS 3:6-7.

You've got to think that if they could have taken it back, they would have. If they could have seen what their sin would cause, they wouldn't have bitten the fruit. Think about it: that one sin gave birth to death, and war, and disease, and poverty, and so on . . . All because Adam and Eve couldn't follow one little rule. If they knew what we know, no way they would have eaten the fruit.

Here's the truth: even if Adam and Eve didn't eat that particular fruit at that particular moment, chances are they would have sinned some other way. Why? Because Adam and Eve were human beings, just like us. And Adam and Eve had free will to make decisions for themselves. You have to think that if Adam and Eve were capable of sin that one time, they would have eventually sinned some other way. There's no way around it.

We have the same sin nature as Adam and Eve. Our hearts are bent toward sin. No matter how good we are at our best, there is darkness in our hearts. That's why it's so amazingly amazing that God loves us as He does. He loves us so much He made a way to bridge the separation sin causes between Him and His children. He sent His perfect, holy Son, Jesus, to die as a sacrifice for our sins. If we believe in Him, His sacrifice is counted for us. From that moment on, God sees us as forgiven and sinless.

Adam and Eve planted the seeds of sin in all people's hearts. But Jesus provides us a way to be free from the penalty of sin.

SOMETHING TO THINK ABOUT . . .

· How aware are you of your sin? Do you feel convicted when you have sinned against God? Or has it just become a part of your life?
· When was the last time you confessed your sins to God and thanked Him for His forgiveness? It wouldn't be a bad idea to stop and do that now.

> **"AND THEY HEARD THE SOUND OF THE LORD GOD WALKING IN THE GARDEN IN THE COOL OF THE DAY, AND THE MAN AND HIS WIFE HID THEMSELVES FROM THE PRESENCE OF THE LORD GOD AMONG THE TREES OF THE GARDEN." — GENESIS 3:8**

Here's a slightly uncomfortable question: How do you act when you've gotten caught doing something you know you shouldn't? You act guilty, right? You may get defensive, or embarrassed. But guilt is at the heart of your response. Guilt is a complex emotion. It's a feeling based on unmet expectations, isn't it? It comes from knowing you were supposed to do one thing (the right thing), but you instead did something else (the wrong thing).

Read Genesis 3:8-12. This is a heartbreaking development. Up to this point in the creation narrative, the environment in which God and Adam and Eve interacted had been so pure. Then sin entered the equation. Look at the results: Adam and Eve, the jewel of God's creation, were shamefully hiding from God, their creator! This is a vivid example of the barrier that sin created between God and people. When faced with a perfect God, Adam and Eve's sin sent them scurrying for a hiding place.

We know what shame and guilt feel like. We've all experienced it. The most beautiful thing about God's plan is that He sent Jesus to take away the shame and guilt of our sin once and for all. Jesus died on the cross to pay the penalty for our sin. When we are saved through faith, the guilt of our sin is wiped away. Because of Christ, and only because of Christ, we can relate to God without the separation sin causes. We don't ever have to hide.

SOMETHING TO THINK ABOUT . . .

· It's OK to feel guilty for letting God down. But that guilt should never be something that creates a wall between you and God. If you're having trouble accepting the forgiveness that God offers through Jesus, go to God in prayer. Ask Him to help you feel the freedom that comes with His grace and mercy.

WEEK 3

WEEK 3, DAY 1

"THEREFORE, AS ONE TRESPASS LED TO CONDEMNATION FOR ALL MEN, SO ONE ACT OF RIGHTEOUSNESS LEADS TO JUS-TIFICATION AND LIFE FOR ALL MEN."
- ROMANS 5:18

This week's memory verse is all about placing Jesus within the context of Adam and Eve's sin in the Garden. Paul puts it pretty straightforward, here. He said that through Adam, sin entered into all of our lives. It brought condemnation from God. But through Jesus' sacrificial death on the cross, all sin was wiped away. Furthermore, through faith in Christ, there is justification and forgiveness for all who come to Him in faith.

This is a powerful message! And a great verse to memorize.

This week, try using the same "5 – 5 – 5" method we used last week. We've pasted it below to remind you how it works.

FIRST, read the verses five times. On the last couple of times, read it slowly and out loud, if possible. Focus on the words.

NEXT, write the verses five times. Some people find it helpful to say the words out loud as you write them. On the last few times, see if you can write the verses without looking at them.

FINALLY, see if you can say the verses out loud five times without looking at your Bible or the page you've written the verses on. (Even if it takes more than five times, stick with it until you can.)

WEEK 3, DAY 2

"AND TO ADAM HE SAID, 'BECAUSE YOU HAVE LIS-
TENED TO THE VOICE OF YOUR WIFE AND HAVE EAT-
EN OF THE TREE OF WHICH I COMMANDED YOU, 'YOU
SHALL NOT EAT OF IT,' CURSED IS THE GROUND
BECAUSE OF YOU; IN PAIN YOU SHALL EAT OF IT ALL
THE DAYS OF YOUR LIFE; THORNS AND THISTLES IT
SHALL BRING FORTH FOR YOU; AND YOU SHALL EAT
THE PLANTS OF THE FIELD.'" - GENESIS 3:17-18

Consequences. They're interesting, if you think about them. Sometimes we love consequences. The consequence of eating well and
exercise is good health. The consequence of studying for a test is a
good grade (usually). The consequence of working up the courage
to ask your crush to the prom is an awesome night you'll never forget
(hopefully). But other times, consequences are something we wish
weren't in play. Like when we're going 12 miles over the speed limit
as we pass a police officer. Consequences can be good, or bad.

READ GENESIS 3:16-19. What you're reading is a list of the consequences for Adam and Eve's sin, pronounced by God Himself. Can
you imagine? Standing in front of God having Him say these things to
you? Knowing that the beautiful relationship God had set in motion
was altered because of what you did. It's not enough that God caught
Adam and Eve sinning. Their sin had consequences.

Our sin has consequences today, too. Sure, if you come to faith in
Christ and are saved from your sins, you are freed from the permanent guilt of your sin. You share in the eternal life that Jesus bought
for you on the cross. You're forgiven. But that doesn't mean that
when you sin all the consequences go away. Your sin can still hurt
others and you. It can have long-term effects. Even the most seemingly insignificant sins can harden our hearts to God's voice. That's
why we're called to fight against sinning.

We'll always be saddled with our sin nature this side of heaven. But striving to resist temptation is part of what it means to be a Christ-follower.

WEEK 3, DAY 3

**"AND THE LORD GOD MADE FOR ADAM
AND FOR HIS WIFE GARMENTS OF SKINS
AND CLOTHED THEM." — GENESIS 3:21**

Yesterday's devotion talked about the consequences of sin. But we want to go a little further in today's devotions to look at the cost of sin.

READ GENESIS 3:20-24. What do these verses show God doing for Adam and Eve? As part of the punishment for their sin, God kicked Adam and Eve out of the Garden. And because He loved them, He didn't send them out naked. What did He do? He made them clothes out of skin. But ask yourself this question: Where did God get the animal skin? Certainly, God could have produced one out of thin air. After all, He's God. But, most people who study these things believe that this isn't what happened. Most people think that what we see here is the first instance where sin earned death. Most people believe God killed an animal from the Garden to make clothes for Adam and Eve.

In Romans 6:23 Paul says that the punishment for all sin is death. So, what we see here is, in a sense, an animal paying for Adam and Eve's sin. This wouldn't be a stretch for God. In His mercy, He set up the sacrificial system so that His people could sacrifice an animal to pay for their sins instead of dying for them themselves. And the sacrificial system points to Jesus, the ultimate sacrifice, who would once-and-for-all pay the price for people's sins.

Sin is costly. It costs us dearly. Which is why we should literally fall on our knees in prayer and praise to Jesus for removing from us our sin-debt. If you have come to faith in Christ, you have been given life. Thank God today for this gift. It's the most important gift you've ever been given.

**THIS DEVOTION SPEAKS TO GOD'S FORGIVING NATURE.
GO TO PAGE 4 FOR A DESCRIPTION OF THIS ATTRIBUTE.**

WEEK 3, DAY 4

"THE LORD SAID TO CAIN, 'WHY ARE YOU ANGRY, AND WHY HAS YOUR FACE FALLEN? IF YOU DO WELL, WILL YOU NOT BE ACCEPTED? AND IF YOU DO NOT DO WELL, SIN IS CROUCHING AT THE DOOR. ITS DESIRE IS FOR YOU, BUT YOU MUST RULE OVER IT.'"
- GENESIS 4:6-7

Our worst decisions are often made when we're upset or angry. Think about it: you don't usually say something you regret when you're having a great day. You're more prone to rebel against God when you're upset, or when things aren't going the way you want them to, right?

READ GENESIS 4:1-16. It's likely that God favored Abel's offering because Cain's was given from past success, i.e., food that he had after the harvest was done. Abel's offering was risky, because by offering firstborns of his flock, he was cutting into his future profits. In short, Cain played it safe, but Abel showed that he trusted God.

When Cain was angry, he had a choice, and God made that choice clear to him: "Sin is crouching at the door. Its desire is for you, but you must rule over it." Cain didn't decide to murder his brother all at once. It was one step at a time. First, he didn't fully trust God. Then he was angry with God. Next, he didn't listen to God's warning. And finally, he killed his brother.

God knows that anger and frustration help us pile one sin on top of another. By the time it's done, we have no way to fix it. As people who reflect God's nature, the idea is to squelch sin in our lives when it's just a temptation. That's the goal. And while we know it doesn't always work out that way, it's something we should shoot for.

SOMETHING TO THINK ABOUT . . .
· What is a choice you've made or something you've done that you wish you could take back? What led you to make that choice?
· In the end (verse 15), God actually protected Cain, even as he suffered the consequence of killing his brother. What does that tell us about God?
· Where is a place in your life where sin is crouching at your door? How do you think God can help you master it?

WEEK 3, DAY 5

"THE LORD SAW THAT THE WICKEDNESS OF MAN WAS GREAT IN THE EARTH, AND THAT EVERY INTENTION OF THE THOUGHTS OF HIS HEART WAS ONLY EVIL CONTINUALLY." - GENESIS 6:5

READ GENESIS 6:5-8. Think for a minute about whether the description of the people in Genesis 6 fits with the popular belief in our culture that people are generally good, even if they make a few mistakes. From God's point of view, people in Genesis 6, and people in general, aren't basically good people who sometimes make a mistake. See, God doesn't care about degrees of goodness or badness. One sin means that the individual is completely sinful. And even the best of us sin more than once (that's the understatement of the century).

But wasn't all God created good? How did it all go wrong, and how could a perfect God ever do something He "regretted" (v .6; some translations say God was "sorry")?

God describes in 6:5-8 how He feels about humankind's rebellion using human terms. God declared His creation to be "very good," but humans had rebelled against Him, resulting in a broken world. But this was no surprise to God, who knows every single word we utter before we even say it (Psalm 139:4)! Even though He saw this coming, God was heartbroken over the sin of his children.

God's attitude toward sin is not flippant; He does not take our sin lightly. It's true that if you trust in Jesus, Jesus has taken the eternal punishment you deserve for your sin. That's how much God loves you. But perhaps it's because God loves us so much that he is so heartbroken over our sin.

SOMETHING TO THINK ABOUT . . .

· When you think about your own sin, do you think of your wrong choices more as casual mistakes, or outright rebellion against God?
· How does thinking of your sin as breaking God's heart impact the meaning of Jesus' sacrifice for you on the cross?

THIS DEVOTION SPEAKS TO GOD'S GREAT LOVE. GO TO PAGE 4 FOR A DESCRIPTION OF THIS ATTRIBUTE.

WEEK 4

WEEK 4, DAY 1

"AND HE TOOK A CUP, AND WHEN HE HAD GIVEN THANKS HE GAVE IT TO THEM, SAYING, 'DRINK OF IT, ALL OF YOU, FOR THIS IS MY BLOOD OF THE COVENANT, WHICH IS POURED OUT FOR MANY FOR THE FORGIVENESS OF SINS."
- MATTHEW 26:27-28

This week, your memory verse is actually two verses. But you got this.

These verses speak to the new covenant Jesus set in motion with His sacrificial death on the cross. A covenant is a binding promise between two parties. God entered into several covenants with various individuals in the Old Testament. But in every case, people were unable to keep their end of the bargain. (Not God. He is faithful to His promises, every time.) God knew this and always planned to send Jesus as a way to provide people with a covenant they could keep: by coming to saving faith in Christ, Jesus' ability to keep His part of the deal counts for us. Pretty amazing, isn't it?

So today, memorize these verses. You can use the "5 – 5 – 5" method you've used the last couple of weeks. Or you can use a Bible app to listen to the verses over and over again until you can say them without any help.

While you're learning the verses, praise God for providing the new covenant in Christ, a way for us to stay in perfect relationship with Him.

WEEK 4, DAY 2

**"BUT I WILL ESTABLISH MY COVENANT WITH
YOU, AND YOU SHALL COME INTO THE ARK,
YOU, YOUR SONS, YOUR WIFE, AND YOUR SONS'
WIVES WITH YOU." - GENESIS 6:18**

It's easy to talk about God's love. So many people in our culture think of God as a fickle, angry God. It can be fun to tell them that God is actually all-loving. So loving, in fact, that the Bible doesn't just say that God loves, but that God *is* love (1 John 4:8). But is that all God is?

READ GENESIS 6:11-22. Not exactly the Sunday school version of a loving God, is it? There are many people who would rather forget the accounts of God in the Old Testament. But how should God respond to this type of terrible injustice? What would you have Him do? The lives of the people God made were characterized by constant violence against one another. From how God relates to Noah in this same passage, it's clear that God wants to be in relationship with the humans He created. Noah wasn't perfect, but he was willing to respond to God when God pursued a relationship with him. The same kind of offer was open to everyone else. But instead of pursuing God, they pursued the worst kinds of violence you can think of.

In the midst of that violence, God made a covenant with Noah, not because Noah was sinless, but because Noah was willing. In the same way, you can experience a relationship with God. You don't have to be perfect (no one is), but you have to be willing.

SOMETHING TO THINK ABOUT . . .
· How does the way God reacts against injustice impact the way you think about your own sin? In what ways do you tend to take your own sin lightly?

**THIS DEVOTION SPEAKS TO GOD'S SENSE OF JUSTICE.
GO TO PAGE 4 FOR A DESCRIPTION OF THIS ATTRIBUTE.**

WEEK 4, DAY 3

"GO OUT FROM THE ARK, YOU AND YOUR WIFE, AND YOUR SONS AND YOUR SONS' WIVES WITH YOU. BRING OUT WITH YOU EVERY LIVING THING THAT IS WITH YOU OF ALL FLESH—BIRDS AND ANIMALS AND EVERY CREEPING THING THAT CREEPS ON THE EARTH—THAT THEY MAY SWARM ON THE EARTH, AND BE FRUITFUL AND MULTIPLY ON THE EARTH." - GENESIS 8:16-17

Have you ever wanted to start over? It would be nice to get a second chance at some aspects of our lives.

READ GENESIS 8:11-22. As you read, think about what Noah and his family may have been feeling as they watched God flood the earth. Usually when this story is told to kids, the teacher skips right to the rainbow. But imagine for a minute what it must have been like to set foot back on dry land after all that time on the boat.

It looked like the same Earth: grass, flowers, even a few small trees that had begun to grow again after the flood. But this time, it was different: There were no cities full of shouting. No screams to announce yet another violent crime that hardly anyone cared about. Just . . . silence. This was a new start.

God had provided a new start, even after showing His anger against a viciously rebellious world. God is a God of fresh starts. It's not that God ignores our sin, or that He isn't heartbroken over our rebellion. But even when we are at our worst, God shows His grace by letting us try again. We may not be able to go back in time and declare a "do over," but we do get the chance to respond to God's grace by doing it differently the next time.

SOMETHING TO THINK ABOUT . . .
· If you could choose one decision or action to take back, or to do differently, what would it be?
· Where in your life do you need a fresh start?
· Spend some time today thanking God that He doesn't hold our sins against us. Praise Him that each day is a fresh start with Him.

WEEK 4, DAY 4

"WHEN THE BOW IS IN THE CLOUDS, I WILL SEE IT AND REMEMBER THE EVERLASTING COVENANT BETWEEN GOD AND EVERY LIVING CREATURE OF ALL FLESH THAT IS ON THE EARTH."
- GENESIS 9:16

Promises are easily broken, right? Think about the last time someone broke a promise they made to you. Because we take promises so seriously, it's pretty painful when they are broken.

READ GENESIS 9:8-17, and keep your eye out for the promise that God is making in this passage. We're barely into the very first book in the Bible, and already we've seen a lot: God's good creation, His creation of human beings, rebellion from those same human beings, terrible cruelty and injustice, God's anger against that injustice, and a terrible flood.

God could have stopped there. We probably would have stopped there if we were God. But God didn't stop there. In fact, God made a promise (a covenant is basically a promise) to Noah and his descendants that He would never flood the entire earth again.

The significance of this promise isn't just that God would never flood the entire earth, but that by even making a promise in the first place, He was saying to the human race, "I'm not done with you yet." Up to this point, the humans God created hadn't exactly shown any love toward God. But still God loved them enough to make a promise.

God's not done with you yet. You may feel like there's not a lot of great stuff in your past. You may have been hurt. Or maybe you've hurt others. Just as God made a covenant with Noah, God has a covenant—His promise—for you: If you trust in what Jesus did for you when He died on the cross, you don't get just a fresh start, you have eternal life.

SOMETHING TO THINK ABOUT . . .
· Do you really believe that God's not done with you yet? Why or why not?

 **THIS DEVOTION SPEAKS TO GOD'S FAITHFULNESS.
GO TO PAGE 4 FOR A DESCRIPTION OF THIS ATTRIBUTE.**

WEEK 4, DAY 5

**"SO THE LORD DISPERSED THEM FROM THERE OVER
THE FACE OF ALL THE EARTH, AND THEY LEFT OFF
BUILDING THE CITY." – GENESIS 11:8**

A few years ago there was this really cute YouTube video where two twin babies were standing in their kitchen "talking" to one another. To anyone else it sounded like baby talk nonsense. However, the babies appeared to have an obvious conversation. It was hilarious to watch the babies babble back and forth in a language only they could understand. This makes us laugh because we can't understand, but did you know there was a time when all of the people on the earth spoke the same language and could understand one another?

READ THE STORY ABOVE IN GENESIS 11:1-9. All of the population of the earth after the flood came together to build a magnificent city with a strong tower that reached high to the heavens. God came down to see their accomplishment and was not happy with what they were doing. God saw that sin had already started to seep into the hearts of humankind. These people didn't even mention the Lord. These were the descendants of Noah and his sons. They should have been spending their days building a tower that praised a God who saved their ancestors. Instead, the city and tower is all about them, and their fame. They were extremely selfish.

God changed their language to save these people from themselves. Through this one act, God could slow down the people's ability to accomplish "anything and everything," even destruction. It's crazy to think that God's act of confusing people's language was actually an act of mercy.

SOMETHING TO THINK ABOUT . . .
· Can you think of a time when you thought a decision you were making was a good one, but looking back you see it wasn't in your best interest? How did God show you mercy to put you on the right path? Thank Him for all of the times He keeps you from destructive choices.

WEEK 5

WEEK 5, DAY 1

"THERE IS NEITHER JEW NOR GREEK, THERE IS NEITHER SLAVE NOR FREE, THERE IS NO MALE AND FEMALE, FOR YOU ARE ALL ONE IN CHRIST JESUS. AND IF YOU ARE CHRIST'S, THEN YOU ARE ABRAHAM'S OFFSPRING, HEIRS ACCORDING TO PROMISE." - GALATIANS 3:28-29

This week your memory verse speaks to the awesome idea of being adopted into God's family. If you have come to a saving faith in Jesus, you've been welcomed to the family as one of God's children. What a cool concept! In this week's devotions, you'll be learning a little about how God started His people, the Jews, with one (unlikely) couple, Abraham and Sarah. God's plan involved calling a people to Himself, then sending a Savior through those people. It started with Abraham and Sarah. But Jesus was always in God's plan.

This week, focus on the pairs of words as you memorize these verses (Jew and Greek, slave and free, etc.). Learning them in pairs will help the verse stick. Try saying them out loud, focusing on the rhythm the pairs create. You'll have it down in no time!

WEEK 5, DAY 2

**"AND I WILL MAKE OF YOU A GREAT NA-
TION, AND I WILL BLESS YOU AND MAKE
YOUR NAME GREAT, SO THAT YOU WILL BE
A BLESSING." — GENESIS 12:2**

Let's imagine you're sitting in your room, just hanging out. Maybe you're texting a friend, reading a book, playing a video game, or just daydreaming. Then God shows up. With a booming voice, He says something like, "Stop what you are doing! You are going to leave your house and everything you know. You are going to pack up your belongings and take a journey. I am not going to tell you exactly where you are going. I will tell you when you arrive. It's alright though: I have a plan for you. Oh, and all of the people in the whole world will ultimately be blessed through you, as well."

How would you react? Well this is exactly what happened to a guy named Abram in Genesis 12:1-4. Take a moment and read it.

Abram had to uproot his entire life. And he was old! He was settled down, and was certainly not expecting God to show up in this way. I'm pretty sure Abram wasn't thinking God was going to ask him to take a crazy adventure. Yet, what was his response? He went. No questions, no concerns, and no wondering. As a matter of fact, Abram said nothing at all. He just obeyed. Abram simply trusted God.

It can seem scary when the Lord asks us to follow Him into the unknown. Chances are, you won't have to wander around in the desert until God says, "you're here." He might just be asking you to tell a friend who doesn't know Jesus what a relationship with Him looks like. Our first response can usually be doubt and excuses. But it doesn't have to be.

SOMETHING TO THINK ABOUT . . .
· Do you struggle to trust God? Why do you think that is?
· How would it look if you just trusted He would take care of you and stepped out in faith?

**THIS DEVOTION SPEAKS TO GOD'S SOVEREIGNTY. GO
TO PAGE 4 FOR A DESCRIPTION OF THIS ATTRIBUTE.**

WEEK 5, DAY 3

"ON THAT DAY THE LORD MADE A COVENANT WITH ABRAM, SAYING, 'TO YOUR OFF-SPRING I GIVE THIS LAND, FROM THE RIVER OF EGYPT TO THE GREAT RIVER, THE RIVER EUPHRATES, THE LAND OF THE KENITES, THE KENIZZITES, THE KADMONITES.'"
– GENESIS 15:18-19

Yesterday we talked about how Abram jumped up and trusted God. Do you remember how we looked at our own trust? We discussed whether or not you would be willing to just take everything you own in a moving truck and go until God says, "You are here."

Imagine you had done this. Imagine that you went on a journey of trust, not knowing where God was taking you. Now imagine that you had arrived . . . and someone else already lived there! That's probably not what you would have had in mind. If God was going to make you move half a world away, why would you show up to a place with other people in it?

READ THE STORY IN GENESIS 15:7-20. Abram is a man of trust, but he has his doubts. God doesn't beat Abram up, or yell at him because he doubts the plan. Instead, God decides to make a covenant with Abram to assure him that He is not going to back out on His promise.

Look back at the story and re-read what Abram did with the animals. Abram set up a sacrifice where God and Abram would walk through together to create a covenant. (In Abram's culture, blood was necessary to seal this type of agreement).

God is described in the Bible as a "consuming fire." This fire solidifies the covenant. In other words, the Lord showed Abram that the covenant wasn't dependent only on what Abram did, but on who God is. It sort of sounds like grace, doesn't it? Our salvation isn't based on what we do to earn God's favor, but what Jesus already did for us on the cross.

SOMETHING TO THINK ABOUT . . .
· Do you ever doubt God's promises? Dwell today on how your salvation relies on Christ's death and resurrection, and not on anything you do.

WEEK 5, DAY 4

**"THE LORD VISITED SARAH AS HE HAD SAID, AND THE
LORD DID TO SARAH AS HE HAD PROMISED."
— GENESIS 21:1**

Have you ever had to wait a really long time for something you were super excited about? Maybe your family announced a trip you'll be taking a year from now. Perhaps you've been saving money for a car or something else expensive. Or you've bought tickets to a concert that is months away. You're so excited! It's easy to feel like that day might not arrive. This is something that happened to Abraham.

READ GENESIS 21:1-7. After the covenant we discussed yesterday, God changed Abram's name to Abraham. You might remember he was 75 when he followed God, and not long after God said he would have a son. After almost 25 years, when Abraham was 100 years old, his wife finally gave birth to a son. That is a long time to wait! But God never gave up on His promise to bless Abraham and Sarah with a son. As a matter of fact, she gave birth just when God said she would.

Following God can be tough. We can forget along the way that God can't break His promises with us. When we have a relationship with Christ, we experience God's faithfulness. God will never leave us. He loves us more than we can ever realize. He takes care of us along the way.

As we look at the lives of people like Noah and Abraham, we can see it didn't mean things would always be easy. Yet, when we look at a man who was given a son at 100 years old-that had been promised to him years before-we can be reminded that God does not forget when He agrees to something. We can't always claim to understand why God works the way He does, but we can trust He will walk with those who belong to Him.

SOMETHING TO THINK ABOUT . . .
· Have you ever thought God forgot about you?
· What is one way you know He is always with you no matter what?

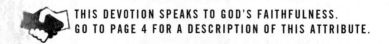
**THIS DEVOTION SPEAKS TO GOD'S FAITHFULNESS.
GO TO PAGE 4 FOR A DESCRIPTION OF THIS ATTRIBUTE.**

WEEK 5, DAY 5

**"ABRAHAM SAID, 'GOD WILL PROVIDE FOR HIMSELF THE LAMB
FOR A BURNT OFFERING, MY SON.' SO THEY WENT BOTH OF THEM
TOGETHER." - GENESIS 22:8**

Think for a moment about the most valuable thing you own. What if some-one came up to you and asked you to destroy it? You'd think they were crazy, right? We value those things in our lives that have meaning. The more they mean to us, the more we value them. This is healthy and normal, for the most part. (If you value your stuff more than people, maybe you need to re-think your priorities.) We don't want people harming the things that matter most in our lives.

READ GENESIS 22:1-14. Can you imagine how Abraham had to have felt about Isaac? He had waited until he was 100 years old to finally have a son. He had to wait 25 years after God's promise for his arrival. It seems certain that Abraham's plan was to protect Isaac, not to harm him. Many biblical scholars believe that Abraham trusted God so much that he never thought it would really happen. Yet, Abraham did as the Lord instructed.

Abraham's willingness to sacrifice Isaac, his only son, is a foreshadowing of Jesus' death on the cross. There would come a point in time when God would send us His only son, and at that point He would be the sacrifice. God loves us so much that He didn't hesitate to send Jesus in order that we might experience freedom from our sins and eternal life in relationship with God.

God was willing to see harm and pain come to His son, all because He loved us. God didn't hold anything back from us. Are you guilty of holding anything back from Him?

SOMETHING TO THINK ABOUT . . .
· Could you have trusted God the same way Abraham did in this story?
· Is there anything in your life that you have tried to keep from God? What area needs to be totally surrender to God?

WEEK 6

**"FOR GOD SO LOVED THE WORLD, THAT
HE GAVE HIS ONLY SON, THAT WHOEVER
BELIEVES IN HIM SHOULD NOT PERISH BUT
HAVE ETERNAL LIFE." — JOHN 3:16**

This week, you'll read about Jacob, and begin reading about Joseph. This is sort of the next stage in God's plan to call a people to Himself. But what you'll learn is that the journey was a bit rocky at times. And not because of anything God did. God kept His promise. But people-people just like us-kept messing things up.

Of all the verses in the Bible, John 3:16 may be the "most memorized," if that's even a thing. But sometimes we can hear something so often that it loses its power. We become too familiar with the words and we overlook the power contained in them. Don't let that happen today.

God's plan was perfect, even if His people aren't. God knew that ultimately, He would send Jesus into the world to provide a once-and-for-all solution for our sin problem. This verse is a perfect expression of what this decision means for us.

If you haven't memorized this verse, do so today and this week. If you're artistic or creative, try writing it down and then illustrating or decorating some of the key words.

WEEK 6, DAY 2

"AND ISAAC PRAYED TO THE LORD FOR HIS WIFE, BECAUSE SHE WAS BARREN. AND THE LORD GRANTED HIS PRAYER, AND REBEKAH HIS WIFE CONCEIVED." - GENESIS 25:21

Let's be honest: movie sequels are often terrible. It's so difficult for directors, producers, and actors to recapture the magic that made the original movie a success. So why do movie studios continue to make sequels? Well, the only thing better than making piles of money off an idea for a movie is making piles of money twice off the same idea! Some sequels definitely feel like the only point is for the studio to make more cash.

READ GENESIS 25:19-28. Wait, haven't we heard this story before? Abraham's son Isaac and his wife, Rebekah, are unable to have children. God intervenes and blesses them with a son. Kind of sounds just like what God did for Abraham and Sarah. In fact it's almost an exact repeat of what God did for Abraham and Sarah. It's like a sequel. But, this sequel is one of the rare ones that are JUST as good as the original! Watching God work His miracles never gets old.

Why did God allow this to happen in consecutive generations? While we can't know His exact reasoning, it seems like maybe God wasn't going to leave any doubt that He is the one responsible for the blessings we experience. God is fully capable of pushing forward with His plan, and is not derailed by things that seem massively impossible to us. There is no challenge too great for God to handle.

SOMETHING TO THINK ABOUT . . .

·What are some ways that you underestimate God and His power? Why do you think we are prone to doubt His power?
·How would your outlook on this week change if you really believed that God was able and willing to change your life? How would your prayers change?

THIS DEVOTION SPEAKS TO GOD'S POWER. GO TO PAGE 4 FOR A DESCRIPTION OF THIS ATTRIBUTE.

**"HIS MOTHER SAID TO HIM, 'LET YOUR CURSE
BE ON ME, MY SON; ONLY OBEY MY VOICE,
AND GO, BRING THEM TO ME.'"
- GENESIS 27:13**

Drama. Welcome to the life of a teenager, right? It can be exhausting trying to keep up with who's with whom, who's fighting whom, who's secretly in love with whom, and who's not supposed to talk to whom. What if I told you that relationship drama is not just a 21st century thing, but that it has always existed? Check out this story from the Bible.

READ GENESIS 27. This story is crazy. It features a mother demonstrating extreme favoritism, a son manipulating his father and stealing from his brother, and it all boils over into one of the biggest sibling rivalries of all time. The worst part is the key figure seems to be Jacob, the con man. This sounds more like a show on the CW, not the Bible. Drama, drama, drama.

Here is the craziest part: God was at work through all of it. Don't be confused. God does not support deception. But His plan won't be thwarted by it, either. God works in spite of our shortcomings. And while our sin has consequences, it can't ultimately stand in the way of God accomplishing what He sets out to do. God had a plan for Jacob. In spite of Jacob's sin, God acted to faithfully see His plan through. God will do the same for you in your life. God will work for your good and His glory, even when you blow it. Which is a pretty good thing to remember.

SOMETHING TO THINK ABOUT . . .
·What are some circumstances in your life that seem insurmountable? What looks as though it will never get better? How does it make you feel to know that God can work through even the most extreme circumstances?
·How do you need to move forward trusting God in your circumstances? Pray that God would help you to trust Him every step of the way.

WEEK 6, DAY 4

"BEHOLD, I AM WITH YOU AND WILL KEEP YOU WHEREVER YOU GO, AND WILL BRING YOU BACK TO THIS LAND. FOR I WILL NOT LEAVE YOU UNTIL I HAVE DONE WHAT I HAVE PROMISED YOU." - GENESIS 28:15

Have you ever been comforted by someone's presence? Maybe they didn't say anything groundbreaking, or do anything amazing. Maybe they were simply there when you needed someone to be there. Your BFF sat with you and ate ice cream when your boyfriend dumped you. Or your dad made you laugh when you were nervous about the big game. There are other examples from your own life. Sometimes, presence can be incredibly powerful.

READ GENESIS 28:10-22. Do you remember the covenant God made with Abraham? Here God extends the same covenant to Abraham's grandson, Jacob, in a dream. Verse fifteen holds the key. God promises He would be with Jacob, and reaffirms that He will do all that He promised.

We could say it another way: God reassures us that He will be faithful to His promises by giving us His presence. Jesus says it this way to His disciples in John 15: "Abide in me, and I in you." As followers of Jesus, we have His presence with us. He goes with us as we go. Here's good news for you today as you go through your life's journey: God is with you.

SOMETHING TO THINK ABOUT...
· How would it change how you lived today if you truly believed that God was going with you? What specific things might be different?
· What is something you could do today to remind you that God is with you?

THIS DEVOTION SPEAKS TO GOD'S FAITHFULNESS.
GO TO PAGE 4 FOR A DESCRIPTION OF THIS ATTRIBUTE.

WEEK 6, DAY 5

**"BUT WHEN HIS BROTHERS SAW THAT THEIR FA-
THER LOVED HIM MORE THAN ALL HIS BROTHERS,
THEY HATED HIM AND COULD NOT SPEAK PEACE-
FULLY TO HIM." - GENESIS 37:4**

We are surrounded by an unbelievable amount of stuff. It's easy to start to evaluate our lives based on what we have: the newest phone, the coolest car, or the cutest date. When we lack what other people have, jealousy can quickly develop.

READ GENESIS 37:1-4, 12-28. Today we're introduced to a new character. In this passage, we meet Jacob's favorite son, Joseph. Talk about one of the worst days of all time. How would you like to be beaten, sold into slavery, and taken off to a foreign country? And by your brothers, of all people! And to top it off, the reason is because they were jealous of the attention you received from your dad, which, by the way, was totally out of your control. Worst. Day. Ever.

Now, everybody wants to be the hero, like Joseph. But the stark reality is that this passage should make us ask if we are being unfair in our assessment of someone else. In other words, do you have a relationship where you resemble Joseph's brothers more than you resemble Joseph? Are you jealous? Envious? Is it leading you to wrong someone else?

It's no fun thinking about our weaknesses. But if we want to live as imitators of Christ, we have to constantly be evaluating our hearts and our actions. Your desire should be to live a life pleasing to God. Don't let envy or jealousy get in the way of that.

SOMETHING TO THINK ABOUT...
· It isn't easy to evaluate yourself. But spend some time today thinking about your attitudes and actions toward others. Is there anything you need to repent of?
· What is the danger of allowing jealousy and bitterness to take hold in our lives? Pray that God would immediately show you when you are being jealous and help you to change.

WEEK 7

WEEK 7, DAY 1

"AND WE KNOW THAT FOR THOSE WHO LOVE GOD ALL THINGS WORK TOGETHER FOR GOOD, FOR THOSE WHO ARE CALLED ACCORDING TO HIS PURPOSE."
- ROMANS 8:28

This week, you'll be looking at how Joseph weathered a hard time in his life. If you recall from last week, Joseph's brothers sold him into slavery. God looked after him, though, and Joseph found himself living as a slave in a house in Egypt. His owner, Potiphar, quickly grew to trust Joseph. But as you're going to find out this week, Joseph's story doesn't end there.

We all experience trials in our lives. Being a Christ-follower doesn't mean that life will be easy. In fact, the opposite is often true. We often experience tough times because we publicly identify with Jesus. But this week's memory verse reminds us that in all things, God is constantly working to make good out of bad, for His glory, and according to His plan. We can be confident in this as we go through the tough times that are bound to come.

This week, try memorizing this verse using the 5-5-5 method we talked about a few weeks ago. It's a great way to hide God's Word in your heart.

WEEK 7, DAY 2

"AND JOSEPH'S MASTER TOOK HIM AND PUT HIM INTO THE PRISON, THE PLACE WHERE THE KING'S PRISONERS WERE CONFINED, AND HE WAS THERE IN PRISON." - GENESIS 39:20

The movie "Unbroken" (Universal Pictures, 2014) is based on the true story of Louis Zamperini, an Olympic athlete who was taken prisoner in Japan during World War II. The movie does an amazing job of illustrating Zamperini's courage, will to survive, and commitment to his fellow prisoners. However, there is more to the story, a side not covered by the movie. Later in life, Zamperini became a Christian, and because of his relationship with Jesus, extended forgiveness to his former captors. His attitude toward his experience has given Zamperini a massive platform to proclaim the good news of Jesus.

READ GENESIS 39. Joseph does the right thing and ends up being thrown in prison for his reward. Perhaps the saying is true, "Good guys never win." The hard truth is that sometimes doing the right thing doesn't get you a trophy, but just pain and suffering. There are times when honoring God is going to result in ridicule, mockery, or persecution. The question we must answer is, "How much is obeying God worth?"

If anyone should have been bitter toward God about his life circumstances, it was definitely Joseph. But he remained obedient and faithful toward God. Much like Louis Zamperini, Joseph fought to maintain a positive attitude, despite his circumstances. In a massive plot twist, we read in verse 23, "And whatever he did, the Lord made it succeed." Even in prison, God was with Joseph and giving him success. Prison normally seems like a dead end, but God used it propel Joseph forward to bigger and better things. The stories of Joseph and Zamperini point us to this truth: Sometimes tragic events lead us to discovering more about ourselves and about God.

SOMETHING TO THINK ABOUT...

What would you be willing to endure in order to do what is right? How can you prepare yourself now to be able to make the right decision later?
How does it change your perspective to know that God can give you success when success seems highly unlikely? In what ways, does that change your attitude for what awaits you today?

WEEK 7, DAY 3

**"THEY SAID TO HIM, 'WE HAVE HAD DREAMS, AND
THERE IS NO ONE TO INTERPRET THEM.' AND JO-
SEPH SAID TO THEM, 'DO NOT INTERPRETATIONS
BELONG TO GOD? PLEASE TELL THEM TO ME.'" -
GENESIS 40:8**

Ruby Falls in Chattanooga, TN is an unusually beautiful waterfall, miles underground. To view the falls, you take an elevator that drops deep into the
earth. The front of the elevator is clear, so that as you ride down into the
caves, the constant view is of a massive wall of rock. For a long time, you
just stare at this rock face as you descend. Finally, the doors open and you
find yourself on a narrow, underground pathway that winds, and winds, and
winds. With every step you start to wonder if you'll ever get there. There's not
a lot to see along the way. But when you finally arrive at the falls, it's well
worth it. The beauty at the end is worth the not-so-spectacular journey to
get there.

READ GENESIS 40. Joseph was sold into captivity, and thrown in jail along
with two of the Pharaoh's employees. One night, each of the king's men had
dreams that perplexed them. Since Joseph's godly character shone through
even in prison, the first asked Joseph for an interpretation. He got a good
report, so the second asked for the same. Unfortunately his was not so good.
Here's the thing: Even while imprisoned, Joseph sought to do the will of God.
He didn't wait for better days. He didn't shrug these guys off. (Furthermore,
he spoke the truth, even in giving bad news.)

SOMETHING TO THINK ABOUT...
· How do bad situations affect the way you treat other people?
· What character traits do you find to be very strong in Joseph?
· What is one practical action you can take next time you are in a bad situ-
ation that will bring honor to God?

Life isn't always great views in good places. The elevator ride to Ruby Falls is
a great reminder of the mundane we must often endure to get to the place
where we can truly shine for Christ. Ask God to help you bring glory to Him,
especially when it's not comfortable.

WEEK 7, DAY 4

"JOSEPH ANSWERED PHARAOH, 'IT IS NOT IN ME;
GOD WILL GIVE PHARAOH A FAVORABLE ANSWER.'" -
GENESIS 41:16

There was once a guy who was a very good drummer. During his junior year, he auditioned better than even the seniors, attaining the coveted position of 1st chair all-county percussionist. The next year rolled around and it was time to try out for all-county band once more. Having the confidence of last year's success, he strode into tryouts and played extremely well . . . in his opinion. A funny thing happened later that afternoon. Everyone's names and chairs were called in front of the entire group of musicians who had tried out for every instrument. Finally, the announcer got to the percussion section. With shock, the confident senior realized it wasn't his name that was called first. It was an eighth grader! An eighth grader! The embarrassed drummer had to play second chair to an eighth grader his senior year because his pride had overtaken his humility.

READ GENESIS 41:14-36. Joseph had gained the attention of Pharaoh because he had accurately interpreted the dreams of two servants. And now Pharaoh had given Joseph his undivided attention in order to have Joseph interpret his two dreams. Go back and look at verse 16. Note that even though Joseph had the opportunity to attempt to interpret the dream by his own power, he did not. Also note that Joseph had the chance to make something up that might free him from prison. He did not. Joseph daringly acknowledged the one true God in front of the most powerful man in the world, a man who did not share the same faith as Joseph.

THINK ABOUT THESE QUESTIONS AS YOU CONSIDER THE VIRTUES OF STRIVING TO BE HUMBLE:

· When have you acted like that drummer and not like Joseph?
· What might have happened if Joseph had approached the Pharaoh under his own power?
· What are some potential outcomes when a person chooses to honor God instead of himself/herself in public?

Remember, everything good comes from glorifying God, not ourselves. Ask God to prevent your pride from overtaking your humility today.

WEEK 7, DAY 5

"YOU SHALL BE OVER MY HOUSE, AND ALL MY PEOPLE SHALL ORDER THEMSELVES AS YOU COMMAND. ONLY AS REGARDS THE THRONE WILL I BE GREATER THAN YOU." - GENESIS 41:40

If you spend enough time driving around the Southeast or the West Coast, you'll no doubt encounter one of these little-known places, tucked off the beaten path, that will sell you a chance to pan for gold in a river or stream. The key to getting the gold and jewels out of a lumpy pile of river sand is in the process of sifting. Sifting involves slowly pouring the sand from the pan into a screen. The sand passes through the screen while the larger particles remain on the screen. If you work at it long enough, you'll begin to see shining minerals. And, if you're incredibly lucky, maybe even some gold!

The sifting process is much like the challenging times we face in our lives. Joseph had gone through a 13-year-long ordeal of slavery and imprisonment because of jealousy in his family. But there is good news for Joseph in the Scripture passage today.

GET YOUR BIBLE AND LOOK UP GENESIS 41:37-45. Take a few moments to read and digest the passage. At this point in Joseph's life, he has been through a long, hard several years. Just like pressure can turn coal into a diamond, long times of hardship can reveal the Christ-like character in a person. Thirteen long years of God "sifting" out the sands of weakness in Joseph's life were over. Joseph's perseverance and obedience to God in the hardest of times had lead to a position as far from slavery as possible. Joseph had been appointed governor over all of Egypt!

SOMETHING TO THINK ABOUT...
· What is the most difficult time of challenge you have ever been through?
· How were you stronger after getting through that challenging time?
· What makes God's "sifting" process in your life so difficult?

Take a moment today to ask God to prepare you to persevere even in the most difficult of times, knowing that He is preparing you to shine brightly for Him like gold or a precious jewel.

WEEK 8

WEEK 8, DAY 1

"BLESSED ARE THOSE WHO ARE PERSECUTED FOR RIGHTEOUSNESS' SAKE, FOR THEIRS IS THE KINGDOM OF HEAVEN." — MATTHEW 5:10

This week, you'll be spending another few days looking at Joseph's life, and then you'll begin looking at what the Israelites' lives were like once Joseph died. In both Joseph's case and in the case of the Israelites, you'll notice that they were treated unfairly even though they did nothing wrong. This is a common thread in the Bible, and a common thread in the lives of modern day Christ-followers.

There will be times when you experience pretty crummy treatment because you publicly identify with Jesus. But take heart. By doing so, you join a centuries-long list of people who have experienced similar treatment.

This week's memory verse will help you find a little strength for those times when you find yourself on the receiving end of others treating you unfairly because of your faith. Memorize this verse. When you need it most, it will be there.

WEEK 8, DAY 2

"AND JOSEPH RECOGNIZED HIS BROTHERS, BUT
THEY DID NOT RECOGNIZE HIM."
- GENESIS 42:8

If you've read *The Hunger Games* books, or watched the movies, you know that the friendship/romance between Peeta and Katniss is central to the plot. Do you remember the part where the rebels stage the daring arena rescue that leaves Peeta behind and at President Snow's mercy? Snow brainwashes Peeta and allows the rebels to rescue him. Katniss finds out the hard way that Snow had programmed Peeta to kill her, which he almost succeeded at doing. But even after this near-successful assassination attempt, Katniss clings to her devotion to Peeta.

Many readers and viewers wanted Peeta to face justice for attempting to kill Katniss. But Katniss showed no such desire. And when they healed Peeta from his brainwashing, Katniss didn't reject his friendship. The brand of forgiveness and compassion shown by Katniss doesn't always happen in real life. Not always. But sometimes it does . . .

READ GENESIS 42:1-17. Joseph had a choice to make. He had the opportunity to exact revenge on those who wrecked the better part of his life. You may have that choice, as well. Whether it's a family member or friend who has betrayed you, or a bully who has made your school or neighborhood feel miserable, you have a choice. You can choose revenge and bitterness. Or you can choose to forgive.

YOU'LL BE LEFT HANGING TODAY ON THE OUTCOME OF JOSEPH'S STORY. SO WHILE YOU ANXIOUSLY AWAIT TOMORROW'S DEVOTION, PONDER THESE QUESTIONS:

· How hard is it for you to forgive those who do wrong to you?
· Could you forgive someone who sold you into slavery or even attempted to murder you?
· What would you have done to your brothers if you were in Joseph's position?

Pray that God will give you the strength in real life to do the right thing by showing compassion and forgiveness when given the opportunity.

 THIS DEVOTION SPEAKS TO GOD'S FORGIVENESS. GO TO PAGE 4 FOR A DESCRIPTION OF THIS ATTRIBUTE.

WEEK 8, DAY 3

"AND GOD SENT ME BEFORE YOU TO PRESERVE FOR YOU A REMNANT ON EARTH, AND TO KEEP ALIVE FOR YOU MANY SURVIVORS. SO IT WAS NOT YOU WHO SENT ME HERE, BUT GOD. HE HAS MADE ME A FATHER TO PHARAOH, AND LORD OF ALL HIS HOUSE AND RULER OVER ALL THE LAND OF EGYPT." - GENESIS 45:7-8

Resiliency. Do you know what that word means? It means that nothing can keep you down. It means you can take a shot and keep on trucking. Back in the day, there were these watches made by Timex. The slogan for these nearly indestructible watches was, "It takes a lickin' and keeps on tickin.'" (Kind of the opposite of, say, your smartphone, as you know if you've ever dropped it on the ground.)

TAKE OUT YOUR BIBLE AND LOOK UP GENESIS 45:1-15. As you read this passage you will discover a remarkable true story of forgiveness, compassion, and even undeserved gifts. Joseph could have had his brothers imprisoned or even executed. Yet, he honored them. How illogical does this seem? When looking at the situation from a human perspective, this seems ridiculous. However, a closer look at verses 7-8 reveals God's perspective.

Joseph was kind of like one of those old Timex watches: He was resilient. And his resiliency came from trusting in God and His plan. God's plan for you is constant, and holds eternal implications for you and those around you. Following God's plan, through faith in Jesus Christ, will lead you to forgive even the harshest of offenders. A relationship with Christ will compel you to show compassion to those who don't deserve it.

SOMETHING TO THINK ABOUT . . .

· Why is it so hard to grasp that your time of suffering might be so you can help someone who doesn't deserve your help?
· How would you have felt if you were in Joseph's shoes, suddenly having it made clear to you how God is always working in and through you?

WEEK 8, DAY 4

**"THEREFORE THEY SET TASKMASTERS OVER THEM TO AFFLICT THEM
WITH HEAVY BURDENS. THEY BUILT FOR PHARAOH STORE CITIES,
PITHOM AND RAAMSES." - EXODUS 1:11**

Imagine being a king. Not just any king, but a self proclaimed "god-king." (That's what the Egyptian pharaohs were thought to be: part god, part king.) Every word you said and every action you took would all carry the weight of deity. If you're honest, don't you think it would be overwhelming? What if you made the wrong decision? No one would be there to check you and get you back on the right path.

READ EXODUS 1:8-14. Imagine the backstory that must have lead the young king to act this way. Imagine how he and his friends would grumble about the fact that a few generations before he came to power, an idiot pharaoh gave these foreigners the best land in the country. We can imagine him complaining about how the Israelites have grown so numerous, and have become strong from all the labor forced on them. Now, the time has come when this young king comes to power. Unfortunately, he decided to act harshly toward the Israelites for no other reason than they weren't Egyptians. He had forgotten the story of how Joseph saved Egypt.

The new king made the wrong call. And in doing so, he caused a ton of pain for the Israelites, who suffered for no reason. But, it was all part of God's plan to ultimately call a people to Himself.

SOMETHING TO THINK ABOUT . . .

· Can you think of something you went through that seemed bad, but looking back, it actually made you stronger? Maybe you owe God an apology for being mad that He allowed that to happen in your life. Now's a good time to make it.
· Think of someone specific in your life that you think is mistreating you. Now switch places with them in your mind. Is there a reason they mistreat you? Perhaps it's his/her own weaknesses, fears, or small mindedness. Is there a way you can change his/her attitude about you by first seeing life through his/her eyes?

**THIS DEVOTION SPEAKS TO HOW GOD KNOWS ALL.
GO TO PAGE 4 FOR A DESCRIPTION OF THIS ATTRIBUTE.**

WEEK 8, DAY 5

"THEN PHARAOH COMMANDED ALL HIS PEOPLE, 'EVERY SON THAT IS BORN TO THE HEBREWS YOU SHALL CAST INTO THE NILE, BUT YOU SHALL LET EVERY DAUGHTER LIVE.'" EXODUS 1:22

Can't you see it now: "What in the world!?! Is she crazy!?! Mom seriously just put our baby brother in a basket and floated him down the Nile?" Crocodile bait, anyone?

READING EXODUS 1:22 AND 2:1-10, it all seems so plain and sanitary; we miss the absolute insanity of it all. Don't just "blah, blah, blah" right over the fact that they were rounding up little baby boys and tossing them into the river! Imagine the horror, the screaming wails of mothers, and the bloodied faces of fathers who tried to fight off the soldiers. Israelite parents had two choices it seems: helplessly watch, or die trying to fight. Except that Moses' mom figured out a third option. With all that going on in the neighborhood, Moses' mom doesn't seem fazed. Instead of fighting only to have her baby ripped from her arms anyway, she calmly surrendered the situation and gave God a chance to be God.

Moses' mother isn't the only heroine. The shrewd decision of Moses' sister shows how awesome she was. She must have been a straight A student because, wow, she played the situation with cool intelligence. She went right up to the sister of the king (the king who's killing her people) and said, "Hey, I get it. He's really cute, but you're a princess. You don't want baby spew on your dress. And then there's all that baby poo and diapers . . . I just happen to know a lady who, if you paid her, might be convinced to raise this kid for you." And then she goes and gets Moses' mom!!! (That's ice-cold, cool-headed thinking.)

The point of this story is that Moses' mom could have tried to do what she thought best according to her own reasoning. But ultimately, she did what God was leading her to do. And the crazy, seemingly half-baked idea just so happened to work. Imagine that . . .

SOMETHING TO THINK ABOUT
· In what ways are you kicking and fighting when you should be calmly surrendering and allowing God to be God?
· When you see your chance to be the hand of God (like Moses' sister) are you brave enough to take a chance? Why or why not?

WEEK 9

WEEK 9, DAY 1

"TRULY, TRULY, I SAY TO YOU, IF ANYONE KEEPS MY WORD, HE WILL NEVER SEE DEATH." – JOHN 8:51

This week you're going to be really picking up the pace with the big-picture story of the Bible. You're about to get into one of the most important narrative threads in Scripture: God delivering His people out of oppression in Egypt. It's a miraculous story full of God's mercy and power. But it's also important because of the relationship we see between God's actions and His Word.

God made Moses His mouthpiece, delivering His Word to Pharaoh. Through God's Word, Moses would warn Pharaoh what would happen if he did not let God's people go. And through God's Word, Moses predicted deliverance for the Israelites. In other words, through God's Word, there was life! The same is still true today.

We are saved from the penalty of our sins when we hear the Gospel-the good news of Jesus Christ-and believe in it. Memorize this verse today. And remember how important it is to know, follow, and share God's Word.

WEEK 9, DAY 2

"THE MIDWIVES SAID TO PHARAOH, 'BECAUSE THE HEBREW WOMEN ARE NOT LIKE THE EGYPTIAN WOMEN, FOR THEY ARE VIGOROUS AND GIVE BIRTH BEFORE THE MIDWIFE COMES TO THEM.' SO GOD DEALT WELL WITH THE MIDWIVES. AND THE PEOPLE MULTIPLIED AND GREW VERY STRONG. AND BECAUSE THE MIDWIVES FEARED GOD, HE GAVE THEM FAMILIES." - EXODUS 1:19-21

READ EXODUS 1:11-25. Look closely at verses 19-21. Those lying cheats! How could they just lie to the Pharaoh and have God bless them anyway? Isn't that against the 10 Commandments or something?

Throughout Scripture, we see people portrayed accurately with no attempt to paint over their sins. David committed murder to deceptively cover his adultery. Abraham lied and sent his wife to be married to the Pharaoh to save his skin. Peter denied even knowing Jesus. The fact that the Bible includes all the flaws of our favorite heroes only makes it that much more believable. God sees the true heart of sinners. He also sees their sin. He loves them and works through them despite their sin.

Now, back to the real question. Should the midwives have lied? No. What would have happened if they had told the truth? Who knows. That's not what happened, and history doesn't give us do-overs. But on to the real lesson . . . God sees beyond your actions to what's in your heart. But God still sees your actions. God never "winks" at sin. But He loves us, and works through us even though we are sinful. The fact that God can achieve His perfect will using imperfect instruments only makes Him that much more amazing!

SOMETHING TO THINK ABOUT . . .
· Are you making excuses for sin in your life when you know you should come clean? Confess and repent. Do it now.
· For a moment, imagine you are God and you can see your true heart. What beauty does He see in you? Make a list.
· Can you think of someone you need to forgive because his/her actions were hurtful even though you know that he/she has a heart of love for you?

THIS DEVOTION SPEAKS TO GOD'S COMPASSION. GO TO PAGE 4 FOR A DESCRIPTION OF THIS ATTRIBUTE.

WEEK 9, DAY 3

"BUT MOSES SAID TO GOD, 'WHO AM I THAT I SHOULD GO TO PHARAOH AND BRING THE CHILDREN OF ISRAEL OUT OF EGYPT?'"
— EXODUS 3:11

It hurts when our best friends fail us. It's inexcusable. Sure, people let you down everyday. But not your best friend. Not the one who sticks closer than a brother or sister. Not the one who's always got your back.

READ EXODUS 3:1-12. Reread verse 11. God came to Moses (the same Moses who was wasting his life in the desert, herding sheep) and spoke in an audible voice. And what did Moses do? He argued with God. But so much is made of the fact that Moses argued with God that we entirely miss Moses' initial response in verse 4. "Here I am."

Heroes of the Old and New Testament echo Moses' response throughout the Bible. Guys like the prophet, Isaiah (see Isaiah 6:8); the prophet, Samuel (see 1 Samuel 3:4); and even in the sentiment of the Apostle Peter (Mark 4:29) who said "Even if all these fall away, I will not." Peter was telling Jesus, "I've got your back no matter what."

But sometimes, "no matter what" is more frightening than we originally thought. That's true for Peter, Moses, and your best friend. In Moses' case, God was asking him to go back to Egypt where he was a treasonous murderer. Then He wanted Moses to speak up to the king, Pharaoh, and demand freedom for the Israelites. That's a big ask. But in the end, Moses does the job.

Of course, this isn't about Moses or Peter. It's not even about your best friend. It's about you.

SOMETHING TO THINK ABOUT

· Is God calling you to action, and you can't believe what He wants you to do? Don't argue, just do it! Reread verse 12: "I will be with you." God's got your back.

· Do you need to forgive a friend? Think of all the times he/she actually did have your back. Forgive him/her. And if possible, restore the friendship.

WEEK 9, DAY 4

"BUT THE MAGICIANS OF EGYPT DID THE SAME BY THEIR SECRET ARTS. SO PHARAOH'S HEART REMAINED HARDENED, AND HE WOULD NOT LISTEN TO THEM, AS THE LORD HAD SAID." - EXODUS 7:22

READ EXODUS 7:14-25. Remember that Moses was probably raised with the Pharaoh. They would have eaten together, studied together, and played pranks together. Maybe they even fought like brothers do. These two guys had a history. Their history also includes Moses abandoning his step-brother. Moses murdered an Egyptian guard, and thanklessly ran out on the whole family. You can imagine Pharaoh feeling like his family gave Moses everything, and yet Moses rejected them all. After all that, Moses has the nerve to come back to Egypt and tell his big brother what to do!? Not a chance.

Can you relate to Pharaoh's pain? Sprinkled throughout the Bible, God warns us to protect our hearts. Check out:
- Psalm 51:10
- Proverbs 4:23
- Luke 6:45
- Philippians 4:6-7

Apparently having a hard heart is something we humans struggle with. Fortunately, in Ezekiel 37:26, God promises: "And I will give you a new heart, and a new spirit I will put within you. And I will remove the heart of stone from your flesh and give you a heart of flesh." God isn't going to force this on you though. You have to be a willing participant in the heart exchange. Are you willing?

SOMETHING TO THINK ABOUT:
· Pray that God's Holy Spirit will expose to you your heart of stone. Beware, He probably will.
· What action is God recommending that will crush your heart of stone? Do it!

WEEK 9, DAY 5

"BUT NOT A DOG SHALL GROWL AGAINST ANY OF THE PEOPLE OF ISRAEL, EITHER MAN OR BEAST, THAT YOU MAY KNOW THAT THE LORD MAKES A DISTINCTION BETWEEN EGYPT AND ISRAEL."
— EXODUS 11:7

Remember what it felt like in elementary school when it was time to pick teams? The waiting was the worst. But being chosen . . . what a sense of relief and belonging! God makes a clear distinction in today's passage that the Israelites are His people, and under His protection.

READ EXODUS CHAPTER 11. The Israelites had come to Egypt in a time of famine and gained refuge under the reign of Joseph. After Joseph's death, they grew in number and were ultimately subdued into slavery. Now, God had raised up Moses to be the one to lead His people to freedom. Nine previous plagues had revealed God's power over nature, and Pharaoh still refused to give in. This new threat would create a dividing line between Egypt and Israel that made it clear: for God's people there was life. Apart from Him there is only death and destruction!

In these days, the firstborn of Pharaoh would have been his successor to the throne. The plague of the firstborn meant not only great anguish to Pharaoh as a father, but a clear threat to his royal line. Preserving the firstborn of the Israelites shows God's fatherly affection for His children, while still remembering His promise to create in them a great and powerful nation.

Look closely at verses 6-7. Why do you think God went so far as to say that "not even a dog shall growl against" His people?

You can look back at Exodus 7:1-4 and see that God predicted Pharaoh's response from the beginning of these plagues. So, what do you think was the point of all the plagues, then?

The line has been drawn in the sand. God's children will live, others will die. And now they wait for Him to show His ultimate power.

SOMETHING TO THINK ABOUT
· How does knowing that God has chosen you for His team give you peace when you face frightening situations?

THIS DEVOTION SPEAKS TO GOD'S POWER. GO TO PAGE 4 FOR A DESCRIPTION OF THIS ATTRIBUTE.

WEEK 10

WEEK 10, DAY 1

"THE NEXT DAY HE SAW JESUS COMING TO-WARD HIM, AND SAID, 'BEHOLD, THE LAMB OF GOD, WHO TAKES AWAY THE SIN OF THE WORLD!'" - JOHN 1:29

This week you'll be introduced to the tragic yet wonderful miracle of the Passover. Sadly, there was a lot of death that resulted from Pharaoh's arrogance. But there was a miraculous saving of lives, as well. God acted to punish the Egyptians for stubbornly enslaving His people. But He acted to deliver the Israelites from slavery and death.

God did this through the blood of the Passover lambs. This event, which you'll read about, foreshadowed the True Passover Lamb, Jesus, who would sacrifice Himself thousands of years later for the sins of all humankind. In John 1:29, we see John the Baptist recognizing Jesus for who He truly was. We gain life when we recognize Jesus for who He is. The Israelites were spared the consequences of the death of the firstborn. When we come to faith in Christ, we are spared death, as well.

Spend some time today and this week meditating on this simple but powerful verse. Memorize it if you can. Write it down and put it somewhere where you will see it frequently. Thank God for providing a way for you to come to life in Christ.

THIS DEVOTION SPEAKS TO GOD'S FORGIVENESS. GO TO PAGE 4 FOR A DESCRIPTION OF THIS ATTRIBUTE.

WEEK 10, DAY 2

"YOU SHALL SAY, 'IT IS THE SACRIFICE OF THE LORD'S PASSOVER, FOR HE PASSED OVER THE HOUSES OF THE PEOPLE OF ISRAEL IN EGYPT, WHEN HE STRUCK THE EGYPTIANS BUT SPARED OUR HOUSES.' AND THE PEOPLE BOWED THEIR HEADS AND WORSHIPED."
— EXODUS 12:27

Think of a moment in your life that required preparation. Maybe you worked all year to prep for an AP exam, or trained for weeks for a track event. Think of those feelings in the moments before "go time." Investing in preparation makes us value the brief moments of action. God has been at work preparing the way for the Israelites to leave Egypt. But in today's reading, they finally have to take their own measures of preparation.

READ EXODUS 12:21-32. God has made the distinction between His people and the rest of humankind. The first nine plagues required nothing from the Israelites but that they stand back and see God's power at work. In this final plague, they are required to mark themselves as God's people. Earlier in the chapter God tells them to choose a perfect lamb, roast it, buckle their belts, put on their shoes, and eat it fast. He is basically telling them, something amazing is about to happen. Get ready!

The celebration of the Passover is a tradition still significant in Jewish customs today. Unfortunately, many Jewish people missed the significance of this symbolism when Jesus arrived. Even after centuries of preparation, many of God's people were still not ready for the realization of His ultimate sacrifice on the cross. What about you? Is your heart a place that accepts Jesus and all He represents?

SOMETHING TO THINK ABOUT . . .
· If God already knew who His people were, why do you think He asked them to mark their homes with the blood of a lamb?
· What do we know from Scripture that the Israelites did not yet know about the blood of the True Lamb, Jesus?
· How have you responded to the blood Jesus shed for you? How has it changed your life and identity?

WEEK 10, DAY 3

> "MOSES TOOK THE BONES OF JOSEPH WITH
> HIM, FOR JOSEPH HAD MADE THE SONS OF
> ISRAEL SOLEMNLY SWEAR, SAYING, 'GOD WILL
> SURELY VISIT YOU, AND YOU SHALL CARRY UP
> MY BONES WITH YOU FROM HERE.'"
> — EXODUS 13:19

Have you ever experienced someone else getting credit for your idea, or your work? It can be really frustrating to see something that should have been yours go to someone else. In today's passage, however, we see how much bigger God's view is than our own. Moses led the Israelites out of Egypt, but we are reminded that this exodus from Egypt was a continuation of the promise made to Joseph's father, Jacob. The generations in Egypt served for God to show Himself as the Savior and Deliverer of His people. Joseph provided temporary salvation from starvation in Egypt, but even at his death, he knew that God would ultimately deliver them and fulfill His promise. His faith in God's steadfastness was strong, even when he knew he would never see that promise fulfilled first-hand.

READ EXODUS 13:17-22. Notice in verse 17 that God chooses to send His people the long way around. He could have led them straight into victorious battle with the Philistines to reclaim their land. But He was still revealing mysteries about His nature. The time would soon come when God showed the Israelites how He could fight through them. But first He wanted them to trust that He would fight for them.

When you think of God's great promises in Scripture, look for how He is leading in your life as you play your part in His great master plan!

SOMETHING TO THINK ABOUT . . .
· Why do you think God chose to lead them with a pillar of cloud by day and fire by night, when He could have just had them follow Moses?
· God still uses pastors and teachers to lead us today. But how does He direct believers individually?

**THIS DEVOTION SPEAKS TO HOW GOD KNOWS ALL.
GO TO PAGE 4 FOR A DESCRIPTION OF THIS ATTRIBUTE.**

WEEK 10, DAY 4

"AND MOSES SAID TO THE PEOPLE, 'FEAR NOT, STAND FIRM, AND SEE THE SALVATION OF THE LORD, WHICH HE WILL WORK FOR YOU TODAY. FOR THE EGYPTIANS WHOM YOU SEE TODAY, YOU SHALL NEVER SEE AGAIN.'"— EXODUS 14:13

Have you ever seen a magic trick that left you obsessed with the question, "How did he do that"? We are conditioned to be skeptical because we live in a world where we trust our own intellect above all else. The early Hebrews had seen genuine miracles, and still found themselves skeptical in trusting God.

READ EXODUS CHAPTER 14 AND PAY CLOSE ATTENTION TO VERSES 13 AND 19. The plagues proved God's power over the Egyptian magicians. This deliverance at the Red Sea showed Israel God's command over earth itself. Throughout Scripture, we see that God's people often reach a point of no hope. It is in these times when God reveals Himself as the ONLY hope.

This is the final contest between the Lord and Pharaoh, proving once and for all, that while others may try to bind His people, God is their true King. The Lord alone is their Savior. The declaration that they will never see the Egyptians again is significant. The Lord is declaring that His deliverance is final. Later, as recorded in John 8:34-38, Jesus would remind the Jews that what He sets free will be free indeed!

SOMETHING TO THINK ABOUT . . .
· Look at verse 13. How does the image of the Red Sea swallowing up Israel's enemies paint a picture of the Gospel?
· Look at verse 19. Why do you think the angel of God and the pillar of cloud moved from the front of the group of Israelites to the back? Think about all that this signifies before you answer. Take some time to write your response below, and thank God for all that He is.

"NOW THEREFORE, IF YOU WILL INDEED OBEY MY VOICE AND KEEP MY COVENANT, YOU SHALL BE MY TREASURED POSSESSION AMONG ALL PEOPLES, FOR ALL THE EARTH IS MINE." – EXODUS 19:5

Have you ever seen the old game Operation? It's hilarious to watch people jump as they touch the sides and the buzzer scolds them for harming their patient. But, it's no laughing matter at all if a real surgeon flinches in an operation. You see, the significance of the rules all depends on the consequences at stake. **CONSIDERING ALL THAT GOD HAS DONE FOR THE ISRAELITES UP TO THIS POINT, READ EXODUS 19:1-6.** Pay attention to the warning He gives them.

The Israelites were at a point of transition. Even though God had met their physical needs and delivered them from slavery, their new freedom was not all they had hoped it would be. They would have to learn how to be God's people, and that was going to mean following rules that they would not always understand. While the 10 Commandments are coming just around the corner, they first had to learn to simply obey God's voice.

God instructed Moses to declare to Israel that He had kept His promise. He had delivered them, and proclaimed that they would be a holy nation of His priests. But, just as with the Passover, there were instructions for keeping up their end of the bargain. The nation of Israel had been publicly established. Now, what they do as that nation will be public as well.

The more publicly you choose to live for Christ, the more significant your obedience to Christ becomes. Following God's voice becomes no laughing matter when others know that you belong to Him!

SOMETHING TO THINK ABOUT . . .

· How do the conditions of God's promise in verse 5 show the difference between God's nature and people's?

· Do you think God's reminder of their past will help prepare them for the laws they will live by in the future? How?

·How does reflecting on your past help you embrace God's commands for your future?

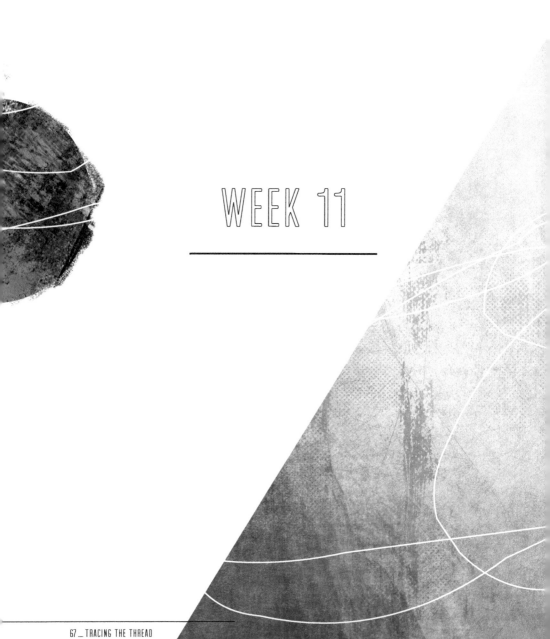

WEEK 11

WEEK 11, DAY 1

**"BUT GOD SHOWS HIS LOVE FOR US IN
THAT WHILE WE WERE STILL SINNERS,
CHRIST DIED FOR US." – ROMANS 5:8**

As we trace the big-picture story of the Bible, we see echoes of the Gospel woven throughout. Nowhere is this more apparent than when we see God giving His people the 10 Commandments, and the rest of the Law. We may be tempted to see this as just a bunch of rules. But it's more than that. And understanding this points to the need of a Savior.

God gave His people rules so that they would be a people who lived out God's character. Following God's commands would separate His people from the surrounding nations that didn't follow God, and who did all sorts of awful stuff. And yet, God's people couldn't follow His rules. The sin that had crept into people's hearts with Adam and Eve's fall kept the Israelites from fully obeying God. And because God is perfectly righteous, this failure to obey is sin. And sin deserves death.

But God in His mercy sent Jesus to cover the sins of all who would believe in Him. Through faith, we can know forgiveness. Keep this in mind as you read the account of God giving His people His Law this week. And maybe, you could memorize Romans 5:8. It's a powerful message for God's children.

**THIS DEVOTION SPEAKS TO GOD'S RIGHTEOUSNESS.
GO TO PAGE 4 FOR A DESCRIPTION OF THIS ATTRIBUTE.**

WEEK 11, DAY 2

"AND GOD SPOKE ALL THESE WORDS, SAYING, 'I AM THE
LORD YOUR GOD, WHO BROUGHT YOU OUT OF THE LAND
OF EGYPT, OUT OF THE HOUSE OF SLAVERY.'"
— EXODUS 20:1-2

Rules, rules, rules. Everyone loves to hate them. When you see a "Caution Wet Paint" sign, you want to touch the wall, don't you? Touching the wall didn't ever cross your mind until you saw the sign. So, you realize that the paint sign (i.e. the rule) showed you where you were messed up. It put a spotlight on your heart's desire to do what you want, despite what anyone else says.

READ EXODUS 20:1-17. In this passage, God gives the most famous list of rules ever: the 10 Commandments. When you look at this list, you realize that it serves to highlight our sin. When you know the rules, you realize you've broken countless of them. You realize just how much you are in need of help, someone who is better at rule keeping than you could ever be.

The 10 Commandments show you your sinfulness, which leads to your great need for a Rescuer. In Jesus, you have the Rescuer your heart longs for. Jesus is the only one who scored 100% on the 10 Commandments. He lived the perfect life that you could not live. He died on the cross the death that you deserved to die. He rose again from the dead, defeating death, and making a way for those whose rule keeping scores are less than the 100% needed to stand as perfect before God.

SOMETHING TO THINK ABOUT . . .

· How do you score on the 10 Commandments? Aren't you glad that your standing before God is not based on your score?
· How does the hope that Jesus scored 100% for you change your life this week?
· Many people have missed the grace of God in rescuing people from trying to work their way to God by keeping rules. Is there someone that you can share the hope of Jesus scoring 100% with today?

WEEK 11, DAY 3

**"MOSES CAME AND TOLD THE PEOPLE ALL THE WORDS
OF THE LORD AND ALL THE RULES. AND ALL THE PEOPLE
ANSWERED WITH ONE VOICE AND SAID, 'ALL THE WORDS
THAT THE LORD HAS SPOKEN WE WILL DO.'"
- EXODUS 24:3**

Weddings are great occasions that are filled with food, fun, and fellowship. And yet, amidst all the fanfare, wedding-goers can lose sight of the importance of the marriage promise. Ultimately, a wedding is not about the festivities, but the marriage promise itself.

READ GENESIS 24:1-8. Here you'll see God's people making a promise-also called a covenant-with God. This is a defining moment for the people of Israel. They have heard and understood the rules surrounding this promise, and they have committed to obey God and keep their end of the covenant.

Like many of us when we make promises, the people of Israel would fail many times in keeping the promises they made to God. That is why, thousands of years later, God would send His Son, Jesus, to be a sacrifice for the people's failures to follow God. Jesus came as a sacrifice that would forever take away the guilt and penalty for our sins.

When we fail to follow God, like we so often do, we can rest on the fact that our standing before God is based on what Jesus did for us at the cross, rather than our performance for Him. When we commit to following Jesus, we know that God's grace is there for us when we fail. It's the only way we can come into relationship with a perfect God.

SOMETHING TO THINK ABOUT...
· What are some things that you will not be a part of since you are committed to following God?
· How can you help those around you to see that you have committed yourself to following Jesus?

WEEK 11, DAY 4

"THEY SHALL MAKE AN ARK OF ACACIA WOOD . . ." - EXODUS 25:10

Where is your most special place to go? Where is that place where you have memories that have helped to shape your life? The place where you feel the safest? The place where you can hear from God? Think about this place. If this place is somewhere near you, go to that place now. No, seriously. Go now.

Now, open your Bible and read Exodus 25:10-22. This is a passage that shows God's commands to His people to make a place where they can hear from God Himself. Since the Israelites moved around a lot awaiting God's promise of a land, God would meet with them not in a physical location, but around a physical object called the Ark of the Covenant.

The Ark of the Covenant would one day be placed in a Tabernacle, and then the Temple. It was hidden from the eyes of the people, and was only approached by the High Priest once a year. The people were also not allowed to touch the Ark of the Covenant because it was holy and set apart for God. This was a very special place. What made it so special is that it was where God would talk to His people (see verse 22).

What if you were to make your own special place where you could seek and hear from God? For many teenagers, one of the challenges with seeking God in prayer is the noise around them. Between the TV, tablet, and smart phone, there is rarely a time when it is quiet enough for you to hear from God. Finding your own special place is a good first step in blocking out the noise, and making room to hear from God.

SOMETHING TO THINK ABOUT...
· Find a special place in or around your home. Go to that special place, and pray that God would speak to you. Consider making this place where you seek God in prayer and devotions every day.
· Take some time today to be silent and pray to God. Turn off the TV, mute the music, and hide the smart phone in order to truly seek God in prayer.

WEEK 11, DAY 5

"BUT CALEB QUIETED THE PEOPLE BEFORE MOSES AND SAID, 'LET US GO UP AT ONCE AND OCCUPY IT, FOR WE ARE WELL ABLE TO OVERCOME IT.'"
- NUMBERS 13:30

Is the glass half full or half empty? Have you ever had a friend that saw everything in a negative light? For them nothing was ever good enough. Friends like this are draining. They can suck the very life out of you. They can take your passion, your excitement, and your energy and run it into the ground. These friends who can't see the good in anything have lost something very important: hope.

READ NUMBERS 13:1-2 AND 26-33. Notice, the spies are divided into two groups: half-full, and half-empty. One group only sees the problems: big people, and city walls. The other group sees the land flowing with "milk and honey" (v. 27). The "glass half full" group hangs on to the hope that with God they would be able to overcome it (v. 30).

The difference between these groups is their respective level of trust in God and His promises. Is God really big enough to come through for His people? Is God's promise of a Promised Land really true? In this passage, you see that the power to believe and trust the promises of God is what allows you to truly follow God into His plans for you.

So what about you? Is the glass half full or half empty? Do you trust God and His promises? Is there a path that God is calling you to take? Which group of spies will you be like?

SOMETHING TO THINK ABOUT...

· What are some promises of God that you need to trust in more fully? Take a notecard and write down these promises. Then, place the notecard on the mirror in your bathroom to remind you of them.
· What are the challenges that you see on the path that God may be calling you to take? Make a list of these promises and spend some time surrendering them to God in prayer.
· What is the next step of faith you can take today in seeking to walk with God in His plans for your life?

WEEK 12

WEEK 12, DAY 1

**"FOR THE GRACE OF GOD HAS APPEARED, BRING-
ING SALVATION FOR ALL PEOPLE."
- TITUS 2:11**

You're going to continue your look at the Israelites' journey to inherit the land promised to them by God. As you continue to uncover the big-picture story of the Bible, keep in mind that the Promised Land represents God's faithfulness to His covenant with Abram. Sure, God has kept His promise to make Abram the father of a great nation. But, that nation needed a home. For the Israelites, the Promised Land was a major part of their salvation as a nation. But the source of our salvation is much different.

God doesn't save nations or people groups. God saves individuals. And as individuals, our salvation comes through faith in Jesus Christ, God's Son. God sent Jesus to die on the cross as payment for the penalty our sins earn for us. If we believe in Christ, His sacrifice counts in our place. We are forgiven.

The cool thing is that God called Israel to Him so that He could send Jesus through them. Pretty cool. And so this week, make it a point to memorize Titus 2:11. It may be a message that someone in your life needs to hear.

WEEK 12, DAY 2

"THEN ALL THE CONGREGATION RAISED A LOUD CRY, AND THE PEOPLE WEPT THAT NIGHT. AND ALL THE PEOPLE OF ISRAEL GRUMBLED AGAINST MOSES AND AARON. THE WHOLE CONGREGATION SAID TO THEM, 'WOULD THAT WE HAD DIED IN THE LAND OF EGYPT! OR WOULD THAT WE HAD DIED IN THIS WILDERNESS!'" - NUMBERS 14:1-2

If you have ever hung out with little kids, many of them love to complain. "It's too hot." "I don't wanna." "Do we have to?" This gets SUPER annoying really quickly. In the Old Testament, this annoying character trait was referred to frequently as "grumbling." And boy did the Israelites like to grumble to God, to Moses, and to others.

READ NUMBERS 14:1-4 AND 26-35. Here the Israelites are tired of walking with God on His journey into the Promised Land. They are hacked off at Moses for leading them. And they are having hallucinations that slavery in Egypt would be better than where they found themselves. They claim to be willing to go back to slavery in Egypt in order to get out of the desert.

At the core, the Israelites' showed that they didn't trust God or believe in His promises. This caused God to respond to them with judgment. The complaining people would never see the Promised Land. God would cause them to wander in the desert until their generation was dead. Their kids ultimately got to experience the blessings of the Promised Land.

The key question for us from this text is, "Do I trust, follow, and believe in God"? As Christ-followers, we so often want our own way. We think we know better than God. But today's passage stands as a clear reminder that we do not. We need to surrender to God's will and plan for our lives. God may not be bringing us into the physical Promised Land, but He is leading us to become who He has made us to be.

SOMETHING TO THINK ABOUT...
· How can you avoid complaining in your own life?
· How is your attitude toward God's leadership over your life?
· What are some areas where you need to more fully surrender to God's plans for your life?

THIS DEVOTION SPEAKS TO GOD'S SENSE OF JUSTICE. GO TO PAGE 4 FOR A DESCRIPTION OF THIS ATTRIBUTE.

WEEK 12, DAY 3

"IT IS THE LORD WHO GOES BEFORE YOU. HE WILL BE WITH YOU; HE WILL NOT LEAVE YOU OR FORSAKE YOU. DO NOT FEAR OR BE DISMAYED."
- DEUTERONOMY 31:8

Have you ever had to take someone else's place? Perhaps you have an older sibling, and you have always felt like you've walked in his/her shadow. Maybe you were elected the next president of your class, or organization. Or maybe you made it onto the team you tried out so hard for, but there was a strong legacy you had to follow.

READ DEUTERONOMY 31:1-8. Moses had just accomplished a lot for Israel, and Joshua was chosen to take his place. Can you imagine the expectations that Israel had for Joshua? Everyone has felt the weight of heavy expectations, even expectations to follow in someone's footsteps. But God promises to Israel and to Joshua: Don't be afraid. I will give you what you need.

Now read Deuteronomy 34:1-9. Israel grieved Moses' death, but look again at verse 9. God gave Joshua wisdom, fulfilling God's promise to never leave him. The result was that Israel followed and respected Joshua. God followed through with His promise to take care of Joshua, miraculously protecting him and Israel.

SOMETHING TO THINK ABOUT...

· What are some of the fears that you woke up with today? What does this promise in Deuteronomy mean for you and your fears?
· How can this passage encourage you to remember that God keeps His promises and does whatever He can to protect you?

WEEK 12, DAY 4

"THIS BOOK OF THE LAW SHALL NOT DEPART FROM YOUR MOUTH, BUT YOU SHALL MEDITATE ON IT DAY AND NIGHT, SO THAT YOU MAY BE CAREFUL TO DO ACCORDING TO ALL THAT IS WRITTEN IN IT. FOR THEN YOU WILL MAKE YOUR WAY PROSPEROUS, AND THEN YOU WILL HAVE GOOD SUCCESS. HAVE I NOT COMMANDED YOU? BE STRONG AND COURAGEOUS. DO NOT BE FRIGHTENED, AND DO NOT BE DISMAYED, FOR THE LORD YOUR GOD IS WITH YOU WHEREVER YOU GO."
- JOSHUA 1:8-9

Have you ever seen a fire alarm and had the irresistible urge to pull it? There is something about a rule or warning that almost provokes you to "test" to see if it's really worth following. I mean, think about it: What happens if you go a little over the speed limit, really? If you walk on prohibited grass, what will really happen?

READ JOSHUA 1:1-9. Rules can be kind of scary. But we know that rules also come with a promise. When Joshua became the leader of Israel, God issued a promise as well as a command in verse 8. Follow God's laws at all times, and you will prosper.

This sounds like a really hard command to follow God's entire Law. But look at the language used in verse 1. God wants you to look at the laws as something that is on your heart and mind all the time. From there, your heart will be drawn to follow God's rules, motivated by love for Him.

This makes perfect sense: Rules are meant to protect you from harm, and show you a better path. Following God's law is the same way; it protects you from harm and provides you with the promise of protection. God goes out of His way to protect His people.

SOMETHING TO THINK ABOUT...
· What are some of God's commands that are hard to follow? What can you lose by avoiding that command? What can you gain?
· Why do you think it means for people to "meditate on the law day and night"? What are some ways that you can begin doing that?

WEEK 12, DAY 5

**"AND JOSHUA THE SON OF NUN SENT TWO MEN SE-
CRETLY FROM SHITTIM AS SPIES, SAYING, 'GO, VIEW
THE LAND, ESPECIALLY JERICHO.' AND THEY WENT
AND CAME INTO THE HOUSE OF A PROSTITUTE WHOSE
NAME WAS RAHAB AND LODGED THERE." - JOSHUA 2:1**

God has a habit of choosing misfits to lead His people. Moses had some sort of a speech impediment-perhaps a lisp-but God chose him to lead the entire nation of Israel out of captivity. Wow!

Have you ever felt called to a task that seemed too big for you? **READ JOSHUA CHAPTER 2.**

Rahab was a prostitute, which was just as controversial then as it is today! God entrusted an entire mission to Rahab's hands, even though Joshua's people typically saw her as an outcast. Picture it: Rahab knows how people feel about her. When she was asked to be a part of the mission, she was probably shaking in her boots. Not only did Joshua put trust in Rahab, but Rahab had to also have an enormous amount of trust that she could be used in a positive way.

Sometimes we don't realize our potential to be used by God. At times, we can feel different from everyone else, like our differences make us so sepa-rate that God can't use us. Today, remind yourself that it doesn't matter what sets you apart: God can use anybody. Whether you have a lisp like Moses that you can't change, or have a history of mistakes in your life like Rahab that you don't know how to change: God can use you.

SOMETHING TO THINK ABOUT...
· What can you tell yourself when you're feeling different, to remind yourself that you are loved by God?
·How could this fact change the way that you treat others?

**THIS DEVOTION SPEAKS TO GOD'S GREAT LOVE. GO TO
PAGE 4 FOR A DESCRIPTION OF THIS ATTRIBUTE.**

WEEK 13

WEEK 13, DAY 1

"AND THE ANGEL SAID TO THEM, 'FEAR NOT, FOR BEHOLD, I BRING YOU GOOD NEWS OF GREAT JOY THAT WILL BE FOR ALL THE PEOPLE. FOR UNTO YOU IS BORN THIS DAY IN THE CITY OF DAVID A SAVIOR, WHO IS CHRIST THE LORD.'" - LUKE 2:10-11

This week you'll continue the story of the Israelites. You'll see them finally enter into the Promised Land. And then you'll continue the story by seeing a little glimpse of life once they've settled in. You may ask yourself, what does this have to do with the angels announcing Jesus' birth? Plenty.

Entering into the Promised Land was one of several essential steps in the timeline of God's plan to rescue humankind from sin. You'll discover over the course of the next few months in this book that there is a sort of thread running from Jesus' birth all the way back to the Israelites inheriting the land God promised them.

When the Israelites entered into the Promised Land, there was much fanfare and pronouncements. It was a time to celebrate their deliverance. When Jesus came, there was also an announcement made (by pretty special messengers). But the deliverance Jesus would bring was far superior to any land. Jesus' deliverance was from sin. It was perfect. It was for all people. And it was once-and-for-all. Reflect on this verse this week. Consider memorizing it if you choose. It's a powerful reminder of the amazing gift of grace Jesus was to all humankind.

WEEK 13, DAY 2

**"THEN JOSHUA SAID TO THE PEOPLE, 'CONSE-
CRATE YOURSELVES, FOR TOMORROW THE LORD
WILL DO WONDERS AMONG YOU.'"
- JOSHUA 3:5**

"Holy, holy, holy. Lord God almighty." Have you ever sang this song in church before? Chances are you probably sing a lot of songs that talk about God being holy. You've probably also heard that just as God is holy, we are to be holy too. (Jesus says this in the New Testament. Peter echoes the sentiment in his first letter.) What does it mean to be holy? Holy means to be set apart, especially in a religious, or sacred way. Another word for holy is "consecrated."

READ JOSHUA 3, AND FOCUS ON IN VERSE 5. Joshua told his people that if they were set apart, then God would do amazing things in and through them. What a cool promise!

It's scary being "set apart" though, especially as a teenager. The last thing anyone wants to do is look different than everyone else. After all, God doesn't want us to ever feel alone, right? He created us for one another. So how can you be set apart? How can you be holy? Holiness is all about following Jesus. For example, when the rest of the world seeks revenge, being holy is following Christ's example to forgive one another. When the students at your school gossip or bully one another, being holy is to stand up for people. Holiness means that you are set apart for God's purposes of grace and justice in the world.

SOMETHING TO THINK ABOUT...
· What are some ways that you can be holy at school? At home? On your sports team or club?
· How can God set you apart to do amazing things through your life? How will being holy impact your life and the world around you?

**THIS DEVOTION SPEAKS TO GOD'S HOLINESS. GO TO
PAGE 4 FOR A DESCRIPTION OF THIS ATTRIBUTE.**

WEEK 13, DAY 3

"AND AT THE SEVENTH TIME, WHEN THE PRIESTS HAD BLOWN THE TRUMPETS, JOSHUA SAID TO THE PEOPLE, 'SHOUT, FOR THE LORD HAS GIVEN YOU THE CITY.'" - JOSHUA 6:16

One of the best board games ever is Quelf. Have you ever played it? In Quelf, when you land on a space, you choose a card. The cards have various activities on them: act something funny out, make something out of dough, answer a trivia question, draw something, or come up with a funny rule.

It sounds simple. But the things Quelf has you come up with are hilarious and random. You may end up with a beard made out of toilet paper, writing a haiku about cat whiskers, or doing an interpretive dance about nachos.

Sometimes God's instructions to His people sound super weird. Read Joshua 6 and check it out for yourself. God's answer to Joshua's problem with Jericho was to march around the city and to sound a trumpet. Almost sounds like a funny game card from Quelf, right?

The people inside Jericho were probably laughing at first. But God pulled through and used the situation to spread Israel's fame across the land, making God's name great. It may have seemed silly at first, but the win in the end was worth it.

SOMETHING TO THINK ABOUT...
· Are there any things that God asks us to do that may seem odd to us at first? How could those things help spread God's name?
· What are some very practical ways that you can use your influence to make God famous?

WEEK 13, DAY 4

"AND JOSHUA THE SON OF NUN, THE SERVANT OF THE
LORD, DIED AT THE AGE OF 110 YEARS. AND THEY BURIED
HIM WITHIN THE BOUNDARIES OF HIS INHERITANCE IN
TIMNATH-HERES, IN THE HILL COUNTRY OF EPHRAIM,
NORTH OF THE MOUNTAIN OF GAASH. AND ALL THAT
GENERATION ALSO WERE GATHERED TO THEIR FATHERS.
AND THERE AROSE ANOTHER GENERATION AFTER THEM
WHO DID NOT KNOW THE LORD OR THE WORK THAT HE
HAD DONE FOR ISRAEL." - JUDGES 2:8-10

If your high school team has a senior athlete who is the leader of the team, not long after the final game of the season people will start talking about how he or she will be missed. Some may even say that the team will just not be as good with the graduation of the great player. It is true that some outstanding players who are great leaders can actually "carry" their team, and help them achieve way above what was expected.

READ JUDGES 2:6-19. Joshua was a great leader for the armies of the Hebrew people. He was a great strategist; one of his basic war strategies, divide and conquer, has been used by military leaders throughout history. When he died, it did not take long for God's people to revert to not trusting God. They seemed to put too much faith in the earthly leader, Joshua, and not enough faith in their heavenly leader, God.

Are you relying on the strength of someone in your church or youth group to give you the courage to live for God each day? What will happen when that leader graduates or moves away?

SOMETHING TO THINK ABOUT . . .

· It is wonderful to have strong leaders around you, but God wants you to learn from these leaders, not depend on them. Your spiritual strength comes from your relationship with God. Have you ever thought that God might be calling you to be a leader in your youth group, in your church, or at your school?

WEEK 13, DAY 5

"AND SHE SAID, 'OH, MY LORD! AS YOU LIVE, MY LORD, I AM THE
WOMAN WHO WAS STANDING HERE IN YOUR PRESENCE, PRAYING
TO THE LORD. FOR THIS CHILD I PRAYED, AND THE LORD HAS
GRANTED ME MY PETITION THAT I MADE TO HIM. THEREFORE I
HAVE LENT HIM TO THE LORD. AS LONG AS HE LIVES, HE IS LENT
TO THE LORD.' AND HE WORSHIPED THE LORD THERE."
- 1 SAMUEL 1:26-28

The word sacrifice should be one you are familiar with. It means to give up something for the sake of something greater. You sacrifice time to be a better student, in order to get a scholarship, so that you can go to a good college. You sacrifice temporary pain to train your body, in order to be a better athlete, so that you can improve your team. You sacrifice endless hours of practice, in order to be a better actor or singer, so that you can make your school play a success.

READ 1 SAMUEL 1. Hannah prayed for a child, and when she was finally able to conceive, she gave her son, Samuel, back to the Lord in service. Her sacrifice took the form of presenting him to the temple priest Eli, when Samuel was around 9 or 10-years-old, to be totally used for the work of God. Hannah actually gave her son to Eli! Can you think of another example of this kind of sacrifice in the Bible?

This journal is called *Tracing The Thread*. The idea is to help you see how the entire Bible all fits together in one beautiful picture of God's plan of redemption. So to answer the question, just as Hannah gave her son to the temple for the work of bringing people to God, the Lord gave His Son Jesus to redeem humankind. The sacrifice of Jesus was for something greater, and made out of God's great love for us. Jesus was sacrificed in order that all people could have a personal relationship with God.

Take a few minutes to thank God for sacrificing His Son, Jesus, for your salvation.

**THIS DEVOTION SPEAKS TO GOD'S GREAT LOVE. GO TO
PAGE 4 FOR A DESCRIPTION OF THIS ATTRIBUTE.**

WEEK 14

WEEK 14, DAY 1

"HOW THEN WILL THEY CALL ON HIM IN WHOM THEY HAVE
NOT BELIEVED? AND HOW ARE THEY TO BELIEVE IN HIM OF
WHOM THEY HAVE NEVER HEARD? AND HOW ARE THEY TO
HEAR WITHOUT SOMEONE PREACHING? AND HOW ARE THEY
TO PREACH UNLESS THEY ARE SENT? AS IT IS WRITTEN,
'HOW BEAUTIFUL ARE THE FEET OF THOSE WHO PREACH THE
GOOD NEWS!'" - ROMANS 10:14-15

The history of God's people is sometimes hard to watch. Over and
over again, they blow it. Big time. (Now before we judge them, if we
were in their shoes, you can bet we'd have a similar track record.)
You'll see a little bit of that this week, and definitely more as you
move on. But in spite of their crummy track record, God managed to
work through His people.

See, God wanted to be the only king His people needed. They were
a nation after Him. They were supposed to be a nation that, by its
very identity, led others to know and fear the Lord. But they weren't
satisfied with God's plan. They wanted a king like other nations. And
God relented and gave them what they wanted. And while God still
used the Israelites to make a name for Himself, it wasn't the same.

The Israelites were supposed to be a testimony to God and His character, and draw people to Him. It didn't work out perfectly. And so
God in His wisdom knew that there would need to be a better way.
God sent Jesus to be that way. And just like you see in this week's
memory verse, God's Word is the way people find out about Jesus.
God's Word is like the more perfect version of the Israelites. It draws
people to God. Memorize these verses this week. They represent one
of the best summaries of evangelism you'll find anywhere.

**THIS DEVOTION SPEAKS TO GOD'S SOVEREIGNTY. GO TO
PAGE 4 FOR A DESCRIPTION OF THIS ATTRIBUTE.**

WEEK 14, DAY 2

"AND THE LORD CALLED SAMUEL AGAIN THE THIRD TIME. AND HE AROSE AND WENT TO ELI AND SAID, 'HERE I AM, FOR YOU CALLED ME.' THEN ELI PERCEIVED THAT THE LORD WAS CALLING THE BOY. THEREFORE ELI SAID TO SAMUEL, 'GO, LIE DOWN, AND IF HE CALLS YOU, YOU SHALL SAY, 'SPEAK, LORD, FOR YOUR SERVANT HEARS.'' SO SAMUEL WENT AND LAY DOWN IN HIS PLACE." - 1 SAMUEL 3:8-9

Some years ago a cell phone company had a very famous advertising campaign built around the phrase, "Can You Hear Me Now." The sales pitch was that their company had better signal coverage, and you never had to worry about not being able to hear or understand what the person on the other end of the line was trying to say.

READ 1 SAMUEL 3. Young Samuel's problem was not that he could not hear a voice calling out to him; he just wasn't sure whom the voice belonged to. Twice he went to Eli thinking he had called him, but both times Eli told him to go back to bed. Eli soon realized Samuel was hearing the voice of God. He told the young boy to say, "Speak, Lord, for your servant hears." Three quick thoughts:

· The voice of the Lord is always distinctive, speaking in peace and in perfect alignment with the Bible.

· Samuel made a declaration, "You are the Lord, I am your servant."

· To be able to hear God we must be listening for Him.

In your prayer time today, declare to the Lord that you are His servant, spend time listening instead of always doing the talking, and learn to distinguish clearly the voice of God.

"BUT THE PEOPLE REFUSED TO OBEY THE VOICE OF SAMUEL. AND THEY SAID, 'NO! BUT THERE SHALL BE A KING OVER US, THAT WE ALSO MAY BE LIKE ALL THE NATIONS, AND THAT OUR KING MAY JUDGE US AND GO OUT BEFORE US AND FIGHT OUR BATTLES.' AND WHEN SAMUEL HAD HEARD ALL THE WORDS OF THE PEOPLE, HE REPEATED THEM IN THE EARS OF THE LORD. AND THE LORD SAID TO SAMUEL, 'OBEY THEIR VOICE AND MAKE THEM A KING.' SAMUEL THEN SAID TO THE MEN OF ISRAEL, 'GO EVERY MAN TO HIS CITY.'"
- 1 SAMUEL 8:19-22

READ 1 SAMUEL 8. Once the Israelites inhabited the Promised Land, they decided they wanted to have a king just like every of other nation. God had led them out of slavery in Egypt, provided their every need while wondering in the wilderness, and given them great military leaders to win victory as they marched to their future homeland. After all God had done for them, they decided they wanted to be ruled by a king.

God's people made an interesting decision. They decided they wanted to be just like everyone else. They wanted a man to fight for them instead of God. And God finally told Samuel to let the people have what they wanted. In many ways the people in Samuel's day, some 3,000 years ago, were much like we are today. Their selfish thinking always led to bad results. As you pray today, ask God to lead your life and put His way of thinking and living ahead of yours. You will never go wrong by letting God be in control of your life.

SOMETHING TO THINK ABOUT . . .

· How often have you stumbled in your Christian life because you wanted to be like others instead of who God uniquely created you to be?
· How often have you trusted in the opinions of people to help you through the tough times of life instead of first praying and seeking God's direction?
· Can you think of a time when things turned out just the way you wanted them to, and the result was a disaster because it was contrary to God's plan? What did that teach you?

WEEK 14, DAY 4

"AND HE SAID TO THE PEOPLE OF ISRAEL, 'THUS SAYS THE LORD,
THE GOD OF ISRAEL, 'I BROUGHT UP ISRAEL OUT OF EGYPT,
AND I DELIVERED YOU FROM THE HAND OF THE EGYPTIANS AND
FROM THE HAND OF ALL THE KINGDOMS THAT WERE OPPRESSING
YOU.'' BUT TODAY YOU HAVE REJECTED YOUR GOD, WHO SAVES
YOU FROM ALL YOUR CALAMITIES AND YOUR DISTRESSES, AND
YOU HAVE SAID TO HIM, 'SET A KING OVER US.' NOW THEREFORE
PRESENT YOURSELVES BEFORE THE LORD BY YOUR TRIBES AND
BY YOUR THOUSANDS." - 1 SAMUEL 10:18-19

It's probably already happened to you a few times in your life. You had a good friend you took places with you, and maybe even bought a gift for at Christmas or on a birthday. Maybe you helped the person out through a bad time in life. Then one day, this friend rejects you and no longer wants to be a friend. You're bummed out, and your thoughts are like, "And after all I did for them!"

READ 1 SAMUEL 10:17-27 AND 1 SAMUEL 11:12-15. Maybe this is what was rolling through the mind of God when the Israelites demanded a king to lead them. (Probably not, but we would understand if it was.) After everything God had done for them, with the parting of the Red Sea and victories in the Promised Land, the Hebrew people more or less rejected God in favor of choosing to follow the lead of an ordinary man.

Do you know what God's ultimate response was to the people and their decision? God chose to keep on loving them! And that should be your response when people reject you. Tough? Yes! But then being a Christian is sometimes a tough thing to do.

SOMETHING TO THINK ABOUT . . .
· Pray today for those people who have rejected you, or treated you badly, and ask God to help your response to be one of love.

**THIS DEVOTION SPEAKS TO GOD'S GREAT LOVE. GO TO
PAGE 4 FOR A DESCRIPTION OF THIS ATTRIBUTE.**

> "BUT THE LORD SAID TO SAMUEL, 'DO NOT LOOK
> ON HIS APPEARANCE OR ON THE HEIGHT OF HIS
> STATURE, BECAUSE I HAVE REJECTED HIM. FOR THE
> LORD SEES NOT AS MAN SEES: MAN LOOKS ON THE
> OUTWARD APPEARANCE, BUT THE LORD LOOKS ON
> THE HEART.'" - 1 SAMUEL 16:7

If you were going to customize a quarterback for your favorite video game, how would you make him look? Tall and fast with a strong and accurate arm? Or short and slow with average arm? What if you were in charge of picking out a lead actor for an upcoming action movie? Would they be handsome and in great shape? Or the average looking with a bit of a gut? Now, what if you were picking a king? What would he look like?

TAKE A SECOND AND READ 1 SAMUEL 15:10-11. Then read 1 Samuel 16:1-13. Samuel was confident that Eliab was going to be God's choice. He just knew it. But God reminded him that while people look at the outward appearance, God looks at the heart. Eliab and all of Jesse's other sons might have been taller and more handsome than David, but those weren't things God was looking for. God was going to use someone that had a heart that would follow Him. That's what was important to Him.

We're no different than Samuel. We all have preconceived notions about what type of person would fit into certain roles. We quickly look at people and size them up by their appearance. If they don't measure up to a certain standard, we write them off in no time. Maybe you should read 1 Samuel 16:7 again.

SOMETHING TO THINK ABOUT . . .
· Why is it so easy for us to focus on people's appearance first?
· How do we begin to look past appearances and look at the heart?

WEEK 15

WEEK 15, DAY 1

"AND THEY SANG A NEW SONG, SAYING, 'WORTHY ARE YOU TO TAKE THE SCROLL AND TO OPEN ITS SEALS, FOR YOU WERE SLAIN, AND BY YOUR BLOOD YOU RANSOMED PEOPLE FOR GOD FROM EVERY TRIBE AND LANGUAGE AND PEOPLE AND NATION, AND YOU HAVE MADE THEM A KINGDOM AND PRIESTS TO OUR GOD, AND THEY SHALL REIGN ON THE EARTH.'"
- REVELATION 5:9-10

This week you'll be learning about David and a little bit about his rule as the king of Israel. As you'll see, while David did lots of awesome things, he made some pretty awful mistakes, as well. Even David, who would later be called a man after God's own heart, wasn't free from sin. And though he was arguably the best leader the Israelites ever had, he fell short of being the godly model they needed.

As we think about David's life, it's hard not to think about Jesus. Jesus Himself identified strongly with David and his kingship. But Jesus is the perfect "David," uniquely capable of redeeming humankind from their sins. David was a king. Jesus is THE King. David couldn't lead his people in godliness. Jesus died so His people could be godly. There is a great difference in the two.

This week's memory verses come from John's heavenly visions as written down in Revelation. Here, we see Jesus being praised for who He is and for what He accomplishes. Why don't you take the time to praise Jesus for who He is? And while you're at it, memorize these verses so you can continue to praise Him all day long.

WEEK 15, DAY 2

"THE PHILISTINE SAID TO DAVID, 'COME TO ME, AND I WILL GIVE YOUR FLESH TO THE BIRDS OF THE AIR AND TO THE BEASTS OF THE FIELD.'" - 1 SAMUEL 17:44

We all love a great underdog story. We want to see upsets during March Madness, right? J.K. Rowling, the author of the Harry Potter series, was an unemployed single mom when she started writing. Now she's one of the most successful writers in recent memory. We all love hearing stories like that.

TAKE SOME TIME AND READ 1 SAMUEL 17. Goliath was a bad, bad dude. No one wanted to mess with him. In fact, everyone was scared to death of him. He didn't scare David, though. David was sent to take his brothers some food, but while he was there, he heard what Goliath had to say. David didn't flinch. He immediately said that he was up for the challenge. His reasoning? He says in verse 37, "The Lord who delivered me from the paw of the lion and from the paw of the bear will deliver me from the hand of this Philistine."

Most of the time, we look at obstacles in our path and analyze them like almost everyone in this story did. If something looks like it's going to be too difficult to deal with, we avoid it. If something looks like it's going to be a challenge, we come up with all sorts of excuses to not face it head-on. But David recognized that how things look on the outside isn't the real issue. The issue with the things we face in life is whether or not we trust in the Lord and are obedient to what He calls us to do. If He's for something, can we really come up with a legitimate reason to avoid it?

SOMETHING TO THINK ABOUT . . .
· What are your biggest fears in life?
· Do you trust the fact that God is bigger and more powerful than your fears?
· How can you begin to move forward in faith instead of being crippled by fear?

WEEK 15, DAY 3

"AT HEBRON HE REIGNED OVER JUDAH SEVEN YEARS AND SIX MONTHS, AND AT JERUSALEM HE REIGNED OVER ALL ISRAEL AND JUDAH THIRTY-THREE YEARS."
- 2 SAMUEL 5:5

Have you ever had to be around people that loved to talk about how awesome they are? Now, have you ever been around someone that is truly humble? Maybe they really are awesome, but they don't flaunt it or talk about it. It's kinda refreshing, isn't it?

TAKE SOME TIME AND READ 2 SAMUEL 5:1-5 AND THEN 2 SAMUEL 7:18-29. At the age of thirty, David began to reign. By the time he was thirty-seven, he reigned over all of Israel and Judah. That's a pretty big deal. Then we come to the end of chapter 7 and we see his humility before the Lord. He essentially asks, "Why have you brought someone like me to this point?" Rather than having a cocky arrogance about him, David recognizes God's greatness and power, and understands his place in relation to the creator and sustainer of the universe.

Out of all the people that could claim some level of awesomeness, David was one of them. He began his rule early in life and experienced a ton of success. But it wasn't his practice to go around talking about how great he was. Why? Because he knew that he really wasn't that awesome. He knew that his success was a result of God's goodness and graciousness in his life. See, David didn't just not talk about himself. He talked about God. He pointed to the Lord and talked about His greatness. True humility isn't just the absence of being arrogant or prideful. It's also recognizing the source of our blessings and all the goodness in our lives.

SOMETHING TO THINK ABOUT . . .
· When good things come your way, is your first reaction to pat yourself on the back or recognize the Lord's goodness in your life?
· What is the best way to combat the sin of pride and arrogance in our hearts?

WEEK 15, DAY 4

"BUT THE THING THAT DAVID HAD DONE DISPLEASED THE LORD." - 2 SAMUEL 11:27

Have you ever felt shame for something you did? Has it ever made you wonder what God thinks about you? Has it ever made you doubt His love for you, or caused you to wonder if He would ever want to use someone like you for His purposes?

TAKE SOME TIME AND READ 2 SAMUEL 11. Oh man! David really messed up here, didn't he? Let's look at how this whole thing went down. First, David noticed Bathsheba, a married woman, bathing on her roof. No harm at this point. All he needed to do was just turn around and go about his business. Instead, David sent his messengers to bring her back to him. David and Bathsheba had sex and she got pregnant. So, this isn't good. David had sinned and made a huge mistake. But he didn't stop there. He decided to bring Bathsheba's husband, Uriah, back from battle in the hopes that they would have sex. This way Uriah would think the baby was his. Uriah refused and said he needed be back with his men in battle. So, David had him sent to the front of the lines of battle, and ordered the commander to draw back from him so he would get killed. Wow!

That's some pretty bad stuff right there, right? I mean, we're talking about adultery and murder. Take a second and read Acts 13:22. God called David "a man after my heart." He used him mightily. So, when we're tempted to feel like God can't use someone as messed up as us, let's all try and remember this story. If God can use David, He can use anyone.

SOMETHING TO THINK ABOUT . . .
· Where do guilt and shame come from?
· Why should guilt and shame be something that Christ-followers are free from?
· What are some things you can do to overcome guilt and shame when the crop up in your life?

THIS DEVOTION SPEAKS TO GOD'S FORGIVENESS. GO TO PAGE 4 FOR A DESCRIPTION OF THIS ATTRIBUTE.

WEEK 15, DAY 5

**"DAVID SAID TO NATHAN,
'I HAVE SINNED AGAINST THE LORD.'"**
- 2 SAMUEL 12:13

Do you have a friend or relative that always complains about things other people do when they do the exact same thing? Doesn't it drive you nuts?

TAKE A FEW MINUTES AND READ 2 SAMUEL 12:1-25. So, Nathan comes to David and breaks down a situation for him. There was a rich man and a poor man. All the poor man owned was a little lamb, and the rich man took it to serve to one of his guests. The rich man had more lambs than he knew what to do with, and he took the poor man's lamb. Boy, David was steaming mad. He went as far as to say that the rich man needed to die. And then Nathan had his chance to call out David's sin. He said to him, "You are the man!" David was the rich man in the story. He had taken Bathsheba, who wasn't his, and then ended up having her husband killed. David could have anything he wanted, and he chose to take from Uriah. He was no different than the rich man in the story. In fact, he was probably worse!

When we thought about that friend or family member that's always complaining about others, but doing the same things himself, we realized how foolish it sounded. But the truth is, we're all the same. We see other people's sin, but we don't acknowledge our own. Or, if we do acknowledge our own sin, we don't think it's nearly as bad as others. We love to maximize other's mistakes and minimize our own. What we really need to focus on is our own sin, and how amazing it is that Jesus chooses to love us, the worst of sinners.

SOMETHING TO THINK ABOUT . . .
· Why do we love to focus on other people's sin?
· Why is it so easy for us to identify sins we don't struggle with as "big sins" but minimize the sins we deal with?
· How can we begin to truly recognize the depths of our own sin as well as the lavish grace of Christ? Why is it necessary for us to truly grasp both?

WEEK 16

WEEK 16, DAY 1

**"I AM THE GOOD SHEPHERD. I KNOW MY OWN
AND MY OWN KNOW ME, JUST AS THE FATHER
KNOWS ME AND I KNOW THE FATHER; AND I LAY
DOWN MY LIFE FOR THE SHEEP."**
- JOHN 10:14-15

The Book of Psalms is one of the true treasures of the Christian faith. The individual psalms capture so many different emotions, and ways of interacting with God. They provide us with beautiful words to use in prayer, in praise, and even when we are questioning God's plan for our lives.

You may know this already, but David wrote most of the psalms. Before he was King of Israel, David was a shepherd. You can almost imagine him sitting alone on a Judean hillside, looking up at the stars, and composing some of these beautiful words of praise to God.

Jesus is the King of Kings, and used a really meaningful metaphor to show how much He loves and cares for us. In John 10, Jesus refers to Himself as the "good shepherd." Like a shepherd who cares for his sheep, Jesus tends to us. He knows us and cares for us. These verses are a tender expression of Jesus' desire to lovingly look after us, His sheep. We even see Jesus referencing making the ultimate sacrifice so that we can experience a life free from the penalty of sin.

Take time to focus this week on John 10:14-15. Write it on a notecard and put it where you will see it when you're getting ready in the morning. Make it the screen saver for your phone. Let the truth of these verses sink in: Jesus knows you. He cares for you. He died so that you may live.

**THIS DEVOTION SPEAKS TO GOD'S COMPASSION.
GO TO PAGE 4 FOR A DESCRIPTION OF THIS ATTRIBUTE.**

WEEK 16, DAY 2

**"FOR THE LORD KNOWS THE WAY OF THE RIGHTEOUS,
BUT THE WAY OF THE WICKED WILL PERISH."
- PSALM 1:6**

Have you ever heard someone say that they are "blessed"? That word gets thrown around a lot. From "God bless America," to "God bless you" when you sneeze, it seems that the word has a very ambiguous meaning. As you read today's passage, carefully consider how Scripture defines someone who is blessed.

READ PSALM 1. This is the beginning of the psalms. This collection of praises shows how, despite our human suffering and troubles, God is to be praised for who He is above all else. While much of the book reveals the nature of God, some, like this one, help us understand our relationship with Him.

This passage opens with 'blessed is the man who', and then gives a nice comparison/contrast to show what it looks like to be blessed by God. It begins by categorizing what a blessed man does NOT do. The first verse here makes it clear that there is no room for God's people to endure advice, influence, or judgment from those who do not love God. Instead, we are to love His law, and make it the priority of our hearts!

Written to people who lived in the desert, the image of the tree planted by a stream in verse 3 makes perfect sense. To be blessed by God is to be placed in connection with Him, drawing our life from His. Throughout Scripture, we see that God's blessing is this: to be rooted in Him and be grafted into His family.

SOMETHING TO THINK ABOUT . . .
· God knows everything. So, what do you think it means to say that the Lord knows the way of the righteous?
· In what ways are you known by God?
· Thank God today for knowing you, and allowing you the blessing of knowing Him through His word!

WEEK 16, DAY 3

"THE LORD IS MY SHEPHERD; I SHALL NOT WANT."
- PSALM 23:1

Can you imagine what it would be like to "not want"? Take a moment and think about the things you want right now. In today's psalm, the author says he does not want. As you read, think about what it would take for you to be able to be that content.

READ PSALM 23. David was very familiar with the role of a shepherd. This imagery was second nature to David, as he grew up tending sheep. The job of a shepherd may not seem like a big deal, but without a shepherd, sheep will surely die. Not only are sheep defenseless against predators, but it is said that they can get so focused on the grass under their noses that they will walk right off a cliff! This is why a shepherd carries a staff. He uses this staff to prod the sheep in the direction they need to go to stay alive. David moves from describing provisions for sheep (green pastures and still water) to those fit for a king (banquets and oils). He ends the psalm by conveying that he could need nothing more than the mercy of God, which allows David to dwell with Him forever.

Think about how this imagery applies to God and us. Are we not ultimately defenseless against evil? Do we not get so focused on what we want that we walk right into danger? God, through His word and His sovereign control of circumstances, prods us back toward the path that leads to life.

When we realize that our greatest need is to be saved from evil, everything else comes into perspective. Because God provided Christ as our substitution, allowing us to dwell with Him forever, we can truly say that we no longer want for anything!

SOMETHING TO THINK ABOUT . . .
· How might your current "wants" be distracting you from being content in Christ?
· How might reevaluating your priorities help you to be more content with God as your shepherd?

WEEK 16, DAY 4

**"RESTORE TO ME THE JOY OF YOUR SALVATION, AND
UPHOLD ME WITH A WILLING SPIRIT."
- PSALM 51:12**

Have you ever gotten lost? When you are little, the solution is always the same. STAY WHERE YOU ARE and call someone to find you. This is because we often make matters worse when we take them into our own hands. That is certainly what David did in his sin. That is, until he realized that his only choice was to stop and cry for God to meet him where he was.

READ PSALM 51. This psalm reveals one of the most beautiful pictures of the Gospel found in Scripture. After being chosen by God and becoming king, David made some pretty big mistakes. When the prophet Nathan confronts him about his actions regarding Bathsheba, David's eyes are open to the seriousness of his sin.

Notice that David doesn't just confess His sin to God and ask for forgiveness. In verse 3-5, he makes it clear that he knows he is deserving of God's judgment. But in verses 6-12, we see the Gospel unfold. David proclaims with certainty that God not only uses our sin to teach us, but that He has the power to remove it from us completely. God sees our sin. Yet when we confess our failures to Him, He removes that sin. That is the joy of our salvation!

Our joy is in remembering what God has taken from us, and sharing His mercy with others. There is no ritual or secret trick to receiving God's salvation, just a sincere heart that genuinely turns to God as its only hope! Just like a lost child, when we find ourselves in sin, we must cry out to our Heavenly Father, and rejoice that only He can make us clean.

SOMETHING TO THINK ABOUT . . .

· Can you think of any areas of your life where you need to cry out to God and confess sin?
· When was the last time you rejoiced in your salvation? What are you waiting for?

WEEK 16, DAY 5

"I WILL SAY TO THE LORD, 'MY REFUGE AND MY FORTRESS, MY GOD, IN WHOM I TRUST.'" - PSALM 91:2

Everybody loves a hero. Think of your favorite hero moment in a movie or book. It's always the same. When there is no other hope, and all seems lost, the hero rises up and shows what they are truly made of. We live for those moments in a fantasy world, but sometimes miss it in real life. Why is that? Believers are called to live bold, courageous lives, and yet so many of us just play it safe. The author of today's psalm had clearly taken risks for God, and in those moments, saw Him as the Ultimate Hero.

READ PSALM 91, and pay attention to the dangers that the author seems to have faced. In this passage, we see that the author of this psalm has clearly seen some troubles. More importantly, in each dangerous instance, the Lord has shown up and provided deliverance. While we do not know for certain the identity of this author, it is clear that there is reference to the Exodus and the Passover. God defined Himself as Israel's refuge and deliverance in those days, and His people trusted His consistency.

The psalmist continues to describe every manner of danger known to him. While the dangers all seem very severe, there is no hint of uncertainty. Throughout this passage, God is presented as a shelter, refuge, fortress, shield, and perhaps most significant, a dwelling place. It is clear that God does not just swoop in and save the day, but that He offers a constant sanctuary for the believer.

When you live boldly for Christ, there will be trouble. But just as the psalmist describes, you will know God as your refuge when the need arises.

SOMETHING TO THINK ABOUT . . .
· Have you ever sought God as your sanctuary or refuge? What was it like?
· How does trusting God as your refuge help you to be bold for him?

THIS DEVOTION SPEAKS TO GOD'S POWER. GO TO PAGE 4 FOR A DESCRIPTION OF THIS ATTRIBUTE.

WEEK 17

WEEK 17, DAY 1

"HAVE THIS MIND AMONG YOURSELVES, WHICH IS YOURS IN CHRIST JESUS, WHO, THOUGH HE WAS IN THE FORM OF GOD, DID NOT COUNT EQUALITY WITH GOD A THING TO BE GRASPED, BUT EMPTIED HIMSELF, BY TAKING THE FORM OF A SERVANT, BEING BORN IN THE LIKENESS OF MEN. AND BEING FOUND IN HUMAN FORM, HE HUMBLED HIMSELF BY BECOMING OBEDIENT TO THE POINT OF DEATH, EVEN DEATH ON A CROSS."
- PHILIPPIANS 2:5-8

David led Israel as it came into the dream of a powerful nation-state. This week, you'll watch the rule of Israel transition from David to Solomon. And you'll see that Solomon started things off on the right track, much as David had done.

The best leaders are servant leaders, leaders who don't use their influence to better themselves, but use their influence to better others. For most of their kingships, David and his son Solomon were these types of kings. They served Israel well. They led their people faithfully. But, as you know, David was not a perfect leader. And over the next two weeks, you'll learn the same about Solomon. But that's not true of the one, true King, Jesus.

Jesus, God's very son, left the royal comfort of Heaven to join His children on earth. Fully God and fully man, Jesus lived the life of a servant King, willingly going to the cross to purchase the life of His people. This is a big passage of verses to remember. But it's one of the most important descriptions of Jesus and His mission in the Bible. Do your best to memorize it this week. You'll be thankful that you did.

WEEK 17, DAY 2

**"I HAVE STORED UP YOUR WORD IN MY HEART, THAT
I MIGHT NOT SIN AGAINST YOU." - PSALM 119:11**

Have you ever almost gotten a high score on your favorite game? Or, do you know that feeling of being one point away from an A? Isn't it frustrating to be so close to your goal and miss it by a hair? The pursuit of holiness can often feel like this.

READ PSALM 119:1-16.

This psalm begins with a familiar concept in this book: the concept of being blessed. The first four verses describe how blessed it is to be blameless and do no wrong. If fact, it is pointed out that God commands His law to be kept diligently. But in verses 5-8, we see the psalmist's heart. It's as if you can hear him shouting, "Don't give up on me. I'm doing my best!"

Throughout Scripture we see that God requires perfect obedience, and yet we cannot deliver. But the passage takes a comforting turn from verse 9 on. There is hope! As we cling to God's Word, and seek Him with our whole heart, we can be kept from evil. Sure we will not be perfect; we will fail from time to time. But this pursuit of holiness is what God desires of His people. He does not desire for us to wallow in our failures, but to get up and try again.

The pursuit of perfection in life can drive you crazy if you're not careful. The difference in our spiritual life is that we cannot earn our reward; it has already been given to us through the grace of Jesus. Instead, we work toward holiness because we have a love for God that drives us to want to please Him.

SOMETHING TO THINK ABOUT . . .
· Is there an area of your life where you need to be "kept pure"?
· How might your love for God drive you to apply His word in that area?
· How would your life look different tomorrow if you fixed your eyes on His ways?

 **THIS DEVOTION SPEAKS TO GOD'S HOLINESS. GO TO
PAGE 4 FOR A DESCRIPTION OF THIS ATTRIBUTE.**

WEEK 17, DAY 3

"AS I SWORE TO YOU BY THE LORD, THE GOD OF ISRAEL, SAYING, 'SOLOMON YOUR SON SHALL REIGN AFTER ME, AND HE SHALL SIT ON MY THRONE IN MY PLACE,' EVEN SO WILL I DO THIS DAY." - 1 KINGS 1:30

It's not fun to admit it, but there are times that we mess up, and we mess up big. Remember David and Bathsheba? David was supposed to be leading his army in battle, but stayed home. Then he caught a glance of Bathsheba bathing. Try as he might, he couldn't get her out of his mind. So he slept with her. Then he tried to cover it up. And when that didn't work, he had Bathsheba's husband killed.

READ 1 KINGS 1:28-36. By now, David was old, and he had seen his family torn apart by his choices. Bathsheba wasn't the only time he messed up. David had shed many tears as he saw how the consequences of his sin affected his family and his kingdom.

It would have been easy for David to just throw in the towel after that. Isn't it easier once you get a reputation based on your sin to just live up to that reputation? But David didn't. He kept his promise to Bathsheba and to God.

When you mess up, and you mess up big, God doesn't want you to throw in the towel. He wants you to renew your relationship with Him and live differently the next time around.

SOMETHING TO THINK ABOUT...
· What is one way that you've done something wrong in a big way? What did it feel like when you realized how big the consequences were for your actions?
· When you rebel against God in some way, do you ever feel like it would just be easier to keep making those kinds of choices than changing? Why or why not?
· Think about a way that you've hurt someone recently, even if it was just a little thing. You can't change the past, but what can you do to change what you do in the future?

WEEK 17, DAY 4

"I AM ABOUT TO GO THE WAY OF ALL THE EARTH. BE STRONG, AND SHOW YOURSELF A MAN, AND KEEP THE CHARGE OF THE LORD YOUR GOD, WALKING IN HIS WAYS AND KEEPING HIS STATUTES, HIS COMMANDMENTS, HIS RULES, AND HIS TESTIMONIES, AS IT IS WRITTEN IN THE LAW OF MOSES, THAT YOU MAY PROSPER IN ALL THAT YOU DO AND WHEREVER YOU TURN." - 1 KINGS 2:2-3

Have you ever had a conversation with someone who is pretty old? Not just old like your parents, but old as in a grandpa or great grandma? People who are older talk about life much differently than you and your friends do. They don't usually care about the newest iPhone, or the latest Fast and Furious movie. They tell stories, and usually give advice. Part of the reason they do is they have a perspective on life you can only get by living a long time—and making a few mistakes along the way.

READ 1 KINGS 2:1-4. David is near the end of his life, and he's giving advice to his son, Solomon. His first piece of advice is to act like a man and be obedient to God. If you know much about David, you might think to yourself, "Yeah, David, maybe you should have taken some of your own advice along the way."

David isn't giving this advice because he lived it perfectly. He's giving it because he knows the consequences of not doing it. Sometimes, you're in a position to give advice not because you're perfect, but because you've made mistakes right? Good advice hasn't changed much since David. Following God is still the best way to live life, because it's the way God designed us to live.

SOMETHING TO THINK ABOUT...
· Whether you're in 6th grade or about to graduate from high school, what is a piece of advice you could give someone based on a mistake you've made?
· Think about being as old as David (or one of your grandparents). How do you want to describe the life you will have lived to your grandchildren?
· Have you ever thought about spending some time with a mentor older than you to learn more about life and following Jesus?

WEEK 17, DAY 5

"GIVE YOUR SERVANT THEREFORE AN UNDERSTANDING MIND TO GOVERN YOUR PEOPLE, THAT I MAY DISCERN BETWEEN GOOD AND EVIL, FOR WHO IS ABLE TO GOVERN THIS YOUR GREAT PEOPLE?" - 1 KINGS 3:9

Imagine that God came to you in a dream, and He promised to grant you one wish. What's the first thing that pops into your mind? (One rule: you can't ask for more wishes.)

READ 1 KINGS 3:4-15. It's easy to read this and assume that Solomon just wanted to be really smart. When you think about it, it's not a bad wish! But Solomon didn't want to be smart just so he could get through Algebra class with an "A." Pay attention to verses 7-9. Solomon asked for the one thing that would help him serve his people the best: wisdom.

God can do anything He wants, but chances are He won't be offering to fulfill any one wish you can think of. But God has given you a different kind of offer: He lets you decide what to do with what He's given you. You have opportunities every day to love, or to be unloving. God has given you abilities that you can use to serve just yourself, or to serve others. And while it may not feel like it at times, you get to choose what you do with your free time.

Solomon had a choice: to spend what God was giving him on himself, or on others. You have the same choice, and it's up to you to decide whether to spend what you're given on you, or on others.

SOMETHING TO THINK ABOUT...
· What is something that God has given you, whether it's a talent, opportunities, or maybe even financial resources?
· How can you spend what God has given you on others?

WEEK 18

"FOR ALL HAVE SINNED AND FALL SHORT OF THE GLORY
OF GOD, AND ARE JUSTIFIED BY HIS GRACE AS A GIFT,
THROUGH THE REDEMPTION THAT IS IN CHRIST JESUS." -
ROMANS 3:23-24

This is an interesting week. You'll be looking at the last days of Solomon's reign, and will be transitioning into a look at some of the proverbs. Proverbs is an awesome book believed to have been written by Solomon. It contains a ton of God-centered, relevant, ultra practical wisdom. Solomon was a pretty smart guy, after all.

Though Solomon was arguably the greatest ruler Israel ever had, Solomon's last days weren't so pretty. As you'll see he kind of blew it at the end. But that doesn't mean that his sinful actions negated the wisdom God gave him. The same can be said for our own lives.

We sin. We are all sinners. And yet, we're saved by the sacrifice Jesus graciously made on the cross. No matter what we do, or have done, Jesus offers us the chance to be redeemed from the penalty of our sins. His blood covers all sins, if we will only profess faith in Him, repenting from our former way of living. What an awesome message! This is an easy verse to memorize, but a powerful one. Take a stab at memorizing it this week.

WEEK 18, DAY 2

"AND SO I INTEND TO BUILD A HOUSE FOR THE NAME OF THE LORD MY GOD, AS THE LORD SAID TO DAVID MY FATHER, 'YOUR SON, WHOM I WILL SET ON YOUR THRONE IN YOUR PLACE, SHALL BUILD THE HOUSE FOR MY NAME.'" - 1 KINGS 5:5

Think about the last time you said (or thought) a desperate prayer to God. What was going on that you needed God's help with? It might have been something as simple as a test you had forgotten about. Or you may have asked God for help in your parents' marriage, or for a friend who was really ill.

But what about when things are going well? It's easy to keep our relationship with God on the backburner when things are well. We know how to ask God for help when we really need it. How do we follow Him when there's nothing much to ask Him for?

READ 1 KINGS 5:1-7. Pay attention to the situation that King Solomon finds himself in: There are no wars, and there are no disasters. Life is good. It would have been easy for Solomon to just go about his business. Instead, Solomon decided to do something to express his gratitude and devotion to God: He built a temple dedicated to worshiping God.

It's ironic, isn't it? We forget that it's God who gives us good gifts when we're enjoying them the most. It's a good thing to lean on God when life is tough. But part of following Jesus is also praising God when life is good.

SOMETHING TO THINK ABOUT...
· What are some things that are going well in your life right now?
· Make a list of 3-5 of those things and spend a few minutes with God thanking Him for the good things in life.

WEEK 18, DAY 3

"FOR WHEN SOLOMON WAS OLD HIS WIVES TURNED AWAY HIS HEART AFTER OTHER GODS, AND HIS HEART WAS NOT WHOLLY TRUE TO THE LORD HIS GOD, AS WAS THE HEART OF DAVID HIS FATHER."
- 1 KINGS 11:4

Think about a time or a place you felt really close to God. When that happens, we can feel like the thing we want most in the world is to continue that relationship with God, and do what He asks of us, right? Sometimes it happens at a retreat or camp. Sometimes it's during a mission trip or service project. Other times, it's simply during quiet times when we're reading the Bible. But what happens to that commitment when life gets in the way?

READ 1 KINGS 11:1-13. We read in yesterday's devotion that there was a time when Solomon was totally committed to following God. Fast-forward six chapters and many years later, and Solomon had lost that desire to follow God in everything he did. To build his nation, he made treaties with other countries. That doesn't sound like a big deal, but in Solomon's day, the way you did that was by marrying women from the countries you were making a treaty with. Those many wives brought with them commitment to false gods. By the end of his life, following God was barely a thought in Solomon's mind.

A relationship with Jesus isn't just about singing songs at camp, or feeling close to Him from time to time. It's about a simple dedication to Him, day after day. It's about following Him, even when you don't "feel" close to Him. It's not always easy, but it's definitely worth it.

SOMETHING TO THINK ABOUT...
· When or where do you feel closest to God? What are those experiences like for you?
· When are the times when you are more likely to do things your own way rather than pursuing a relationship with God?

WEEK 18, DAY 4

**"THE FEAR OF THE LORD IS THE BEGINNING OF KNOWLEDGE;
FOOLS DESPISE WISDOM AND INSTRUCTION." - PROVERBS 1:7**

If you ever enter military service and go through basic training, you will meet someone called the "DI," or the drill instructor. The DI will be tough and relentless, and ultimately his or her very presence invokes a sense of fear in the recruit. The DI has to be feared to teach the new soldiers, or Marines, not only what they need to learn, but how to respect those in authority. Many recruits actually develop a feeling of closeness and love for the DI over time.

READ PROVERBS 1:7. Solomon was the third great king of Israel, and the son of King David. He was the wisest man who ever lived, and his wisdom came from God. The book of Proverbs is a collection of his wise sayings. Solomon begins the book with the statement that fearing the Lord is the beginning of wisdom. The word fear means to respect and to respect out of love.

As a child of God, you are not to live your life being afraid of God, but rather you are to love and respect Him. When you see God in this light, and live your life worshipping and serving Him, King Solomon says this is the beginning point of real knowledge.

Meditate on this concept today during your prayer time.

SOMETHING TO THINK ABOUT . . .
· In your own words, how do you think that a loving, healthy respect for God empowers your knowledge and wisdom?

**THIS DEVOTION SPEAKS TO GOD'S RIGHTEOUSNESS. GO TO
PAGE 4 FOR A DESCRIPTION OF THIS ATTRIBUTE.**

WEEK 18, DAY 5

"TRUST IN THE LORD WITH ALL YOUR HEART, AND DO NOT LEAN ON YOUR OWN UNDERSTANDING. IN ALL YOUR WAYS ACKNOWLEDGE HIM, AND HE WILL MAKE STRAIGHT YOUR PATHS." - PROVERBS 3:5-6

Have you ever been part of a trust fall? That's when you fall backwards and trust someone to catch you before hitting the ground. It can be a frightening experience, especially if you have trust issues. But usually the experience actually does help in the ability to trust others.

READ PROVERBS 3:5-8. Yesterday you discovered that respect for God is the beginning of knowledge. Today's passage teaches that trust is the basic quality in a relationship with God. It's easy to believe that we have each situation in life completely figured out, but we must learn to trust God's understanding and not our own. Notice that if we always acknowledge the fact that God is the Lord of our lives, He will make straight our paths. In other words, He will remove obstacles that stand in the way of what He wants us to do.

In your prayer time today ask God to teach you to trust Him and to lean on Him. Thank Him that He will always remove the obstacles that stand in the way of His will for you.

SOMETHING TO THINK ABOUT...

· Describe a time when you felt like God was leading you to do something but there were obstacles in the way.
· Did you attempt to navigate the obstacles based on your own knowledge and understanding? Or did you trust God to remove them in His way and in His time? What was the result?

WEEK 19

WEEK 19, DAY 1

"I AM THE GOOD SHEPHERD. THE GOOD SHEPHERD LAYS DOWN HIS LIFE FOR THE SHEEP." - JOHN 10:11

This week, you'll be continuing with your look at the Proverbs. Remember, the proverbs are all about living a life of God-inspired wisdom. Many people say that knowledge is more about information, where wisdom is more about application. Wisdom is how your knowledge impacts your actions. This is interesting to keep in mind as you transition out of your look at Proverbs, and back into the timeline of the big-picture of the Bible.

Why is it interesting? Because Solomon was known for his wisdom, but his son quickly made a name for himself as someone who acted with no wisdom at all! The poor leadership of Solomon's son led to disaster for Israel. But, as we know now, there would come a day when the leader of Israel, and all of God's children, would be perfect in His wisdom and leadership.

John 10:11 paints the picture of a leader who goes to the greatest lengths to care for His people. Jesus, the King of Kings and Lord of Lords, leads us as one who has already made the greatest sacrifice. Jesus laid down His life so that we might enjoy freedom from the penalty of sin. Memorize this verse today. Hide it in your heart. Let it lead to wisdom, not just knowledge.

THIS DEVOTION SPEAKS TO GOD'S COMPASSION. GO TO PAGE 4 FOR A DESCRIPTION OF THIS ATTRIBUTE.

WEEK 19, DAY 2

**"THE WAY OF A FOOL IS RIGHT IN HIS OWN EYES,
BUT A WISE MAN LISTENS TO ADVICE."
- PROVERBS 12:15**

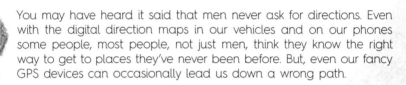

You may have heard it said that men never ask for directions. Even with the digital direction maps in our vehicles and on our phones some people, most people, not just men, think they know the right way to get to places they've never been before. But, even our fancy GPS devices can occasionally lead us down a wrong path.

READ PROVERBS 12:15. Here are some questions to help you ponder this verse:

- Can you think of a time when you thought you absolutely had a situation figured out and it turned out that you were wrong?
- Are there some people in your life you can trust to give you good advice or directions in life?
- What are some ways you can discover God's advice for various situations you may face?

In your prayer time today, ask God to help you become a moldable person who will listen to wise advice. Thank God for His ultimate wisdom and ask Him to help you see the world through the eyes of Christ.

WEEK 19, DAY 3

**"WHOEVER WALKS IN UPRIGHTNESS
FEARS THE LORD, BUT HE WHO IS
DEVIOUS IN HIS WAYS DESPISES HIM."
- PROVERBS 14:2**

Have you ever tried to bake something from a recipe? What components make up a recipe? On a recipe, you not only find the ingredients needed, but also the order that things are to be added. Some recipes can only turn out right if you use the exact amount of the ingredients and add them at just the right time. Good results comes from doing things in the right order.

READ PROVERBS 14:2. The devotions from Proverbs, this week and last, have been like a sort of spiritual recipe:

- Respect the Lord
- Trust the Lord and acknowledge Him in your ways
- Act on these spiritual truths and walk uprightly

When the Bible talks about walking uprightly, it's talking about an outward expression of what's going on in our lives spiritually. So loving God has to be expressed in the way we live and treat others. That's a pretty good recipe for impacting the world for the sake of Christ.

SOMETHING TO THINK ABOUT...
· Is your walk with God matching what you say you believe about God?
· What are your trouble areas?
· Pray today and ask the Lord to help you walk uprightly for Him each day.

WEEK 19, DAY 4

"THE EAR THAT LISTENS TO LIFE-GIVING REPROOF WILL DWELL AMONG THE WISE. WHOEVER IGNORES INSTRUCTION DESPISES HIMSELF, BUT HE WHO LISTENS TO REPROOF GAINS INTELLIGENCE." - PROVERBS 15:31-32

READ PROVERBS 15:30-33. Sometimes we have to look a little deep to glean the truth out of some of the proverbs of Solomon. In this passage, note the following:

- Life-giving reproofs are those words that would bring a person into a relationship with God.
- Those who ignore the life-giving reproof are people who have no regard for their soul or the eternal things of God.
- Listening to this instruction causes the person to gain the knowledge of God, which in turn, leads to a relationship with God.

For the New Testament believer the message is simple. Listening to the Gospel message with open ears leads to making a decision to follow Christ. Those who ignore the message are, in a way, committing spiritual suicide.

Have you ever shared the Gospel with people who simply ignore it? It can be a harsh truth to deal with. After all, you care enough about them to talk with them about Jesus and the difference He makes in our lives. Seeing them turn from God is a tough pill to swallow. But, don't let this discourage you. Pray for those friends who don't know Christ as their Savior, and pray that they will soon have "listening ears."

SOMETHING TO THINK ABOUT . . .
· Today, simply spend time in prayer for the people in your life who desperately need Jesus.

WEEK 19, DAY 5

"HE SPOKE TO THEM ACCORDING TO THE COUNSEL
OF THE YOUNG MEN, SAYING, 'MY FATHER MADE
YOUR YOKE HEAVY, BUT I WILL ADD TO YOUR
YOKE. MY FATHER DISCIPLINED YOU WITH WHIPS,
BUT I WILL DISCIPLINE YOU WITH SCORPIONS.'"
- 1 KINGS 12:14

Parents and grandparents are fairly amazing. And sometimes we can accidentally find ourselves forgetting this truth. How many times have you thought your own parents were simply out of touch? Maybe they don't understand their smartphone, or can't get along with their computer. It makes you curious how they can possibly get through the day! But it's weird how as we grow older, our parents suddenly start to grow smarter. ☒

READ 1 KINGS 12:1-17. The gist of the story is that when King Solomon died, his son, Rehoboam, took over. Rehoboam did not heed the advice of his father's old counselors. Instead, he listened to the words of his young buddies. As a result, the people rebelled, and the kingdom was lost to another king.

So how did Rehoboam go wrong? Didn't he ask both young and old advisors? What can we learn from this? The story of Rehoboam's advisors is really a story about motives. Read the story again. This time, try to guess what motives were behind the advice.

SOMETHING TO THINK ABOUT . . .
· How is a friend's advice impacted by their motive?
· Older advisors are particularly keen when it comes to interpersonal relationships. Younger advisors might be better innovators. When you have a problem, consider the nature of what kind of advice you're looking for before you decide whom to ask.

**THIS DEVOTION SPEAKS TO GOD'S GREAT LOVE. GO TO
PAGE 4 FOR A DESCRIPTION OF THIS ATTRIBUTE.**

WEEK 20

WEEK 20, DAY 1

"JESUS ANSWERED HIM, 'IF ANYONE LOVES ME, HE WILL KEEP MY WORD, AND MY FATHER WILL LOVE HIM, AND WE WILL COME TO HIM AND MAKE OUR HOME WITH HIM.'" - JOHN 14:23

The prophets came on to the story of Israel at a peculiar time. God used them to try and call people back to repentance. God spoke through the prophets, using their words to attempt to draw people back into faithfully following God. The prophets encouraged, warned, scolded, and preached. Many people turned back to God. More didn't.

Our relationship with the Word of God is similar. God gave us His Word to guide us, and to teach us about Him and His ways. When we are in a relationship with Jesus, we want to obey Him. Our motivation is not that He would love us more, or think we're better Christ-followers than the next guy or gal. Our motivation is love for Him. We obey because we love Jesus.

Memorize this verse today. It's a powerful reminder of what it means to obey Jesus within the context of a relationship with Him.

WEEK 20, DAY 2

"AND THE WOMAN SAID TO ELIJAH, 'NOW I KNOW THAT YOU ARE A MAN OF GOD, AND THAT THE WORD OF THE LORD IN YOUR MOUTH IS TRUTH.'" - 1 KINGS 17:24

What do you think when someone uses the word, "radical?" Really, write it down.

READING 1 KINGS 17, it may be easy to lose the pizzazz of this story. If we read Bible stories enough, the substance may get lost. Look at this story with fresh eyes, like someone who's never been to church.

So there is this unemployed woman. Her husband is dead. She can't work, and her son is too young to work. She's living in a country experiencing an economic depression. No one cares about this woman. Everyone is hungry and poor. Many are dying from hunger. There's no food stamps, charity organizations, or social workers. The woman scrounges up her last scraps of food. She knows this will be the last meal for herself and her son. After this meal (if you'd call it that), they will both die.

Now, along comes some wandering homeless guy. Scruffy beard, dirty smelly clothes . . . this guy smells and looks like he's been living in a cave. And he has the gall to ask for the last tiny scrap of food! Amazingly, this woman gives the homeless guy her last scrap of food. I don't know about you, but I'm shocked! What about her son? Isn't she going to act responsibly and be a real parent? Seriously, a homeless guy she doesn't even know? The truth is that she practiced radical compassion, the same kind modeled by Jesus. And in the end, God miraculously provided for her.

SOMETHING TO THINK ABOUT . . .
· Has God challenged you to radical (foundation shaking) generosity? Is there anything you are holding back, "just in case"?
· Get some $5 gift cards from Subway or McDonalds, etc. Next time you see someone begging for money, give them the gift card and tell them about 1 Kings 17.

THIS DEVOTION SPEAKS TO GOD'S POWER. GO TO PAGE 4 FOR A DESCRIPTION OF THIS ATTRIBUTE.

WEEK 20, DAY 3

**"AND AT THE TIME OF THE OFFERING OF THE OBLA-
TION, ELIJAH THE PROPHET CAME NEAR AND SAID, 'O
LORD, GOD OF ABRAHAM, ISAAC, AND ISRAEL, LET IT
BE KNOWN THIS DAY THAT YOU ARE GOD IN ISRAEL,
AND THAT I AM YOUR SERVANT, AND THAT I HAVE DONE
ALL THESE THINGS AT YOUR WORD.'" - 1 KINGS 18:36**

READ 1 KINGS 18. Look closely at verses 32-39. If I were Elijah, I would be afraid that God wouldn't answer. Imagine if the great prophet Elijah called on God and nothing happened. How embarrassing would that have been?

Sometimes when we pray, that's how we feel. We pray, and nothing happens. And that's precisely what happened in this story. The people expected Baal to answer, and nothing happened. The people learned that Baal is no god at all. So then what do we make of our unanswered prayer? Everywhere in the Bible, we read about God's protection and provision. God consistently provides for the people He loves. God miraculously protects His people from lions, fire, war, and natural disasters. Again, what do we make of our unanswered prayer?

This is exactly the question Paul wrestled with in 2 Corinthians 12:8-10. Paul prayed, and nothing happened. He prayed a second and third time. Nothing. Paul concluded that God is no god at all. No, wait! That's not how the story goes. Paul concluded that God's grace was sufficient! In other words, Paul learned to be satisfied in knowing that God in fact loves, cares, provides, and protects, even when we don't think He's doing it the right way.

Paul adjusted himself and his expectations instead of doubting God.

SOMETHING TO THINK ABOUT . . .
· Get a box. Write down an unanswered prayer and pack it in the box. Wrap the box like a gift and "give" that prayer to God. He will handle it His way in His time, and you might not like it. Pray that His grace will be sufficient for you.
· Pray for wisdom. We aren't promised that God will answer very many prayers in specific ways. But we are promised that if we humbly ask for wisdom, God will give it to us (James 1:5).

WEEK 20, DAY 4

"AND HE SAID, 'GO OUT AND STAND ON THE MOUNT BEFORE THE LORD.' AND BEHOLD, THE LORD PASSED BY, AND A GREAT AND STRONG WIND TORE THE MOUNTAINS AND BROKE IN PIECES THE ROCKS BEFORE THE LORD, BUT THE LORD WAS NOT IN THE WIND. AND AFTER THE WIND AN EARTHQUAKE, BUT THE LORD WAS NOT IN THE EARTHQUAKE." - 1 KINGS 19:11

What are the most urgent things competing for your attention? What toll does all the "noise" around you take on your life? Now consider, if your best friend whispered a secret in your ear, would you listen?

READ 1 KINGS 19:9-18. Focus on verses 11-13. It's awesome! Here's Elijah up on a mountain waiting for the God of the universe to show up. There's a wind that blows in so strong that rocks are exploding! That's outstanding! But God wasn't there. Elijah waits. A massive earthquake shakes. Trees are falling over and dirt is flying everywhere. But God wasn't there. Elijah waits. A catastrophic fire engulfs the mountain. The heat, the deafening roar, flames so bright he can't look at it. But God's not there. Elijah waits.

Shhhh. I thought I heard . . . What was that . . . In a gentle quiet whisper, God says, "I'm here. Let's talk."

So again, what are the most urgent things clamoring for your attention? Turn them off. Find a retreat. Get away from it all and listen for the whisper of God's voice. He wants desperately to connect with you. But He won't often shout or jump up and down. That would just make Him sound like another TV commercial. Instead, He's waiting for you to listen.

SOMETHING TO THINK ABOUT . . .

· This week, find time to escape where there is absolutely no distraction. Find your quiet spot and wait quietly for a conversation with God.
· Pick one thing clamoring for your attention. Maybe it's an app on your phone or a fun game. Maybe it's a sport or a musical instrument you obsess over. It could even be something good like church activities. Carve a piece of the time you devote to that, and give it to God. Make it a quiet time to wait for His whisper.

WEEK 20, DAY 5

"AND AS THEY STILL WENT ON AND TALKED, BEHOLD, CHARIOTS OF FIRE AND HORSES OF FIRE SEPARATED THE TWO OF THEM. AND ELIJAH WENT UP BY A WHIRL-WIND INTO HEAVEN." - 2 KINGS 2:11

READ 2 KINGS 2:1-12. Elijah was the main prophet of God in Israel. Elisha was chosen by God to become the main prophet after Elijah (don't get confused by their names being practically the same). Here's the thing about this scripture that's really unbelievable: two people in the Bible didn't actually die. Enoch "walked with God" (Genesis 5:24) and Elijah "went up to heaven in a whirlwind (2 Kings 2:11)." There are songs written about this stuff!

Here's what's often missed in this verse though: Elisha (the younger one) got a double dose of God stuff in his spirit! Elijah (the old guy) was The Man as far as prophets go. But Elisha was given "a double portion of [God's] spirit!" Whatever it was that made Elijah such a man of God, Elisha got two of. Apparently Elisha was going to become twice as amazing as his mentor!

The hard part was that Elisha had to do so in the absence of his mentor and dear friend. To become the prophet that God made him to be, Elisha had to go through a very sad and frightening time. Elisha had the humongous job of being the voice of God to the Nation Israel. But as long as Elijah was that voice, Elisha couldn't be.

SOMETHING TO THINK ABOUT . . .
· Can you think of painful things that have shaped you into the person God needs you to be? Thank Him for those things you used to be mad at Him about.
· Where is your life headed in the near future? Just like Elisha, probably everyone is reminding you, in subtle ways, that painful transition is just around the corner. Can you face that transition thankfully clinging to God?

WEEK 21

WEEK 21, DAY 1

"COME TO ME, ALL WHO LABOR AND ARE HEAVY LADEN, AND I WILL GIVE YOU REST. TAKE MY YOKE UPON YOU, AND LEARN FROM ME, FOR I AM GENTLE AND LOWLY IN HEART, AND YOU WILL FIND REST FOR YOUR SOULS. FOR MY YOKE IS EASY, AND MY BURDEN IS LIGHT." - MATTHEW 11:28-30

We're continuing the big-picture story of the Bible this week with another look at the prophets. The prophets were sent by God to warn Israel of what would happen if they continued to turn from Him. See, after Solomon died, Israel was split in two, resulting in a Northern Kingdom and a Southern Kingdom, each with their own king. This was not God's vision of how His people would live. And so He sent the prophets to convict them to turn from their rebellious ways.

Sin wears us down. If you could go back to the moment the Israelites entered the Promised Land and could tell them how the future would wind up, there's no way they would feel OK about that. Sin wrecks our lives. And the Israelites' sin drove them away from God. That's the beauty of Jesus' offer in Matthew 11. Jesus says that when we are dragged down by sin, and worn out from running from God, we can turn to Him for rest. He promises to take our burdens and lead us toward spiritual freedom.

The Israelites were worn out from their sin. Maybe you are too. But instead of the prophets, you have Jesus calling to you, the One who can ultimately make the most difference in your life. Memorize these verses this week. And if you haven't already, take Jesus up on His offer.

WEEK 21, DAY 2

**"AND I SAID: 'WOE IS ME! FOR I AM LOST; FOR I
AM A MAN OF UNCLEAN LIPS, AND I DWELL IN THE
MIDST OF A PEOPLE OF UNCLEAN LIPS; FOR MY
EYES HAVE SEEN THE KING, THE LORD OF HOSTS!'"
- ISAIAH 6:5**

Have you ever had an experience that you could not explain? Maybe it was something you saw that was so beautiful and breathtaking that you couldn't put it into words. Maybe it was something that caused your emotions to take over to the point that you couldn't remember much of the details. In today's passage, you're going to see such a moment in the life of the prophet Isaiah.

READ ISAIAH 6:1-7. In this passage, Isaiah truly encounters God. He sees God in His greatness on a throne. Isaiah, seeing the holiness and perfection of God, sees his sin as darker than he ever has before. This leads him to cry out, "Woe is me." He feels lost and utterly naked before a perfect God. God then provides Isaiah grace by symbolically taking away his sin.

Isaiah's encounter with God is a great mirror of what Jesus does for us in the Gospel. Jesus stands as perfect, and as we compare ourselves to Him we realize how imperfect we are. Instead of leaving us lost in our sinfulness, Jesus died on the cross to purchase our redemption and to take our place. This gives us hope. One day when we, like Isaiah, stand before God, we will stand as perfect because Jesus took our sin and gave us His perfection.

SOMETHING TO THINK ABOUT . . .

· Have you ever had an encounter where you felt God's presence? What was that like? How did you feel?
· Have you ever been in a situation where your sin made you feel lost? What was that situation?
· Spend some time today praising God and thanking Him for the greatness of grace that you can one day stand before God perfect because of Jesus.

 **THIS DEVOTION SPEAKS TO GOD'S HOLINESS. GO TO
PAGE 4 FOR A DESCRIPTION OF THIS ATTRIBUTE.**

WEEK 21, DAY 3

**"FOR TO US A CHILD IS BORN, TO US A SON IS GIVEN; AND THE GOVERN-
MENT SHALL BE UPON HIS SHOULDER, AND HIS NAME SHALL BE CALLED
WONDERFUL COUNSELOR, MIGHTY GOD, EVERLASTING FATHER, PRINCE
OF PEACE." - ISAIAH 9:6**

Have you ever made a prediction? Many people like to make predictions around sporting events. Imagine all of your friends predicting
scores to the next big game, and someone getting it right. That would
be impressive, wouldn't it? Now lets imagine someone makes a prediction of what someone would be like hundreds of years before that
person's birth. That would be insane! Yet that is what we see in today's
passage.

READ ISAIAH 9:6-7. This is a prediction about Jesus (what Bible scholars call a prophecy). So how is Jesus described: son, ruler of the government, wonderful, counselor, mighty God, everlasting father, and prince
of peace. Jesus is all of these things.

Even before Jesus came to this earth, His resume was very impressive.
As you study the New Testament, you will see how Jesus fulfills each
of these things. Also, this passage tells us that Jesus will bring peace,
rule on David's throne forever, and rule with justice and righteousness.
Jesus didn't just come to be a baby in a manger. He came to rule and
reign as Lord over everything. Jesus is a God who a relationship with
impacts our lives here and now, and our lives throughout eternity. Jesus
is a great God who is worthy of your worship today.

SOMETHING TO THINK ABOUT...
· How does the fact that Jesus' birth and character were predicted hundreds of years before His birth strengthen your faith?
· What characteristic of Jesus from today's passage encourages you the
most? Why?
· Write the characteristic that stood out to you today somewhere where
you will see it (on your hand, phone background, on your binder, etc.).
Every time you see that word today, take a second to praise Jesus for
being that for you.

WEEK 21, DAY 4

**"THEN I SAID, 'AH, LORD GOD! BEHOLD, I DO NOT KNOW
HOW TO SPEAK, FOR I AM ONLY A YOUTH.'"
- JEREMIAH 1:6**

What is a person worth? We live in a culture where everyone is trying to tell you your worth. You will be cool, pretty, popular, accepted if you do this, or buy that, or look like her. Everyone is trying to tell you who you have to be. What if God told you who you were to be, and what His plans were for your life? This is exactly what happened to Jeremiah in today's Bible passage.

OPEN YOUR BIBLE AND TURN TO JEREMIAH 1:1-10 AND READ THE PASSAGE. Once the setting for the book is established, Jeremiah has a crazy conversation with God. In this conversation, God tells Jeremiah that He knew him before he was born, and had a special plan for him. Did you realize that the same God who spoke to Jeremiah is the same God who knows you and has a plan for you?

So many times we feel lost and unimportant. In verse 6, Jeremiah reminds God that he is only a teenager, just like you. Yet, God tells Jeremiah that He is in the business of using teenagers for His purposes and His plan. God then challenges Jeremiah to follow Him as He leads him.

God's purposes for Jeremiah's life and His purposes for your life are likely to look different. But that does not change the fact that the same God knows you, loves you, has plans for you, and leads you to become who He created you to be. Which is pretty cool.

SOMETHING TO THINK ABOUT...
· What are some things that try to define your worth?
· How can you remind yourself today that your true worth is found in Jesus and your relationship with Him?
· What are some steps that you can take today to more closely follow Jesus?

WEEK 21, DAY 5

What does it mean to be a Christian? Christians go to church. Christians try to do the right thing. Christians go on mission trips. Christians go to Bible studies. Some Christians wear cross necklaces. Many times the things we think of being "Christian things" are things that simply involve outward actions. But what if following God is more about what's on the inside than the outside?

READ MICAH 6:6-8. The passage begins with examples of worship in Old Testament times (burnt offerings, calves, rams, oil) as outward expressions of what a person might give God in worship. Then in verse 8, the passage shifts from these outward things to the inward things. What the Lord truly wants from us is living justly, loving kindly, and walking humbly with God.

These three things are inward attitudes and focuses of the heart. To live justly means to stand up for what is right and to do right. "Loving kindly" is to love and care for others in the way that Jesus would. Walking humbly with God is realizing that you are not God, and submitting to Him to lead you every day.

These are all heart attitudes, but notice that these heart attitudes don't just stay in the heart. They overflow into life. So being a Christian is about the outward things. But those outward things are not just done to do them; they flow from a transformed heart that pleases God.

SOMETHING TO THINK ABOUT...
· What are some examples of outward things that you can do that are separated from your heart?
· Pick one of the three heart attitudes (living justly, loving kindly, or walking humbly with God) from today's passage. How can you live that attitude today?
· How would the attitude that you picked change your actions today?

WEEK 22

"THE LORD IS NOT SLOW TO FULFILL HIS PROMISE AS SOME
COUNT SLOWNESS, BUT IS PATIENT TOWARD YOU, NOT
WISHING THAT ANY SHOULD PERISH, BUT THAT ALL SHOULD
REACH REPENTANCE." - 2 PETER 3:9

This week you'll learn what happens when people don't take God seriously. God had been speaking through the prophets to warn his people for a long time. But they weren't listening. It had been generations since David and Solomon ruled. And still people rebelled. God had been lovingly and undeservingly patient. But that patience had come to an end. You'll see what God allows to happen to His people. It's not pretty.

God demonstrates the same patience with us today. Many people may not believe in God simply because He doesn't seem to be active in the world. And the Bible, especially the New Testament, talks a lot about God's return. Is He coming back or not?

Peter addresses this in 2 Peter 3. He says that we shouldn't take God's delay in returning as slowness, or as evidence that He isn't real. Peter says God is waiting, just like He did with the Israelites. God is giving people every last chance to turn to Him before He returns. Have you turned to God? Do you have friends who need to come to faith in Christ? Memorize this verse. Maybe you'll get a chance to speak to your friends about it and explain what it means.

WEEK 22, DAY 2

"THE LORD YOUR GOD IS IN YOUR MIDST, A MIGHTY ONE WHO WILL SAVE; HE WILL REJOICE OVER YOU WITH GLADNESS; HE WILL QUIET YOU BY HIS LOVE; HE WILL EXULT OVER YOU WITH LOUD SINGING."
- ZEPHANIAH 3:17

Everyone loves a happy ending. The movie or book comes to a close as the characters, though walking through difficult times, come to a place of peace and rest. The only thing better than a happy ending in a book or movie is a happy ending that is true. In today's passage, you will see God promise His people, Israel, a happy ending. This will be a time of celebration because the people's relationship with God will be restored resulting in the people's great joy. (But, before this could happen, the people would experience God's judgment because of their sin.)

READ ZEPHANIAH 3:14-17. Take a minute to underline all of the words that show happiness, excitement, or joy. The passage is filled with words of excitement and joy (sing, shout, rejoice, exult). The people were rejoicing because of the promise of God's judgment being lifted from them.

Israel's hope of restoration is the same hope of restoration we have in the Gospel. Jesus has taken our guilt, shame, and fear and set us free to rejoice in a new relationship with Him. Our God is a God of great joy, and He invites you, just like His people Israel, to join Him in the hope of the coming celebration. Because one day He will make all things right again. Happy endings are coming. Are you excited for that? Are you living for that day?

SOMETHING TO THINK ABOUT...
· Spend some time writing a prayer to God praising Him for saving you.
· Play your favorite worship song, and spend some time praising God and rejoicing with singing, just like Israel did in today's passage.

THIS DEVOTION SPEAKS TO GOD'S FAITHFULNESS.
GO TO PAGE 4 FOR A DESCRIPTION OF THIS ATTRIBUTE.

"BUT HE ABANDONED THE COUNSEL THAT THE OLD MEN GAVE HIM, AND TOOK COUNSEL WITH THE YOUNG MEN WHO HAD GROWN UP WITH HIM AND STOOD BEFORE HIM." - 2 CHRONICLES 10:8

Think about some key leaders you have been under the authority of in your life. Stop and give yourself time to think about each of these questions:

· Does a particularly oppressive authority figure come to mind?
· Did that person help you grow or kill your motivation?
· Have you ever had a coach, teacher, or boss who was relentless in driving you to do more?
· Would you listen to someone much older and more experienced than you for advice over someone you have grown up with as a friend?

Today's passage is review. But, after taking a break for the prophets, looking back at what originally caused Israel's downfall sets the stage for God's judgment. Recall, Rehoboam's reign as king followed the four-decade reign of his father, Solomon. Solomon reigned with great authority and little concern for how his harsh rulings affected his people. When his son became king, some viewed it as an opportunity to ease the oppression.

GRAB YOUR BIBLE AND READ 2 CHRONICLES 9:29-10:19. Rehoboam was essentially asked for more merciful leadership while being offered unwavering loyalty in return. As you read, the wise older advisors recommended Rehoboam listen to the people in order to create a mutually beneficial partnership. The young advisors challenged him to threaten even harsher workloads and rules. This ended in utter failure.

SOMETHING TO THINK ABOUT . . .
· Think about the kind of leader you want to be. Do you want to be resented for your merciless dictatorial style, or do you want to earn the respect needed to get those you lead to give you great results?
· Ask God today to help you listen to wise advisers and to lead Christ-like qualities.

WEEK 22, DAY 4

"IN THE NINTH YEAR OF HOSHEA, THE KING OF ASSYRIA CAPTURED SAMARIA, AND HE CARRIED THE ISRAELITES AWAY TO ASSYRIA AND PLACED THEM IN HALAH, AND ON THE HABOR, THE RIVER OF GOZAN, AND IN THE CITIES OF THE MEDES." - 2 KINGS 17:6

Back in the late 1980's there was a senior class of students at a local high school made up of a very intelligent group of young minds. All had earned entry into the National Honor Society. All would walk at graduation proudly wearing gold honor cowls. But before that happened, there was an issue that had to be addressed.

A special meeting of all National Honor Society members was called outside the regular monthly meeting. With a serious tone, the teacher sponsor issued a stern warning: "All of your GPAs are teetering on the brink of getting you removed from National Honor Society. If you don't make drastic changes in your study habits over the next semester, then you won't walk with honors." This was a sobering wake-up call to this group of students who were part of a long tradition of academic excellence at this school. The group was collectively and individually embarrassed.

These students had grown weary of doing what it took to achieve high academic honors and were in danger of paying an embarrassing price for their diminished efforts.

TAKE YOUR BIBLE OUT AND LOOK UP 2 KINGS 17:1-6. What happens when a people start shirking responsibilities? Eventually it catches up with them. If you aren't faithful in the things you've been tasked to do, although you may not fall victim to an invasion and oppressive takeover, you just might have to deal with some embarrassment.

SOMETHING TO THINK ABOUT...
· Spend a few moments today thinking about your responsibilities in life.
· Take a few moments to pray to God. Commit to God to keep steadfast in offering every responsibility in your life to Him as an act of worship.

> "AND THIS OCCURRED BECAUSE THE PEOPLE OF
> ISRAEL HAD SINNED AGAINST THE LORD THEIR GOD,
> WHO HAD BROUGHT THEM UP OUT OF THE LAND OF
> EGYPT FROM UNDER THE HAND OF PHARAOH KING
> OF EGYPT, AND HAD FEARED OTHER GODS."
> - 2 KINGS 17:7

It was Joe's senior year. He was a bit of a goof-off, yet generally polite and well-liked by his teachers. One day in social studies class Joe had an idea. While first-year teacher Ms. Smith was lecturing, Joe quickly made a paper airplane to throw at his friend. When Ms. Smith turned her back, Joe launched it directly at his friend in the opposite corner of the classroom. In an odd twist of events, this seemingly well-engineered jet took a sharp turn and lodged itself in Ms. Smith's curly hairdo. This resulted in Joe being sent out into the hall—a senior sent out in the hall like an elementary school kid.

GRAB YOUR BIBLE AND READ 2 KINGS 17: 7-22. In a nutshell, an invasion came because God's people had turned their backs on Him and His ways, and had begun to worship other gods. Despite God's many warnings, the people continued to deviate from His path for them. Throughout the Bible it's clear what happens when other things are prioritized over God.

Joe and his classmates had been warned time and time again by Ms. Smith that her patience was dwindling. After a stern lecture by Ms. Smith, and a heartfelt apology by Joe, their relationship was restored. Unfortunately for the people of Israel, years of pain, suffering, and death would come from their delinquent lack of respect for God's authority. Restoration would come, but not for generations down the road.

SOMETHING TO THINK ABOUT . . .
· Can you name an area of your life in which you struggle with God's authority?
· Ask God to help you with this area as you go through your week.

THIS DEVOTION SPEAKS TO GOD'S SOVEREIGNTY. GO TO
PAGE 4 FOR A DESCRIPTION OF THIS ATTRIBUTE

WEEK 23

WEEK 23, DAY 1

"BUT GOD SHOWS HIS LOVE FOR US IN THAT WHILE WE WERE STILL SINNERS, CHRIST DIED FOR US." - ROMANS 5:8

This week is going to be an interesting look at some highs and lows in the big-picture story of the Bible. You're going to be watching the last few moments of Israel's days as a great nation. You'll be introduced to some awesome characters, and some that are not-so-awesome. Over all, it's kind of a summary of the way that the story has gone up to this point. Highs and lows. Wins and losses. Great moral victories, and great moral defeats.

The amazing thing is that this is God's story of His people. It's no surprise to Him. None of this caught Him off guard. He saw how it would go, and knew how He would interact and intervene. God knew that His people were sinful, and that they would turn from Him. Knowing this, He still planned to send Jesus to rescue all humankind from the results of their sinfulness. That is amazing love.

This is an easy, and an important verse to memorize. Memorize it this week and look for opportunities to meditate on it, praising God and thanking Him for His great love.

THIS DEVOTION SPEAKS TO GOD'S GREAT LOVE.
GO TO PAGE 4 FOR A DESCRIPTION OF THIS ATTRIBUTE.

WEEK 23, DAY 2

**"AND HE DID WHAT WAS RIGHT IN THE EYES OF THE
LORD AND WALKED IN ALL THE WAY OF DAVID HIS
FATHER, AND HE DID NOT TURN ASIDE TO THE RIGHT
OR TO THE LEFT." - 2 KINGS 22:2**

At age 14, a creative young man published his first picture of a dog.
That man's name was Charles Schulz. The dog's name was Snoopy.
At age 15 a young man named Louis Braille invented the Braille system so the blind could read. Defending her faith while an atheistic
gunman aimed his weapon at her, 17-year-old Cassie Bernall was
gunned down at the Columbine School Massacre in Colorado. And
at age 18, UCLA student Lila Rose went undercover to expose the
atrocities happening inside an abortion clinic. Can young lives make
a huge impact on the world? You better believe it.

GRAB YOUR BIBLE AND READ 2 KINGS 22. Then imagine being an
8-year-old king. Would you feel small? Might you feel overwhelmed?
Go back and look at verse 2. This says a great deal about a guy
who began his 31-year reign as king when he was only eight! This
unlikely hero would usher in a new era of obedience to God's law
that literally changed the course of history. Idols would be removed
and destroyed, and God would once again be central to the life
of a nation. Not bad for a guy who began his rule as a pre-teen.

Surely King Josiah had feelings of insignificance due to age. Surely
he had detractors who didn't think that they would rise up when it
mattered. But they all overcame. What do you need to overcome today in order to be utilized by Christ to do great things for His glory?

SOMETHING TO THINK ABOUT . . .
· How did you think Josiah knew to honor God at such a young age?
· Was there a time in which you were given what you felt was a huge
responsibility considering your age?
· What are some ways you can do what is pleasing in God's sight in
your various roles in life?

WEEK 23, DAY 3

"THEREFORE HE BROUGHT UP AGAINST THEM THE KING OF THE CHALDEANS, WHO KILLED THEIR YOUNG MEN WITH THE SWORD IN THE HOUSE OF THEIR SANCTUARY AND HAD NO COMPASSION ON YOUNG MAN OR VIRGIN, OLD MAN OR AGED. HE GAVE THEM ALL INTO HIS HAND." - 2 CHRONICLES 36:17

Vernal Falls is an awe-inspiring creation of God found at Yosemite Park. Despite more than adequate warning signs from park entrance to the overlook at the site itself, many people have died there. Hikers jump into the pools at the top of the falls, only to be swept away by the fast-moving current. Heeding the warnings could save lives. Yet hikers don't listen, and jump in the water anyway.

Choosing to ignore the warning signs before being overcome by fast-moving water is much like what happened to Israel. Take out your Bible and read 2 Chronicles 36:11-21. To say King Zedekiah was rebellious toward God would be quite the understatement. God sent many prophets to warn him that he was on a crash course with judgment. Zedekiah did not listen, and continued to rebel against any authority other than his own. In the latter part of the passage you can see that the Babylonians mercilessly invaded, killing many people, and destroying everything of value. Death and destruction came as a result of disobedience.

God always warns people of the consequences of disobeying Him. This is true for every human being, including you. Is there a path you have been taking in some area of your life that has many warning signs? Are you passing those signs because the risk seems worth it? Or, do you plan to get on the right path later, and do as you wish for now? These are hard questions that may even seem unfair. The reality is that if you don't heed the warning signs, you'll end up with living far outside God's will for your life.

SOMETHING TO THINK ABOUT . . .
· Today, get real about obedience to God. Apologize for any warning signs you've ignored. Ask for wisdom and strength to turn away and flee from anything that would come between you and Him.

THIS DEVOTION SPEAKS TO GOD'S SENSE OF JUSTICE. GO TO PAGE 4 FOR A DESCRIPTION OF THIS ATTRIBUTE.

WEEK 23, DAY 4

"'AND LET THE YOUNG WOMAN WHO PLEASES THE KING BE QUEEN INSTEAD OF VASHTI.' THIS PLEASED THE KING, AND HE DID SO." - ESTHER 2:4

For the next few days, we are going to talk about Esther, an unlikely queen. Imagine living in a day and age where kings reside as the ultimate Lord over all. As a matter of fact, they can pretty much do what they want, any way they want. This is where we find King Xerxes at the start of our story.

TAKE A MOMENT AND READ THE START OF THIS STORY IN ESTHER 1 AND 2. This story already has the set up for a great movie plot. The king throws a party where he and his friends get drunk for a week. Then, he decides he wants to show the queen off. The queen, who is throwing her own party at the time, does not want to be treated like this, and refuses. Xerxes feels like he needs to show off his power. The king wakes up with a hangover and thinks, "What have I done?"

Enter Esther. She is asked to leave her home, her family, and all that she knows. She has to spend a year being made more beautiful, and for one day she will meet the King. If he likes her he may ask her back. If he doesn't she will live with other women who have seen the king and been cast aside. Did you catch that? There is a chance Esther will spend her life unmarried in the King's palace just because she didn't catch the eye of the man on the throne.

This is a complicated story to read right from the start. But it's one that helps us understand the power a king holds. It's pretty amazing that God as our Lord and King doesn't rule the way Xerxes did. His decisions are not made on a whim or to prove His power. He is a just King, and a worthy ruler.

SOMETHING TO THINK ABOUT . . .
· Compare King Xerxes to God as King. What are the differences and why?
· If you were Esther and called to the king's palace, how would you feel?

WEEK 23, DAY 5

"FOR IF YOU KEEP SILENT AT THIS TIME, RELIEF AND DELIVERANCE WILL RISE FOR THE JEWS FROM ANOTHER PLACE, BUT YOU AND YOUR FATHER'S HOUSE WILL PERISH. AND WHO KNOWS WHETHER YOU HAVE NOT COME TO THE KINGDOM FOR SUCH A TIME AS THIS?" - ESTHER 4:14

Think about a time when you have felt like an authority in your life just was unfair. Maybe it was a parent who decided to enforce a hard rule. It could be a teacher who has ridiculous expectations. What did you do? How did you react?

This is where we find Esther's cousin Mordecai. A man who isn't even the king lets power go to his head, and wants the world to bow down to him (literally). This is against everything Mordecai believes in so he refuses.

READ ESTHER CHAPTERS 3 AND 4. Sometimes people with power can use it in a way that's unfair and downright cruel. Haman got so angry that when Mordecai wasn't doing what he wanted, Haman conspired to kill all of the people of an entire nationality. What? That's just downright crazy. This is where it's important to remember that while Israel may have strayed, God had never left them. It wasn't Esther's beauty that really led to her position as queen. Actually, the Lord put her there. Do you remember that Mordecai told her to not let anyone know she was Jewish? In Esther 4:14 he had changed his tune.

Esther had a decision to make. Did she use her position for the Lord, or did she hide? Could she trust that God would take care of her and her people? Look at how chapter 4 ends. Before she does anything else, she takes the time to seek the Lord and see what He wants her to do. Haman may have thought he had power. Xerxes believed himself to be king. But God had another plan.

SOMETHING TO THINK ABOUT...
· Could you trust that God has a bigger plan than Haman if you were Esther? Why or why not

THIS DEVOTION SPEAKS TO HOW GOD KNOWS ALL. GO TO PAGE 4 FOR A DESCRIPTION OF THIS ATTRIBUTE.

WEEK 24

WEEK 24, DAY 1

"HE HAS DELIVERED US FROM THE DOMAIN OF
DARKNESS AND TRANSFERRED US TO THE KING-
DOM OF HIS BELOVED SON, IN WHOM WE HAVE
REDEMPTION, THE FORGIVENESS OF SINS."
- COLOSSIANS 1:13-14

You'll be reading this week about God's deliverance, or rescue, of two people. You'll be wrapping up your look at Esther's life, and beginning a look at Daniel's. Both of these stories take place after God has allowed Israel to be conquered by outside empires. God allowed this as a form of judgment for His people, who had turned from their worship of Him.

God delivered Esther and Daniel through troubling circumstances. But, their situations were mostly physical in nature. The greatest act of deliverance God ever achieved was delivering people from the consequences of their sin. Our sin separates us from a holy God. The punishment for sin is death. But God, in His grace and mercy, planned for Jesus, His Son, to pay our sin debt on the cross. Through faith in Jesus, and only through faith, we can experience salvation. Through Christ, God brought us from death to life.

Memorize these awesome verses from Colossians this week. They paint a beautiful picture of the gift God gave us through Jesus.

WEEK 24, DAY 2

"AND THE KING SAID, 'WHAT HONOR OR DISTINCTION HAS BEEN BESTOWED ON MORDECAI FOR THIS?' THE KING'S YOUNG MEN WHO AT- TENDED HIM SAID, 'NOTHING HAS BEEN DONE FOR HIM.'" - ESTHER 6:3

When you find yourself in a jam, what's the first thing you stop and do? Do you panic? Do you ask God what to do? There are times when we create bad sit- uations for ourselves. And in those moments we need to take ownership of our choices. Yet, there are other times when people hurt us, and we need help in knowing what to do.

READ ESTHER 5 AND 6. After Esther seeks the Lord, He helps her come up with a plan. She knows she could die by asking to see the king uninvited. Therefore, she approaches him in a way that she knows is respectful and inviting. She knows the king likes to be treated in a way that acknowledges his power. So she offers to make him dinner.

In the meantime, do you remember a strange story at the end of Esther 2? Mordecai stops a couple of guys from murdering the King and it goes unnoticed. It seems especially unfair since the very next thing that happens is that Haman plots to kill Mordecai. God didn't forget though. In the midst of all that is going on, the king wakes up in the middle of the night and decides to do some reading. Realizing Mordecai was never honored, he decides to do something about it. Haman gets called in, and his selfish greedy ways cause him to believe the king wants to do something for him. Instead, Haman the one out to kill Mordecai, has to honor him.

Just when we may think God doesn't care about our little problems, or at the very moment we believe He might have forgotten us, He shows up. God does not forget those who belong to Him. God demonstrates His great power in this situation. Who else could have lead Haman to reveal himself, and in the same time set the stage for saving Mordecai and the Jews? God can and will work in your life to bring you out of your tough situation.

SOMETHING TO THINK ABOUT...
· Think about a time when you might think God has forgotten about you, but in- stead He has taken care of you in a huge way.
· How did this strengthen your faith in God?

 **THIS DEVOTION SPEAKS TO HOW GOD KNOWS ALL.
GO TO PAGE 4 FOR A DESCRIPTION OF THIS ATTRIBUTE.**

WEEK 24, DAY 3

"AND IN EVERY PROVINCE AND IN EVERY CITY, WHEREVER THE KING'S COMMAND AND HIS EDICT REACHED, THERE WAS GLADNESS AND JOY AMONG THE JEWS, A FEAST AND A HOLIDAY. AND MANY FROM THE PEOPLES OF THE COUNTRY DECLARED THEMSELVES JEWS, FOR FEAR OF THE JEWS HAD FALLEN ON THEM." - ESTHER 8:17

Have you ever seen a movie that has a bad guy everyone loves to hate? We watch the film, and wait for the moment when they get found out and "taken care of." When they get caught, the moment is so sweet. Sometimes, it's even sweeter because they've been able to hide their bad side from other characters. FINALLY everyone wakes up to the plot. There is something deeply satisfying about this time in the film.

TAKE A MOMENT AND READ ESTHER 7 AND 8. Haman walks right into God's plan. His pride finally catches up with him. He believed himself to be even more powerful than the king, in many ways. Haman was the ultimate bad guy, and his selfishness caught up with him. In the end, Haman ends up dying on the same gallows he built for Mordecai. Not only that, Mordecai takes his position and his wealth. God knows that no matter how we feel about it, He is the King of all. He especially is the Lord of those who are His.

Unfortunately, there were consequences to the misuse of power. Xerxes knew that others would try and kill the Jews according to plan. Yet, as king he had the power to change the plan. He allowed the Jews to defend themselves. There are times when, if it were up to us, we would not choose the path we find ourselves on. People around us can abuse their position, and hurt others. Yet, when we know we are God's, we can know there is no plan so horrible that it will destroy us. Instead, we can trust that the Lord will not let us down.

SOMETHING TO THINK ABOUT...

· Spend some time in prayer today thanking God that He works through all situations to care for those He loves (that includes you). Even when we can't understand HOW He goes about it, we can know that God is always acting for our good and His glory.

WEEK 24, DAY 4

"THE JEWS GATHERED IN THEIR CITIES THROUGHOUT ALL THE PROVINCES OF KING AHASUERUS TO LAY HANDS ON THOSE WHO SOUGHT THEIR HARM. AND NO ONE COULD STAND AGAINST THEM, FOR THE FEAR OF THEM HAD FALLEN ON ALL PEOPLES." - ESTHER 9:2

Take a moment and think about the best birthday you've ever had. When was a time you felt totally and completely celebrated just for being born? It felt pretty amazing right? It may seem strange that we spend so much effort on one small thing. Yet, every year you get to be alive is actually huge!

TAKE A MOMENT AND READ ESTHER CHAPTERS 9 & 10. The Feast of Purim isn't well known unless you are Jewish. However, it is a celebration that is observed to this day. God could have chosen to allow this group of people to be killed. Instead, He delivered them from their enemy in a powerful way. Not only did He save them, He put a humble man in a position of power. All the plans one man had crafted to kill God's people were turned around. It was a HUGE deal. God showed once again that He is the true King who holds more power than any person.

When God comes through and takes care of us, we can have the tendency to move on quickly. However, it's important to find ways to remember who God is, and how He takes care of us. Esther and Mordecai created an entire festival that actually serves as an echo of what salvation looks like. God saved the lives of His people here on earth. Jesus came and saved our lives for all eternity. This is something amazing to celebrate.

It doesn't have to be Christmas or Easter to celebrate how God takes care of us. We can take the time every day to remember who the Lord is, and how He loves those of us who belong to Him.

SOMETHING TO THINK ABOUT...
· Reflect today on ways that God takes care of you every day. How would your life be different if you didn't know the Lord and His guidance in your life?

WEEK 24, DAY 5

"BUT DANIEL RESOLVED THAT HE WOULD NOT DEFILE HIMSELF WITH THE KING'S FOOD, OR WITH THE WINE THAT HE DRANK. THEREFORE HE ASKED THE CHIEF OF THE EUNUCHS TO ALLOW HIM NOT TO DEFILE HIMSELF." - DANIEL 1:8

Life is complicated, right? The days when life was simple are long gone. Your life is filled with difficult decisions, and often there doesn't seem to be an easy answer. It's easy to feel stuck between pleasing God and pleasing others.

READ DANIEL 1. Imagine being in the shoes of these four friends. Enemy forces had occupied their homeland, and they had been taken into captivity far from home. They were surrounded by an unfamiliar culture. Then, they were placed into a development school so that the country that had destroyed their lives could capitalize on their intelligence. What would you do? Most would probably just try to blend in. A few might push back, rebelling against the oppressive government that had destroyed their lives. Daniel and his friends chose another way, God's way.

They didn't give in to all the demands of their captors. They decided not to eat food that violated their God-given convictions. However, this was not an all out rebellion. They fully participated in their training, and worked for the good of the Babylonians. They wisely worked out a deal with the chief eunuch, believing that if they followed God's ways then He would grant them favor with the chief. They wanted to please God AND be a blessing to the Babylonians.

Life is hard and confusing. At times, it seems like we must chose between passively accepting our culture, or running around telling everyone how wrong they are. But there is another way. Look to the example of these four friends. Work for the good of others AND follow God's way. Be diligent in serving others and in serving Christ.

SOMETHING TO THINK ABOUT...
· What are some ways that you passively accept your culture? Do you have any convictions that you've pushed to the side in order to fit in?
· What are some ways that you can work for the good of those around you?

WEEK 25

WEEK 25, DAY 1

"AND I HEARD A LOUD VOICE FROM THE THRONE SAYING, 'BE-HOLD, THE DWELLING PLACE OF GOD IS WITH MAN. HE WILL DWELL WITH THEM, AND THEY WILL BE HIS PEOPLE, AND GOD HIMSELF WILL BE WITH THEM AS THEIR GOD.'"
- REVELATION 21:3-4

This week you'll continue your look at the big-picture story of the Bible by wrapping up the story of Daniel. It's a pretty awesome story, and you may be familiar with some parts of it. But there are going to be new things you learn about God and about Daniel (and hopefully about yourself) as you read.

One of the coolest things about Daniel's story is how God worked over and over again to protect Daniel. Remember, Daniel was a prisoner. He had been taken from his home in Israel and forced to work in the service of the Babylonian empire. God worked to honor Daniel's faithfulness, and made Daniel's life better as a result. But, Daniel was still in a land far from home, unable to return to his people or country.

This week's memory verse points to a time when God will completely, 100%, perfectly redeem the lives we all live. God has saved us from our sins. But we live in a fallen world full of sin, temptation, and wickedness. But one day, God will make a dwelling for all believers that is completely redeemed from the brokenness of our world. At that point, our redemption will be complete. We'll be WITH God. Forever.

Memorize these verses today. Hold on to them as a reminder that one day, all will be restored.

THIS DEVOTION SPEAKS TO GOD'S FAITHFULNESS.
GO TO PAGE 4 FOR A DESCRIPTION OF THIS ATTRIBUTE.

WEEK 25, DAY 2

"THEN DANIEL WENT TO HIS HOUSE AND MADE THE MATTER KNOWN TO HANANIAH, MISHAEL, AND AZARIAH, HIS COMPANIONS, AND TOLD THEM TO SEEK MERCY FROM THE GOD OF HEAVEN CONCERNING THIS MYSTERY, SO THAT DANIEL AND HIS COMPANIONS MIGHT NOT BE DESTROYED WITH THE REST OF THE WISE MEN OF BABYLON." - DANIEL 2:17-18

Have you ever been watching a movie and thought, "No way! That's impossible!" Special effects, C.G.I. and camera tricks can make the impossible possible in the world of film. Unfortunately, we live in the real world without the benefit of Hollywood tricks. What do we do when we're facing a seemingly impossible situation? Where can we turn?

READ DANIEL 2. Have you ever had tried to tell a friend about a dream, but you have trouble remembering the details? Probably most have. Now how crazy would it be if you said to your friend, "I'm having trouble remembering my dream. How about you tell me what my dream was?" Now that is an insane request! Nebuchadnezzar does just that when he asks the wise men of his court to tell him what his dream was, and then to interpret it for him.

Notice their response to him in verse 10, "There is not a man on earth who can meet the king's demand." Not quite. Enter Daniel. Daniel hears of Nebuchadnezzar's request and volunteers himself. Daniel knew it was an impossible task; he says so in verse 27. So why would Daniel sign up for this impossible task? Because he knew who could accomplish the impossible: God.

So what did Daniel do? He looked to God for the answer. He pulled together his friends that knew God and asked them to "seek mercy from God." In other words, they prayed that God would reveal the answer. And He did. He is a God who makes the impossible possible.

SOMETHING TO THINK ABOUT...
· What are you facing that seems impossible? What has you feeling helpless and hopeless?
· How does it make you feel to know that God "reveals mysteries," and is able to accomplish the impossible? How can you "seek mercy from God?"

WEEK 25, DAY 3

"IF THIS BE SO, OUR GOD WHOM WE SERVE IS ABLE TO DELIVER US FROM THE BURNING FIERY FURNACE, AND HE WILL DELIVER US OUT OF YOUR HAND, O KING." - DANIEL 3:17

Have you ever been asked, "Was it worth it?" Maybe you took a risk, maybe you left a relationship, or maybe you made an unpopular decision. Whatever the circumstances, you had to evaluate if what you gained was actually worth what you gave up.

READ DANIEL 3. This is one of the most famous stories in all of the Bible. Shadrach, Meshach, and Abednego refused to bow down to King Nebuchadnezzar's idol, and were thrown into a fiery furnace. God rescued them from the furnace, proving to all He is the God above all other gods (and kings), and causing even Nebuchadnezzar to proclaim His greatness.

But did you catch how Shadrach, Meshach, and Abednego first responded to Nebuchadnezzar's treat to throw them in the furnace? Read verses 16-18 one more time. In verse 17, they make sure that Nebuchadnezzar understands that their God is able to save them. The implication is that their God is greater than Nebuchadnezzar. The essence of what they are saying to Nebuchadnezzar was, "We trust our God more than we fear you."

Then, they said something truly shocking. In verse 18 they tell Nebuchadnezzar, that even if God doesn't save them, they would rather die obeying Him than live obeying Nebuchadnezzar. Wow! They were willing to say it was worth it, even if they died. They refused to be gripped by fear, trusted God, and were willing to face the consequences believing the entire time that it was worth it. Or more specifically, that God was worth it.

SOMETHING TO THINK ABOUT...

· Take a few moments to honestly ask yourself this question: "Do I trust God more than I fear other people?" What does the answer tell you about your faith?
· Do a quick inventory of your life. What do you spend your time on, invest your money in, and occupy your thoughts with? Is it worth your investment? How much does your life reflect God's worth?

WEEK 25, DAY 4

**"THEREFORE, O KING, LET MY COUNSEL BE ACCEPTABLE
TO YOU: BREAK OFF YOUR SINS BY PRACTICING
RIGHTEOUSNESS, AND YOUR INIQUITIES BY SHOWING
MERCY TO THE OPPRESSED, THAT THERE MAY PERHAPS
BE A LENGTHENING OF YOUR PROSPERITY."
- DANIEL 4:27**

Have you ever had to deliver bad news? Not fun, right? Maybe you had to tell your friend that you saw her boyfriend with a different girl. Maybe you had to confront a friend about his destructive choices. Whatever the situation, delivering bad news is hard.

READ DANIEL 4:4-27. We've seen this scene before. Nebuchadnezzar turns to Daniel for dream interpretation. This time is different though. In verse 19 Daniel is "dismayed," and "his thoughts alarm him." Why? Unlike the last dream, which spoke favorably of Nebuchadnezzar, this dream is a word from God against Nebuchadnezzar. The message? Nebuchadnezzar will face personal difficulty until he embraces the reality that God the Most High, not Nebuchadnezzar, is the ultimate ruler of all.

Delivering bad news is never fun, but delivering bad news to the most powerful man in the world is frightening. What did Daniel do? He boldly told Nebuchadnezzar the truth. He spoke to the king of Babylon on behalf of the King of Heaven, even though it was a difficult message for him to deliver. He told Nebuchadnezzar to change his ways to advert the coming judgment of God.

More than likely, you are never going to need to deliver bad news to the most powerful man on the planet. But you probably will need to tell a hard truth to a friend or family member. What will you do? Hopefully, you'll follow Daniel's example of telling the truth. Remember, Daniel didn't enjoy sharing bad news, but he did muster up the courage to do it. Later, God's judgment against Nebuchadnezzar came to pass. And guess what? He remembered Daniel's words, repented of his pride, and God restored him. While it was difficult at the time, Daniel's bold words actually saved Nebuchadnezzar down the road.

SOMETHING TO THINK ABOUT...
· What would have happened if Daniel had not told Nebuchadnezzar the truth?
· Would it have changed the truth? Would it have possible changed Nebuchadnezzar's response later?
· Do you have a difficult message to give to someone? How can you do it lovingly and boldly?

WEEK 25, DAY 5

"THEN THE KING COMMANDED, AND DANIEL WAS BROUGHT AND CAST INTO THE DEN OF LIONS. THE KING DECLARED TO DANIEL, 'MAY YOUR GOD, WHOM YOU SERVE CONTINUALLY, DELIVER YOU!'" - DANIEL 6:16

In 1892, Francis Bellamy wrote the Pledge of Allegiance. His purpose was to help foster a sense of patriotism for our country by creating a short, memorable recitation. Maybe it works, maybe it doesn't. But we all have allegiances, even if we don't have chants to reinforce them. In today's devotion, Daniel's allegiance to God is tested.

READ DANIEL 6. You know the story: King Darius is tricked by devious men into passing a law with the sole purpose of eliminating Daniel. Daniel breaks the law, and is punished by being thrown in a den of lions. God shows up and protects Daniel from the lions. We've heard it all before. But did you catch verse 10? Daniel is caught because he prays where he can be seen. Why did Daniel continue his practice of praying in front of open windows three times a day? Couldn't he pray just as effectively behind closed doors? Why would Daniel risk his position and even his life to continue his routine?

Why? Because Daniel's ultimate allegiance was to God. The Book of Daniel shows clearly that Daniel was loyal to King Darius. But ultimately Daniel was loyal to God. He understood that he was in his current position because God placed him there. God was in control, not Darius. Daniel was clearly displaying that his first allegiance was to his God. He was not afraid of the new law, the lions, or a group of liars.

I doubt Daniel had a pledge he recited to remind him of his allegiance to God. But his actions demonstrated his allegiance. When your allegiance to God is tested, how will you respond?

SOMETHING TO THINK ABOUT...
· What are your allegiances? What are you committed to regardless of the cost? Honestly assess your allegiance to God.
· How would being ultimately loyal to God change your other loyalties?

WEEK 26

"FOR TO THIS YOU HAVE BEEN CALLED, BECAUSE CHRIST ALSO SUFFERED FOR YOU, LEAVING YOU AN EXAMPLE, SO THAT YOU MIGHT FOLLOW IN HIS STEPS." - 1 PETER 2:21

This week is a big week in your journey through the big-picture story of the Bible. You'll be really close to finishing up the Old Testament part of the story. The Old Testament holds its challenges for modern readers, that's for sure. But, it's such a powerful backstory! And while people can come to faith in Christ without understanding, or even having heard the stories of the Old Testament, when you do know the backstory, it makes Jesus' life, death, and resurrection even more awesome. But you're not quite done yet.

This week you'll look at the story of Nehemiah, and through this story, you'll get a glimpse at what it was like to try and rebuild Jerusalem. Let's just put it this way: it was no easy task. Nehemiah and the remnant of God's people were facing a major uphill battle, one with a ton of emotional implications. But, they recognized that this was the Lord's will. And they persevered and finally succeeded.

Our life as Christ-followers is similar. If we strongly and faithfully live out our faith, we will experience tough times as a result. God will call us into difficult seasons. But the goal is always for our good and His glory. And we can never forget that Jesus faced every hardship you can face, and overcame them all. He is our example. He is our strength. Meditate on 1 Peter 2:21 this week, especially when things are kind of tough. God will see you through it.

"AS SOON AS I HEARD THESE WORDS I SAT DOWN AND WEPT AND MOURNED FOR DAYS, AND I CONTINUED FASTING AND PRAYING BEFORE THE GOD OF HEAVEN." - NEHEMIAH 1:4

Have you ever been so overwhelmed by problems in your community, that it caused you to weep? Maybe you experienced some really rough relational issues. Or maybe someone you know personally had to deal with an illness. Or maybe there was an issue or conflict of some sort that divided your school, church, or city. When we face these types of conflict, it can be really hard.

When we think of prophets, we probably think of tough guys who were privileged to know God personally, and do what He commands. **READ NEHEMIAH 1.** Nehemiah saw the issues of his world, and faced with the realities of what had happened to himself and his people, he sat down and wept. He mourned the sin of his community, and fasted before God.

When is the last time that you took some time to pray, and even fast, about the issues going on in your community? Has it ever occurred to you to see them in this way? It may seem like these issues aren't spiritual issues at all. But if all strife and suffering are a result of sin, then ALL the pain caused by these issues has its roots in sin. It IS a spiritual issue. Have you considered what it's like to take your pain and confusion to God?

SOMETHING TO THINK ABOUT...
· What are some of the big issues in your community that need addressing?
· What's keeping you from taking time to pray for them?
· What is your role in helping to address these issues?

THIS DEVOTION SPEAKS TO GOD'S SENSE OF JUSTICE. GO TO PAGE 4 FOR A DESCRIPTION OF THIS ATTRIBUTE.

"THEN I REPLIED TO THEM, 'THE GOD OF HEAVEN WILL MAKE US PROSPER, AND WE HIS SERVANTS WILL ARISE AND BUILD, BUT YOU HAVE NO PORTION OR RIGHT OR CLAIM IN JERUSALEM.'"
- NEHEMIAH 2:20

Have you ever had a really huge idea, an idea that others didn't understand? If so, you understand what it's like to have so much excitement and nervous energy building inside of you. You want to tell others, but you can't . . . not yet. There is the urge to hold on to the idea until it is far enough along that others will share your enthusiasm. The worst thing that can happen, it seems, is that you let the cat out of the bag too soon. If you've ever felt this way, you'll be able to relate with Nehemiah.

READ NEHEMIAH 2. God gave Nehemiah some very big, very bold plans. Nehemiah knew no one else would understand. So he kept them to himself until it was time. When he finally revealed his plans, the others laughed at Nehemiah, and didn't believe that he could rebuild the wall. And yet, Nehemiah remained strong and confident in the plans God had laid out for him.

It's easy to let others influence our opinions. It doesn't make you weak. It's just human nature. And so we hide our ideas for fear that others will laugh at us. But Nehemiah went on to do incredible things, whether people would support him or not. He's a great example of what it looks like to act out the plans God has for our lives, regardless of what others think.

How many times have you let someone shoot an idea of yours down? How many times have you let people determine your happiness or self-worth? What can you do to carry out your plans with confidence?

SOMETHING TO THINK ABOUT...
· How can you stand by what you believe in, even when others don't understand it?
· Take some time today to pray to God, asking Him to make His will for your life clear to you, and to give you strength to pursue His will regardless of what others think.

WEEK 26, DAY 4

"AND I LOOKED AND AROSE AND SAID TO THE NOBLES AND TO THE OFFICIALS AND TO THE REST OF THE PEOPLE, 'DO NOT BE AFRAID OF THEM. REMEMBER THE LORD, WHO IS GREAT AND AWESOME, AND FIGHT FOR YOUR BROTHERS, YOUR SONS, YOUR DAUGHTERS, YOUR WIVES, AND YOUR HOMES.'" - NEHEMIAH 4:14

It's no fun being made fun of. The embarrassment and pain it causes feels like one of the worst things in the world, especially in the moment. And when it's someone you are friends with, it's even worse. It never feels good. The feelings of self-doubt, anger, and confusion stick around a while.

READ NEHEMIAH 4. Imagine working SUPER hard on something. Imagine it's a huge task, something like rebuilding a once-powerful city by hand. Imagine people see the hard work you've done, and then imagine they laugh at you. They call you names. They insult your project and say it's going to fall apart. Wouldn't that make you furious? Wouldn't that make you afraid? Would you want to give up? Nehemiah didn't give up. Nehemiah encouraged his people to remember that God is AWESOME. He encouraged them to stay strong, reminding them that God would fight for them.

We all have insecurities that we fight every day. Keep in mind that God loves you just the way you are, and is fighting for you. He made you and called you to Him. He is on your side, always. Remember that God is awesome. And no matter what life throws at you, God is greater.

SOMETHING TO THINK ABOUT...
· How can you remind yourself that God loves you, even the parts of you that others make fun of?
· Pray to God today and thank Him for His plan for your life, His unconditional love for you, and His undying faithfulness. Praise Him that He is always in your corner.

THIS DEVOTION SPEAKS TO GOD'S FAITHFULNESS.
GO TO PAGE 4 FOR A DESCRIPTION OF THIS ATTRIBUTE.

WEEK 26, DAY 5

"AND WHEN ALL OUR ENEMIES HEARD OF IT, ALL THE NATIONS AROUND US WERE AFRAID AND FELL GREATLY IN THEIR OWN ESTEEM, FOR THEY PERCEIVED THAT THIS WORK HAD BEEN ACCOMPLISHED WITH THE HELP OF OUR GOD." - NEHEMIAH 6:16

READ NEHEMIAH 6:16-19.

This week you've been reading about the challenges associated with God calling Nehemiah to rebuild Jerusalem. It was a task that was full of problems - some external, some internal. But the task was God-given, and God-empowered. Ultimately, it succeeded. Nehemiah and the people did in fact rebuild the wall. And in doing so, God got the credit for the work. But it's an interesting moment to pause and think about how Nehemiah might have reacted.

Could we blame Nehemiah if he wanted revenge? Could we blame him if he wanted to brag and boast? "I told you so," would have been something that was very easy for Nehemiah to say. He could have put it in the face of his enemies. But it seems like he didn't. It seems like he let the work speak for itself.

It's easy to want to get even with people who have wronged us. So often we want to take revenge into our own hands. But throughout the Old Testament, God reminds us that vengeance is His. We have to trust His sense of justice and judgment. We're not God. We have to let go of our issues, trusting that He will work all things out according to His plan.

Letting God handle our problems doesn't get us the immediate solutions we want. So we often ignore His promise to take care of us, and try and take care of it on our own. What Nehemiah accomplished was so much greater that any one person could have accomplished on his or her own. Nehemiah gave God the credit He deserved, and then trusted God to deal rightly with His enemies. That's not a bad model for us.

SOMETHING TO THINK ABOUT...
· Why is it so hard to let God take care of our problems?
· What is the result of giving our problems to God? Why is it greater than handling it on your own?

WEEK 27

WEEK 27, DAY 1

**"AND THERE IS SALVATION IN NO ONE
ELSE, FOR THERE IS NO OTHER NAME
UNDER HEAVEN GIVEN AMONG MEN BY
WHICH WE MUST BE SAVED."
- ACTS 4:12**

This is a fun week. It's a transition week. You're transitioning from the Old Testament to the New Testament. Remember, the Old Testament was dominated by a few themes: Creation, Adam and Eve's sin, God's covenant to call a people to Himself, God's great care for those people, those people turning from God, God's patient concern for His people, and then God's judgment of His people. But even in God's judgment, there was grace. With every harsh warning the prophets gave, they promised a hopeful future. What we see in Jesus is that hope made flesh.

Tomorrow you'll read one last excerpt from Nehemiah. While Nehemiah isn't the last book of the Old Testament, it's the final chronological account of God's people in the Old Testament. It serves as a great starting point to set up Jesus coming onto the scene. And come onto the scene He does. In dramatic fashion!

Jesus represented the hope for Israel, and for all humankind. As you prepare to begin to focus on Jesus' arrival into the story, memorize Acts 4:12. It is a short, powerful verse that really does sort of encapsulate the Gospel in just a few words. It's a useful verse to know as you share the love of Jesus with others.

WEEK 27, DAY 2

**"AND THE PRIESTS AND THE LEVITES PURIFIED
THEMSELVES, AND THEY PURIFIED THE PEOPLE AND
THE GATES AND THE WALL." - NEHEMIAH 12:30**

New Year is an interesting time, if you think about it. We get su-per-pumped, and spend a ton of energy celebrating. But what are we celebrating? We're really celebrating two things. First, we're cel-ebrating the possibilities of a new year. Second, we're looking back and honoring all that has happened in the previous year. New Year's resolutions are all about the future. But there is at least a small bit of reflection about the ups and downs of the year that just was.

READ NEHEMIAH 12:27-33. After the Israelites built a new wall around Jerusalem, they wanted to have a huge party. But first, they wanted to set it apart as God's. They wanted to take a moment to praise God for following through on His promises, and performing yet another miracle in their land.

It's so easy to move on "business as usual." The Israelites probably had other things to do. But they knew they should stop and honor God. They not only honored God, but they purified everything in the land. They took a moment to realize that this was a new season in their life and in their journey. They were super-excited about looking to the future and the possibility of all that was to come. They puri-fied everything to symbolically make a "blank slate" for the things to come. But there was also great reflection about all that God had done for them. It was a looking back, and a looking forward.

SOMETHING TO THINK ABOUT...
· Take some time today to look back honor God for the things He has done. Write down three to five things God has done in your life over the last year or so.
· Ask God to create a blank slate so that He can continue to work in your life. Welcome Him in to start a new work in you.

WEEK 27, DAY 3

"AND THE ANGEL SAID TO HER, 'DO NOT BE AFRAID, MARY, FOR YOU HAVE FOUND FAVOR WITH GOD. AND BEHOLD, YOU WILL CONCEIVE IN YOUR WOMB AND BEAR A SON, AND YOU SHALL CALL HIS NAME JESUS.'" - LUKE 1:30-31

Has there ever been a time when you felt like God was distant? There are many times in life when it just doesn't seem clear what God wants from us, and we wish He would be a little clearer, or at least louder. Maybe you've said something like this to God before: "God, if you would just talk to me or show me a sign, I'll listen!" But what about the times when God is clear, and we don't have to wonder what He's thinking or what He wants? How do we respond then?

READ LUKE 1:26-38. This must have been a terrifying experience for Mary. First, angels are not the sweet, baby-faced messengers we sometimes imagine them to be. They are more like warriors. Second, if what the angel Gabriel told Mary was true, Mary's life was about to get really complicated.

This was not a time when God's desires were unclear. Mary knew exactly what God was asking her to do. It was a task full of honor; but it was difficult, too. People—even her soon-to-be husband—wouldn't understand, or perhaps even believe her. But how did she respond? "I am the Lord's servant. May your word to me be fulfilled."

What the angel told Mary was probably very scary to her. And we know she didn't completely know what it all meant. But God had been clear to her, so she was willing to do what He said.

SOMETHING TO THINK ABOUT...

· Is there something you know that you should do—maybe even something you know that God wants you to do—that you're avoiding or scared to do?
· What would it mean in that situation to tell God, "I am your servant" and be obedient in what He's asking?

WEEK 27, DAY 4

"AND BLESSED IS SHE WHO BELIEVED THAT THERE WOULD BE A FULFILLMENT OF WHAT WAS SPOKEN TO HER FROM THE LORD." - LUKE 1:45

Have you ever wondered where you fit in? Not just in school, or with your friends, but in our world? If God's really moving in this world, what part do you play? Does it really matter that you're here? Maybe it feels at times like God has a role for everyone to play—expect you.

READ LUKE 1:39-56. If you've been around church much—especially around Christmas—you've heard the story of Mary giving birth to Jesus so often that it's easy to forget one really important detail: Mary was a young teenager, and she was engaged. Back then, people got married pretty young.

We don't really know much about Mary's life before the whole "big-scary-angel-told-her-she'd-miraculously-give-birth-to-the-Messiah" thing happened. We don't know if she ever wondered at her place in this world, if she ever wanted to get out of her small town, or if she even wanted to be married at all. But what we do know is how she responded.

In Mary's song that you just read, she sings about God's greatness and mercy. But there's one line that's easy to skip over: "For behold, from now on all generations will call me blessed; for he who is mighty has done great things for me, and holy is his name."(1:48-49). Mary considers it "great" that she gets to be a part of what God is doing in our world. She marvels at the fact that God would use her in this way.

God has a place for you, too. It may not be clear now, but God is up to something, and He desires to use those who follow His Son Jesus in His plan.

SOMETHING TO THINK ABOUT...
· Why do you think God uses imperfect people to carry out His perfect plan?
· Have you ever wondered whether God could use you?
· What is one way that God has ever used you to make someone's life better? How do you think you can let Him do more of that through you this week?

WEEK 27, DAY 5

"AND ALL WHO HEARD THEM LAID THEM UP IN THEIR HEARTS, SAYING, 'WHAT THEN WILL THIS CHILD BE?' FOR THE HAND OF THE LORD WAS WITH HIM." - LUKE 1:66

Sometimes, things work out for us in a really good way. Maybe it was that time you forgot to study for a test, and you still got a really good grade. Or perhaps someone you loved was really ill, and they got better. We often wonder what God is doing when life is hard, but have you ever considered what God is up to when life is good?

READ LUKE 1:57-66. For the vast majority of Elizabeth and Zechariah's marriage, they had been unable to have kids. In their culture, having kids was a huge deal. They had prayed, wept, and probably even had times when they were angry with God. But now things were different. Elizabeth gave birth to a healthy baby boy. God had answered their prayer, and life was good.

The thing is, God didn't give them this awesome gift just for them. Everyone was happy for Elizabeth: "Her neighbors and relatives heard that the Lord had shown her great mercy, and they shared her joy." God had done something great, and they loved their baby boy. But was God up to something else? When Zechariah named the boy "John" and suddenly regained his ability to talk, everyone began to wonder what exactly God was up to.

When God does something great in your life, chances are He's not doing it just for you. It's true that God loves you and loves pouring His goodness out on you. But it could be that when He gives you an incredible gift, He's not just doing something for you; He's also interested in doing something through you.

SOMETHING TO THINK ABOUT...
· What is something good in your life that has happened recently, or perhaps is happening now?
· What are some ways that God could use that good thing He's given you to bless others?
· If that's true, is there something you can do to make that happen?

THIS DEVOTION SPEAKS TO HOW GOD'S SOVEREIGNTY GO TO PAGE 4 FOR A DESCRIPTION OF THIS ATTRIBUTE.

WEEK 28

WEEK 28, DAY 1

**"FOR OUR SAKE HE MADE HIM TO BE SIN WHO
KNEW NO SIN, SO THAT IN HIM WE MIGHT BE-
COME THE RIGHTEOUSNESS OF GOD."
- 2 CORINTHIANS 5:21**

This week you'll be continuing to look at the big-picture story of the Bible by looking at more of the birth narrative of Jesus. When we consider all Jesus was and is, Paul's words from 2 Corinthians 5:21 speak volumes. For the sake of sinners like us – people who were lost in their sin, separated from God – God sent His Son Jesus. Jesus was perfect. And yet, Jesus took on our sin in order that He might pay the price our sin deserves. And all of this was done so that we may become righteous in God's eyes, freed from the stain our sin earns for us.

This would be a great time to memorize this powerful verse. Maybe you have been ignoring this part of your devotions lately. Take the time today to dig back in. Try the "5-5-5" method we talked about in the beginning of the year. Do whatever it takes to memorize this verse. It's such a wonderful description of God's love, mercy, and grace.

**THIS DEVOTION SPEAKS TO GOD'S RIGHTEOUSNESS. GO TO
PAGE 4 FOR A DESCRIPTION OF THIS ATTRIBUTE.**

WEEK 28, DAY 2

"BUT AS HE CONSIDERED THESE THINGS, BEHOLD, AN ANGEL OF THE
LORD APPEARED TO HIM IN A DREAM, SAYING, 'JOSEPH, SON OF DAVID,
DO NOT FEAR TO TAKE MARY AS YOUR WIFE, FOR THAT WHICH IS CON-
CEIVED IN HER IS FROM THE HOLY SPIRIT. SHE WILL BEAR A SON, AND
YOU SHALL CALL HIS NAME JESUS, FOR HE WILL SAVE HIS PEOPLE FROM
THEIR SINS.'" - MATTHEW 1:20-21

Embarrassing situations are not a lot of fun. You probably try to avoid them when-
ever you can, right? And when we do something that causes people to make fun
of us, we want to do everything we can to either make it stop, or to find a place to
hide. But what about the times when doing the right thing is what causes people
to make fun of us? What do you do when you have a choice between doing what
you know is right and being well liked by others?

READ MATTHEW 1:18-25. Joseph had found out that the woman he was engaged
to was pregnant. And he was 100% sure he was not the dad, since they had never
slept together. Even though they had not been through a ceremony, in their culture
they were as good as married. The choice was easy for Joseph: she had cheated
on him, so they could not be married.

That all changed when Joseph had a dream. An angel told him that Mary had
not cheated on him, but rather that her pregnancy was a miracle since she was a
virgin. Now, he had a tougher choice: stay with Mary and face public ridicule (because who would believe Mary was still a virgin), or do the right thing. Put yourself
in Joseph's shoes. Can you imagine a tougher decision?

SOMETHING TO THINK ABOUT...
· If you were Joseph, what would you have done?
· Have you ever had to choose between the right choice and the popular choice?
What was that like?
· Is there a situation you're facing now where you need to make that choice?

WEEK 28, DAY 3

"AND THE ANGEL SAID TO THEM, 'FEAR NOT, FOR BEHOLD, I BRING YOU GOOD NEWS OF GREAT JOY THAT WILL BE FOR ALL THE PEOPLE. FOR UNTO YOU IS BORN THIS DAY IN THE CITY OF DAVID A SAVIOR, WHO IS CHRIST THE LORD.'" - LUKE 2:10-11

Think about the time that you were doing something and were interrupted. Maybe you were playing video games and your mom or dad made you stop and do chores. Or perhaps you were hanging out with a friend and he or she had to leave early. It's annoying, right?

READ LUKE 2:1-21. The shepherds were doing their job, minding their own business. It wasn't a glamorous job, but it was at least a steady source of income—at least if they did their job right and didn't lose any sheep.

Then, their night gets interrupted. An angel breaks into the sky and surprises them with great news, and his angel friends follow the great news up with a song. God is up to something new, and they were the first ones to hear about it (besides Mary and Joseph). When the angels leave, they jump at the opportunity and go see this baby who would be their savior.

God uses interruptions in our life to point us to Him. In our day-to-day lives, we don't always see God. These interruptions aren't always welcome. Sometimes our routine is disrupted with bad news, like an illness or an unexpected move. But there are times when God breaks into our lives, and you have a choice: jump at the opportunity to see God, or let it pass.

SOMETHING TO THINK ABOUT...
· When is a time when your "normal" life was interrupted?
· Was your life interrupted with a good thing or a bad thing?
·What is one "interruption" going on in your life that God might use to help you see Him?

WEEK 28, DAY 4

**"AND BEING WARNED IN A DREAM NOT TO RETURN TO HEROD,
THEY DEPARTED TO THEIR OWN COUNTRY BY ANOTHER WAY."
- MATTHEW 2:12**

Jake was entering his sophomore year at school. With the freedom of a driver's license and a car, he expected this year at school to be the best yet. A few of the guys saw him drive up on the first day of school. They came over to welcome him (and his car) into their circle. This year was looking spectacular for Jake—except that two weeks later he was pulled over for speeding. He was trying to make curfew after dropping his friends off at their homes.

Jake knew his friends had been acting a little strange and laughing at the tiniest things that shouldn't even have been funny. The officer smelled something familiar in Jake's car. It was the smell of marijuana smoke in the fabric. Then he saw a baggie with what appeared to be a couple of joints in it. The bag had fallen out of Jake's friend's pocket.

After a long night of truth-filled lectures from the police and his parents, Jake realized how much more careful he should have been in choosing his friends. The guys he thought made him look popular were the reason he almost got arrested. Although he continued to be kind to those guys, and prayed for them, Jake steered clear of them when it came to social activities the rest of that year.

GRAB YOUR BIBLE AND READ MATTHEW 2:1-12. Herod was a wicked man. His plans involved all manner of selfishness, and all manner of sin. The wise men realized rather quickly that he did not want to worship Jesus; he wanted to have him executed. So, they heeded God's warning and took the way home that kept them at a safe distance from Herod.

SOMETHING TO THINK ABOUT . . .
· Is there someone you need to continue loving, yet distance yourself from socially because of the danger he or she might be pulling you toward? ·
· Ask God to make it clear to you today.

WEEK 28, DAY 5

"NOW WHEN THEY HAD DEPARTED, BEHOLD, AN ANGEL OF THE LORD APPEARED TO JOSEPH IN A DREAM AND SAID, 'RISE, TAKE THE CHILD AND HIS MOTHER, AND FLEE TO EGYPT, AND REMAIN THERE UNTIL I TELL YOU, FOR HEROD IS ABOUT TO SEARCH FOR THE CHILD, TO DESTROY HIM.' AND HE ROSE AND TOOK THE CHILD AND HIS MOTHER BY NIGHT AND DEPARTED TO EGYPT." - MATTHEW 2:13-14

April 27th 2011 was a tragic day in the city of Tuscaloosa, AL. When a massive tornado hit, many died, and the landscape of much of the sprawling college town was changed permanently. Public officials warned of the coming destruction for several hours leading up to this horrific weather event. And while warning systems are fairly advanced in tornado-prone areas now, unfortunately they still rely on human alertness. If someone doesn't hear or see the warnings, then death may be imminent for them.

TAKE YOUR BIBLE OUT AND LOOK UP MATTHEW 2:13-23. God sent an angel to warn Joseph of imminent danger. Joseph could have ignored the warning. Instead he listened and escaped, saving Jesus from Herod's slaughter of baby boys, which was intended to kill Him. After Herod died, his son took over the throne. Once again God warned Joseph of danger, this time through a dream. Joseph heeded the warning and fled once more.

Tuscaloosa was just one of many towns struck by tornadoes on that infamous day. In every location, warning signs were sent out multiple times. Similarly, God always sends out warning signs to you through the Bible, the Holy Spirit, and even other Christ followers when dangerous sin choices are ahead. Ask God to help you see and hear His warnings more clearly today and to give you the strength to heed them more effectively.

SOMETHING TO THINK ABOUT . . .

· Have you ever narrowly escaped grave danger?
· How many times have you regretted heeding the warning about a sin after it was too late?
· What can you do to be more alert to the warnings God gives you through the Holy Spirit?

WEEK 29

WEEK 29, DAY 1

**"FOR WE DO NOT HAVE A HIGH PRIEST WHO IS UNABLE TO
SYMPATHIZE WITH OUR WEAKNESSES, BUT ONE WHO IN EVERY
RESPECT HAS BEEN TEMPTED AS WE ARE, YET WITHOUT SIN."
- HEBREWS 4:15**

Your journey through the big-picture story of the Bible continues. This week you'll transition from Jesus' birth narrative and will begin looking at Jesus' life and ministry. In doing so, you'll begin to see quite a few awesome things about Christ. But one thing that you'll hopefully see is that, while Jesus was fully God, He was fully human too.

The humanity of Jesus is one of the key things that shines through the gospel accounts of His life. Jesus didn't live His life separated from those He came to save. He lived among us, His children. And because He was both fully God and fully human, Jesus dealt with the same temptations we deal with. When you read that Jesus was sinless, it wasn't because He was a spiritual robot, or something like that. He was tempted. And He overcame temptation without sinning.

This should change the way you view Jesus. Jesus understands what you're going through. He's been there. Memorize this verse this week to help remind you that your Savior understands what it's like to face the things you face. There's great power in this understanding.

**THIS DEVOTION SPEAKS TO GOD'S FAITHFULNESS.
GO TO PAGE 4 FOR A DESCRIPTION OF THIS ATTRIBUTE.**

WEEK 29, DAY 2

**"AND HE SAID TO THEM, 'WHY WERE YOU LOOKING FOR ME? DID
YOU NOT KNOW THAT I MUST BE IN MY FATHER'S HOUSE?'"
- LUKE 2:49**

Arden Hayes is a five-year-old. But he's not like other little kids. He wowed the audience on Jimmy Kimmel Live with his wit and charm. His knowledge of geography astounded the crowd. If you're able to look up YouTube clips, check him out. You'll be as amazed as the crowd at how much this little guy knows.

NOW, GRAB YOUR BIBLE AND READ LUKE 2:41-52. When Jesus was twelve years old, His family left their small town to attend the Passover Festival in the big city of Jerusalem. On their way home from the festival, Jesus' parents realized He was missing. Traveling back to Jerusalem, they found Jesus in the temple, where for three days He had been aweing the religious leaders with His intimate knowledge of God.

Imagine how concerned Joseph and Mary were up until they found Jesus in the temple. In verse 49, Jesus gently reminded them of His purpose on earth, and how easy it would have been to find Him had they not gotten caught up in other activities. Jesus said, "Didn't you know that I must be in my Father's house?" It is amazing enough that a twelve-year-old can teach seemingly wiser, and certainly older, adults about the things of God. In fact, it is much more amazing than a five-year-old who is an expert in geography. Yet how many times do teens focus on things of the world, which will not matter eternally, over the things of God? Do you desire to be more about God and less about the world? Ask God to help you overcome your struggle, and be a shining reflection of Christ even to those much older than you.

SOMETHING TO THINK ABOUT . . .
· What is one practical way you can be more consistent in being in your "Father's house?"
· Look up and read 1 Timothy 4: 12. What area of life listed in this verse do you struggle with most?

WEEK 29, DAY 3

**"AND THE CROWDS ASKED HIM, 'WHAT THEN SHALL WE DO?' AND HE AN-
SWERED THEM, 'WHOEVER HAS TWO TUNICS IS TO SHARE WITH HIM WHO
HAS NONE, AND WHOEVER HAS FOOD IS TO DO LIKEWISE.'"
- LUKE 3:10-11**

Faith was a stereotypical 15-year-old girl going on her first mission trip. She loved selfies, spending money, getting noticed by guys, and feeling accepted. She also had a longing for something more meaningful in her life, which is why she signed up for a 1,000 mile bus ride to another part of the country.

While her mission team was leading a Bible club in a low-income apartment complex, she met a quiet little girl nicknamed Muffin. And, after a couple of days of getting to know this bright-eyed 7-year-old, Faith discovered that the day's Bible club snack was the first food Muffin had eaten since the snack 24 hours earlier at the last Bible club gathering. This broke Faith's heart.

TAKE OUT YOUR BIBLE AND READ LUKE 3: 1-20. John was an extremely bold Christ follower. His life was dedicated to sharing the love of Jesus, and warning of impending judgment for those who rejected Him. He challenged people to help the needy, be honest in their dealings, and be content with what they had. Most of all, He pointed people to Jesus.

Now, apply John's ministry to Faith's situation with Muffin. Faith's whole perspective on life was shaken to the core by meeting a hungry child face-to-face. Selfies, shopping, and making guys' heads turn suddenly seemed very small to her. She had encountered a situation that God used to break her heart for the needs of others. (As for Muffin, the local mission provided three heaping bags of groceries to her family the next day along with a commitment to follow up with them as long as the need was there.)

SOMETHING TO THINK ABOUT . . .
· John's ministry was all about expanding the glory of God in people's lives.
· Ask God to open your spiritual eyes to the physical and spiritual needs around you today. Who knows: your world may just be rocked like Faith's world was when she met Muffin.

WEEK 29, DAY 4

"BUT JESUS ANSWERED HIM, 'LET IT BE SO NOW, FOR THUS IT IS FITTING FOR US TO FULFILL ALL RIGHTEOUSNESS.' THEN HE CONSENTED."
- MATTHEW 3:15

When is the last time your mind was genuinely blown by an illusion or some other stunt performed at a big event? Have you sever seen an illusionist in person? Or watched one on TV? Some of the things they seemingly do defy logic. Many times, they leave you with your mouth open, saying to yourself, "How in the world did they do that"? Sometimes things happen that no one is expecting.

GRAB YOUR BIBLE, FIND MATTHEW 3: 13-17, and carefully read this passage. John had been proclaiming to everyone that Jesus was coming. Imagine talking about this great Messiah to people passionately every day, only to have Him actually show up one day and want you to baptize Him! You can imagine John thinking, "I'm not worthy! I'm not worthy!" Wouldn't you feel that way too?

Reread verse 15. Jesus reminded John that He came to earth as a living example of how to live for God. That included publically acknowledging a life dedicated to God through baptism. Through His own baptism, Jesus was identifying with sinners, and foreshadowing the sin that the sinless Savior would take upon Himself on the cross.

As if it wasn't exciting and humbling enough to baptize Jesus, John and the others at the riverbank witnessed the Holy Trinity all in the same place at the same time! God the Father audibly affirmed God the Son's baptism, while the Holy Spirit was also present in the form of a dove. This was truly a moment to treasure!

Remember that, just like any other person, John was only righteous because of his faith in Christ. Here's what's great about that: If you realize what Jesus did for you on the cross, and follow Him with your life, then you too are righteous in God's eyes!

SOMETHING TO THINK ABOUT . . .
· Have you devoted your life to following Christ?
· Have you been baptized?

WEEK 29, DAY 5

"AND THE TEMPTER CAME AND SAID TO HIM, 'IF YOU ARE THE SON OF GOD, COMMAND THESE STONES TO BECOME LOAVES OF BREAD.'" - MATTHEW 4:3

"If you are the Son of God..."
"If you are the Son of God..."
"If you are the Son of God..."

AS YOU READ MATTHEW 4:1-11, notice each temptation comes with this prompt for Jesus to prove Himself.

Fast-forward about three years. Jesus will be dying in agonizing pain after being up all night and receiving a solid scourging. Matthew 27:39-40 tells us that as people passed by Jesus on the cross, they hurled insults at Him. Among other things, they would say, "If you are the Son of God, why don't you get yourself off that cross"?

Think of a time you've been challenged to prove yourself. Maybe you're the first chair flute, starting forward, or lead vocalist. Imagine if you took the time to teach your 5-year-old nephew your skill. After several attempts to put the ball in the hoop, he throws out the challenge, "if you're so good, why don't you make a basket?" The hoop is seriously like 4 feet off the ground. You wouldn't even have to try. That's Jesus in the face of His own creation mocking Him. Satan? Jesus made him. Those people at the cross? Jesus formed them from dirt. From absolute nothingness, Jesus created the idea of sun, photosynthesis, trees . . . all the things necessary to custom the crude cross He was nailed to.

How did Christ respond to challenges to His truth? How do you respond to challenges to your faith?

SOMETHING TO THINK ABOUT . . .
· If Christ had come down off the cross, if He had given the people exactly what they wanted, we would be facing eternity in Hell. What is God withholding from you? Is it possible, just perhaps, that He has a very good reason?
· Pray for the courage to be a Christian instead of merely acting like one.

WEEK 30

> **"THEN HE SAID TO HIS DISCIPLES, 'THE HARVEST IS PLEN-
> TIFUL, BUT THE LABORERS ARE FEW; THEREFORE PRAY
> EARNESTLY TO THE LORD OF THE HARVEST TO SEND OUT
> LABORERS INTO HIS HARVEST.'" - MATTHEW 9:37-38**

So you're well on your way to digging-in to the story of Jesus' life. One of the things you'll notice quickly is how committed to people Jesus was. You may say to yourself, "Well, yeah. Of course He was. He's God." But don't be too quick to jump to conclusions. Recall that pretty much all of creation is in rebellion against God (that's the effects of sin at work in the world). God could have said, "You know what? We're doing Noah and The Flood, Part 2. Except this time, no Noah." We deserve nothing but punishment for our sin. But God is amazingly, wonderfully merciful. He gives us grace when we deserve judgment. This is why Jesus' unwavering compassion is remarkable.

What you'll see as you trace Jesus' story is that He was tirelessly engaged with people. Whether it was the Pharisees He was trying to set straight, or sick people He was healing, Jesus was deeply involved with people. These verses from Matthew 9:37-38 show the heart behind Jesus' involvement: His compassion. Jesus was motivated to reach those who needed reaching because of His compassion.

Take the challenge to memorize, or at least meditate on these verses this week. Let them move your heart to compassion as well, motivating you to show the love of Christ to those in your life who need it the most.

THIS DEVOTION SPEAKS TO GOD'S COMPASSION.
GO TO PAGE 4 FOR A DESCRIPTION OF THIS ATTRIBUTE.

WEEK 30, DAY 2

AND THEY ROSE UP AND DROVE HIM OUT OF THE TOWN AND BROUGHT HIM TO THE BROW OF THE HILL ON WHICH THEIR TOWN WAS BUILT, SO THAT THEY COULD THROW HIM DOWN THE CLIFF. BUT PASSING THROUGH THEIR MIDST, HE WENT AWAY. - LUKE 4:29-30

Jesus is amazing. If He's trying to win the world for God, why did He start off by insulting the people in His own hometown?

READ LUKE 4:16-30. You'll see what we mean. The people whom Jesus grew up around got so furious that they tried to throw Him off a cliff! Apparently there's something else going on here. For starters, it helps to understand that Jesus practically came right out and said, "I am the Messiah." The verse Jesus read from Isaiah would be very familiar to His listeners. They would have known that it referred to the Messiah. And when He said, "Today this is fulfilled in your hearing," it would have caused a major stir. The people simply couldn't believe that the little boy, Jesus, Mary and Joseph's son, could be the Messiah. They watched Him grow up. So yeah, it was probably a little much to ask these people to believe that Jesus is the Messiah. Or is it?

Now, back to you. What about the whole Christian thing is hard for you to believe. Why? Really examine your motives. If you struggle with the idea of creation vs. evolution, is it really the evidence? Or do you really struggle wanting not to be that kid? If you struggle with the idea of miracles actually happening, is it really the concept that the Being who created space, time, and matter could actually apply them according to His will? Or do you really struggle because you've never seen it? How are you different than the people accusing Jesus of lying?

SOMETHING TO THINK ABOUT . . .

· Jesus spit-up on Mary. He had to learn to walk. Jesus even experienced awkward teen years. Jesus was fully God. But He was 100% human. What does it mean to you that Jesus grew up human?
· Look around at the students in your school. Is it hard to believe one of them may be the next Bill Gates, Albert Einstein, or Abe Lincoln? Why or why not?

> "AND IN THE SYNAGOGUE THERE WAS A MAN WHO HAD THE SPIRIT OF AN UN-CLEAN DEMON, AND HE CRIED OUT WITH A LOUD VOICE, 'HA! WHAT HAVE YOU TO DO WITH US, JESUS OF NAZARETH? HAVE YOU COME TO DESTROY US? I KNOW WHO YOU ARE—THE HOLY ONE OF GOD.' BUT JESUS REBUKED HIM, SAYING, 'BE SILENT AND COME OUT OF HIM!' AND WHEN THE DEMON HAD THROWN HIM DOWN IN THEIR MIDST, HE CAME OUT OF HIM, HAVING DONE HIM NO HARM." - LUKE 4:33-35

When you read verses like Luke 4:31-41, do you ever wonder where the demons go? Is an interaction with Jesus fatal for a demon? Remember, the first one asked Jesus if He intended to destroy him. Who knows? (Well, other than God.)

Yesterday, you were asked to think about any struggle you might have with disbelief. Today, let's focus on belief, particularly the belief of the demons. One thing that's really amazing about these types of interactions is that the demons knew exactly who Jesus was. They don't struggle with disbelief like we do. Even though they are in constant rebellion against God, they still knew the truth. Imagine the shrieking demon announcing, "You are the Son of God!" These demons didn't just politely give in to Jesus' instructions; they were scared out of their little demon minds!

We need to put our belief into action by letting Jesus be the ruler of our lives. That's the part the demons are not willing to do. But Galatians 4:6 tells us that we are the children of God. We know who He is, and in our struggle to let Him rule us, we alone -not demons, not angels - get to call Him Father.

SOMETHING TO THINK ABOUT . . .
· Are you keeping a tiny piece of your life under your own leadership and rule? Give it to God let Him be Lord of all.
· Maybe it's weird, but next time you pray, imagine you are sitting on the couch next to God. He wants a relationship like you might share with your dad (if your dad could be perfect). Talk to Him like this and see what happens.

THIS DEVOTION SPEAKS TO HOW GOD'S SOVEREIGNTY GO TO PAGE 4 FOR A DESCRIPTION OF THIS ATTRIBUTE.

WEEK 30, DAY 4

"AND GOING ON FROM THERE HE SAW TWO OTHER BROTHERS, JAMES
THE SON OF ZEBEDEE AND JOHN HIS BROTHER, IN THE BOAT WITH
ZEBEDEE THEIR FATHER, MENDING THEIR NETS, AND HE CALLED
THEM. IMMEDIATELY THEY LEFT THE BOAT AND THEIR FATHER AND
FOLLOWED HIM." - MATTHEW 4:21-22

"Zebedee." What a cool name. So imagine you're Zebedee. (That's fun to say!) **WHEN WE READ MATTHEW 4:18-22,** there's so much that is left un-written. What was Zebedee's thinking, for example? If you live in the city, this may be hard to get. But if you live on a farm, you can picture it. Fishing was a family business. Zebedee absolutely depended on his sons to make a living. So what was Zebedee thinking when this guy Jesus, who got run out Nazareth, tells his sons to leave their old dad and go off with Him? What was going through his mind when his sons actually did it?

Without a second thought, Zebedee's sons dropped what they were doing and followed Jesus. Where were they going? What would they do? How about food, money, shelter? Is there a strategic plan? Who else is coming? Wouldn't you have legitimate questions that Jesus should answer?

Today, we don't have to wonder much about things. Lost the instruction manual? Google it. Didn't listen in class? Wikipedia knows what you're missing. Want to know how to build a fingerprint scanning garage door opener? There's an Instructable for that. Unfortunately, when you search the Web for "what's on God's mind?" you only find more questions. Fortunately, you do know what's on God's heart. We have His Word to guide us, and the Holy Spirit to help.

SOMETHING TO THINK ABOUT . . .
· Is God calling you to something that scares you? You might not know all the answers, but you know the heart of the One who's asking. Trust Him.
· If Jesus were walking through your town, whom would He pick to follow Him? He apparently selected you. What are you going to do about it?

> "AND HE WENT THROUGHOUT ALL GALILEE, TEACH-
> ING IN THEIR SYNAGOGUES AND PROCLAIMING THE
> GOSPEL OF THE KINGDOM AND HEALING EVERY DIS-
> EASE AND EVERY AFFLICTION AMONG THE PEOPLE."
> - MATTHEW 4:23

READ MATTHEW 4:23-25.

Today is going to be really different. Today, the challenge for you is to write the Gospel - the good news - in your own words. See if you can write the Gospel message down as if you were explaining it to someone for the first time. Use the space below to do it, or grab a journal.

SOMETHING TO THINK ABOUT...
· Was that hard? What was hard about it?
· When was the last time you verbally shared the Gospel with someone? What steps can you take to make sure you share the Gospel more with more people?

WEEK 31

WEEK 31, DAY 1

"AND YOU, WHO WERE DEAD IN YOUR TRESPASSES
AND THE UNCIRCUMCISION OF YOUR FLESH, GOD
MADE ALIVE TOGETHER WITH HIM, HAVING FORGIV-
EN US ALL OUR TRESPASSES, BY CANCELING THE
RECORD OF DEBT THAT STOOD AGAINST US WITH ITS
LEGAL DEMANDS. THIS HE SET ASIDE, NAILING IT TO
THE CROSS." - COLOSSIANS 2:13-14

As you continue to read through the big-picture story of the Bible, this week you'll spend time watching as Jesus encounters various people. As Jesus is going about His ministry - healing, preaching, and performing other miracles – He's doing so with the cross in mind. Jesus' mission had multiple purposes. Much of why Jesus came to earth was wrapped up in demonstrating His identity to His creation. He was proving He was God's Son. But the primary reason Jesus left Heaven was to rescue us from our sins. The cross was the foundation for so many of Jesus' interactions with others.

As you read this week's memory verses focus on that last phrase. How powerful it is! Through Jesus, God nailed our sins to the cross. That's a concept that should lead us to praise and thank God with all that we are. Make it your goal to memorize these verses this week.

WEEK 31, DAY 2

**"ON THE THIRD DAY THERE WAS A WEDDING AT
CANA IN GALILEE, AND THE MOTHER OF JESUS WAS
THERE. JESUS ALSO WAS INVITED TO THE WEDDING
WITH HIS DISCIPLES." - JOHN 2:1-2**

Have you ever been put on the spot by a well-meaning friend or parent? Jesus sure was. Jesus knew that once He began to show what He could do, life would never be the same, and the events leading to His death would be set in motion. But, He also understood that He was here to provide evidence of His power and identity.

READ JOHN 2:1-12 and imagine what it would have been like to have witnessed this event.

At this point in time, Jesus had lived a pretty quiet life. Those who knew what to look for certainly had seen the signs of His deity. But most regarded Him as a prophet of God. His mother, however, knew that there was more to Him that had not yet been revealed. You can just imagine her beaming with pride as she urges Him to show what He can do! She barely notices His hesitation as she begins organizing everyone to do whatever He says.

Notice that Jesus chooses a simple, flesh-pleasing miracle as His first public sign of His deity. He doesn't begin with a bold, controversial feat, but rather one that would instantly please those around Him. The time would come where His deeds would defy the status quo, and would set His enemies on edge. But this was not that day. In fact, this miracle was only noticed by a handful. While the crowd all benefited from it, Jesus was not yet ready for the general public to flock to Him with their demands. Instead, He strategically allowed His disciples to see His power so their faith would be strengthened for all that was in store for them ahead.

SOMETHING TO THINK ABOUT . . .
· Has God ever done a work in your life that only you noticed?
· How have those intimate moments with God strengthened your faith?
· How can seeing God's power at work help prepare you for the future?

WEEK 31, DAY 3

"FOR GOD SO LOVED THE WORLD, THAT HE GAVE HIS ONLY SON, THAT WHOEVER BELIEVES IN HIM SHOULD NOT PERISH BUT HAVE ETERNAL LIFE." - JOHN 3:16

Can you define cliché? It's simply a phrase that is dulled in meaning because it is over used. Unfortunately, many people who have grown up around church may subconsciously feel this way about John 3:16. As you read today's passage, consider the context of this verse, and see if you can gain a new insight on this familiar truth.

READ JOHN 3:1-21. The entire conversation between Jesus and Nicodemus centers on the fact that the Gospel requires a response. Jesus was not formally trained as a Jewish religious teacher, so Nicodemus clearly shows his respect for Jesus when he refers to Him as rabbi. But despite this, Nicodemus seems to be unsure of his allegiance to Jesus since he felt the need to come to Him by night.

Jesus immediately points out that believing His words is not the same as becoming a new creation in Him. Nicodemus doesn't understand this metaphor of being born again, so Jesus explains the Gospel to him more clearly. This is where we pick up John 3:16: "For God so loved the world that He GAVE." Jesus is showing this man-of-the-law that the Gospel is about love and action. If we love God, we respond to Him and begin a new life. In the same way, because God loved us, His Son was born as a man to take our place on the cross, making that new life possible!

When you look at it in context, it's no wonder that Nicodemus didn't understand being born again. Apart from understanding the full work of Christ, being born again isn't possible. Even if the words are familiar, don't let the astounding miracle of the Gospel become a cliché in your life! Christ accomplished what we could never have done for ourselves!

SOMETHING TO THINK ABOUT . . .
· How would you explain the power of the Gospel to someone in a way they could understand?

WEEK 31, DAY 4

"WHOEVER BELIEVES IN THE SON HAS ETERNAL LIFE; WHOEVER DOES NOT OBEY THE SON SHALL NOT SEE LIFE, BUT THE WRATH OF GOD REMAINS ON HIM." - JOHN 3:36

Have you ever been to a concert and been blown away by the opening act? The stature of the opening band is directly related to the main event. The bigger the band, the more of an honor it is to open for them, allowing less popular bands to play for massive audiences. John the Baptist's ministry was like an opening act for the ministry of Christ. He knew that his significance was only linked to the importance of Christ, not himself.

READ JOHN 3:25-36. Look closely at verse 36. This is the essence of John the Baptist's message! When John's followers became territorial, he quickly revealed the heart of a true Christ follower with his reply: "He must increase, but I must decrease" (v. 30). He understood that pointing others to Christ was his only mission, which he sums up nicely in verse 36.

It must have been an exciting time in history to witness the beginning of a movement as large as the onset of Christianity. People were eager to respond to this new message, and followers were gathering everywhere. It would have been easy for John to let this go to his head. Thankfully, John knew the bigger picture. His role was to be sent before the Christ. This was prophesied in Malachi 3:1, and later affirmed in Matthew 11:10. Because He understood his purpose, his joy was complete in the fact that many of his own followers were flocking to Jesus.

A good opening act might give a great show, but they know that the stage belongs to the featured band. Their job is to prepare the crowd for the main event. This is what John the Baptist did for the people in Jesus' time.

SOMETHING TO THINK ABOUT . . .
· How does the story of your life point others to Jesus?
· How do you decrease so that Jesus can increase in your circle of influence?

WEEK 31, DAY 5

**"BUT THE HOUR IS COMING, AND IS NOW HERE,
WHEN THE TRUE WORSHIPERS WILL WORSHIP THE
FATHER IN SPIRIT AND TRUTH, FOR THE FATHER
IS SEEKING SUCH PEOPLE TO WORSHIP HIM."**
- JOHN 4:23

Changing the subject is one of the oldest tricks in the book when it comes to dodging uncomfortable conversations. No doubt you've done it, and had it done to you. When Jesus encounters a woman immersed in sin, He doesn't let her off so easily.

READ JOHN 4:4-26 and watch how Jesus masterfully directs this conversation. The setting of this particular story reveals everything about Jesus' ministry. First, He stops off in Samaria. The Samaritans were a mixed race of Jews and Gentiles, and the subjects of extreme racism. Secondly, Jesus engaged a woman in conversation. This was considered inappropriate at this time in history. Lastly, this woman was at the well during the hottest time of the day. This tips us off to her scandalous reputation that would have excluded her from congregating at the well when all the other women gathered there in the cooler hours of the day. So Jesus' encounter with this woman was a triple-header of social "no no's." And yet, He still offered her eternal life!

At every turn, it seems that this woman was trying to change the subject, and keep the conversation away from her sin. Even when she perceived that Jesus was a prophet, she tried to bring up a general religious question. But Jesus kept focused on the heart of the matter. He IS truth, and we can only come to Him when we acknowledge the truth of our sin. We can't deceive Jesus with fancy talk and fake religion.

SOMETHING TO THINK ABOUT . . .
· In what way do people hide behind religion as a way to cover up their sin?
· How have you used distraction and misdirection to avoid coming clean before God?
· How might your worship be impacted if you consistently repented before God?

**THIS DEVOTION SPEAKS TO GOD'S PERFECT KNOWLEDGE.
GO TO PAGE 4 FOR A DESCRIPTION OF THIS ATTRIBUTE.**

WEEK 32

WEEK 32, DAY 1

"HE IS THE IMAGE OF THE INVISIBLE GOD, THE FIRST-
BORN OF ALL CREATION. FOR BY HIM ALL THINGS
WERE CREATED, IN HEAVEN AND ON EARTH, VISIBLE
AND INVISIBLE, WHETHER THRONES OR DOMINIONS OR
RULERS OR AUTHORITIES—ALL THINGS WERE CREATED
THROUGH HIM AND FOR HIM. AND HE IS BEFORE ALL
THINGS, AND IN HIM ALL THINGS HOLD TOGETHER."
- COLOSSIANS 1:15-17

Healing. Teaching. Calling. This week, as you continue reading through the big-picture story of the Bible, you're going to see Jesus in His element. This is what He came to do! He was radically disturbing the normalcy of our life here on earth. He was shaking things up in the most glorious ways. Nothing would ever be the same.

Jesus could do these things because of who He was. He could heal the dying. He could preach about the Kingdom. He could call people away from their careers to follow Him. Why? Look what Paul said in Colossians 1:15-17. Jesus created all things. And He holds all things together. He can alter the laws of biology and physics because He created them. It's that simple.

This week, work to memorize, or at least meditate on these verses. Focus on what they say about Jesus and His identity. Be amazed and moved by who Jesus is. And let it deeply impact your life and faith.

WEEK 32, DAY 2

"THE FATHER KNEW THAT WAS THE HOUR WHEN JESUS HAD SAID TO HIM, 'YOUR SON WILL LIVE." AND HE HIMSELF BELIEVED, AND ALL HIS HOUSEHOLD.'" - JOHN 4:53

Have you ever discussed your faith with someone who doesn't believe? Often, you will find that people question God. Do not be afraid of this! Christianity is the only faith that invites people to question freely, knowing that all will eventually arrive at the same truth. (After all, at some point in the future, all will stand before God. At that point, there will be no doubt who God is.)

READ JOHN 4:46-54. Jesus' earthly ministry was about much more than just teaching. As He performed His miracles, He was establishing His power over the physical world, and ultimately over death. We see that this man had some faith in Jesus when he first approached Him, but he did not fully believe until he questioned what he was told. When he learned that Christ's power was not just in his deeds but in His very word, he understood Jesus on a whole new level.

How often do we miss what God is doing around us? This situation could have been seen as a coincidence by most people. After all, the son began to recover while Jesus wasn't even around. But, because the father had been with Jesus, he was in-tune to what God was doing. He was looking for the power of God, and so he did not miss it when it was displayed. The father asked what time his son's fever broke, because he already trusted the promise that Jesus had given him.

Don't be afraid to search for God at work. Whether you're in conversations with an unbeliever, or wrestling with questions of your own, know that seeking answers in Jesus is always a worthy endeavor. Don't worry, you'll find Him to be true every time!

SOMETHING TO THINK ABOUT . . .
· Is it possible that you have missed out on giving God credit for working around you?
· What questions can you ask about your circumstances that might help you see what God is up to?
· How does being with Jesus help you notice when He is at work?

THIS DEVOTION SPEAKS TO GOD'S POWER. GO TO PAGE 4 FOR A DESCRIPTION OF THIS ATTRIBUTE.

WEEK 32, DAY 3

"AND SO ALSO WERE JAMES AND JOHN, SONS OF ZEBEDEE, WHO WERE PARTNERS WITH SIMON. AND JESUS SAID TO SIMON, 'DO NOT BE AFRAID; FROM NOW ON YOU WILL BE CATCHING MEN.' AND WHEN THEY HAD BROUGHT THEIR BOATS TO LAND, THEY LEFT EVERYTHING AND FOLLOWED HIM." - LUKE 5:10-11

There's fishing and then, well, there's another kind of fishing. You're probably most familiar with taking a fishing pole, baiting a hook, then putting the line in the water and waiting until a fish nibbles on the bait. The kind of fishing done in Jesus' day was done differently. The men would lower nets into the water, then draw the nets together and pull up the fish that were caught in their nets.

Read Luke 5:4-11. This is a pretty cool story. And while we definitely shouldn't pass over the miracle Jesus performed, it's important to focus on what Jesus ultimately did in the lives of Peter and James and John. Jesus ultimately called them away from their careers. Many think Peter was a prominent fisherman, probably more well-off than your average person in that day. But Peter left it all behind to follow Jesus. Jesus changed Peter's mindset. His purpose was shifted from earthly work to Heavenly work.

Jesus' call to catch people is still His call for today. Our nets are God's Word and the testimony of our faith, which are both to be put out into the world each day. The idea is for people to come to know Jesus as personal Savior. Now here is the cool part: It's not your job to save people. That is the work of the Holy Spirit. God is the one who draws the net. But Jesus has tasked us with doing the work to cast the nets into the water.

SOMETHING TO THINK ABOUT . . .
· During your time of prayer today ask God to help you take seriously the call to be a fisher of people.

WEEK 32, DAY 4

"AND JESUS STERNLY CHARGED HIM AND SENT HIM AWAY AT ONCE, AND SAID TO HIM, 'SEE THAT YOU SAY NOTHING TO ANYONE, BUT GO, SHOW YOURSELF TO THE PRIEST AND OFFER FOR YOUR CLEANSING WHAT MOSES COMMANDED, FOR A PROOF TO THEM.'" - MARK 1:43-44

People who find their way to fame and fortune soon discover that everyone wants to be their friend. It's easy to get caught up in all of the glamour and popularity brought on by success. Sometimes these people learn that the large crowd following them loves them for what they do, not for who they are. This may be what Jesus was addressing in today's Bible passage.

READ MARK 1:40-45. Don't you find it odd that Jesus told the leper not to tell anyone about his healing except for a Jewish priest? Here are two possible reasons for Jesus' command:
Jesus wanted the priest to know that the leper's healing was a miracle from God instead of a result of obeying the Old Testament law.
Jesus wanted people to follow Him because of His teachings, not because of His celebrity status as a miracle worker.

We all want people to love us for who we are instead of how well we can play a sport, or ace a test at school. Our culture puts a ton of emphasis on success and excellence. It's easy to get caught up in the popularity game. But our goal should be to draw people to us who are attracted by our characters, not by any other measure of worldly "success." Pray today that God will surround you with people who love you because you are you, like He does.

SOMETHING TO THINK ABOUT . . .
· Are you a little guilty of being drawn to others because of what they do, or what they have, and not because of who they are?
· Why is popularity oftentimes more of a hassle than a good thing?
· Who in your life values you for who you are? What can you do to strengthen these relationships?

WEEK 32, DAY 5

**"SEEING THE CROWDS, HE WENT UP ON THE MOUN-
TAIN, AND WHEN HE SAT DOWN, HIS DISCIPLES
CAME TO HIM. AND HE OPENED HIS MOUTH AND
TAUGHT THEM . . ." - MATTHEW 5:1-2**

Most people have game-changing moments in their lives. Game-changing moments are those events or occurrences that radically change the state of things. Maybe it's when all your hard work pays off and you make the big play, or nail the dance routine, or hit that score you wanted on your college entrance test. Whatever the case, life is different afterward.

READ MATTHEW 5:1-15. Today's Bible reading is the beginning of what has been called the greatest sermon ever preached. We call it Jesus' Sermon on the Mount. And the Sermon on the Mount was a game-changing moment. It put the world on notice that this Galilean carpenter was a lot more than He might have first seemed. The sermon spans three chapters in the book of Matthew, and includes some of Christ's most important teaching. It is essentially a description of what the life of a Christ-follower looks like.

As you read through parts of this sermon over the next three days notice first the placement of Jesus and the people He spoke to. First, Jesus was sitting on a hillside, which was the posture of rabbi's when they taught their students. Also from where Jesus was sitting, those passing by could hear His voice. Second, the disciples were right by His feet listening to every word, while others passing by may have moved in closer to hear Jesus speak.

And yet, some people either heard Jesus and kept on walking, or ignored Him altogether. Think about those people who heard Jesus speak but decided to keep on walking. They missed the greatest sermon ever preached. They missed one of the many game-changing moments in Jesus' ministry.

SOMETHING TO THINK ABOUT . . .
· The powerful words of God are available to you every day in your Bible. Are you reading it?

WEEK 33

WEEK 33, DAY 1

"SO THEN YOU ARE NO LONGER STRANGERS AND ALIENS, BUT YOU ARE FELLOW CITIZENS WITH THE SAINTS AND MEMBERS OF THE HOUSEHOLD OF GOD, BUILT ON THE FOUNDATION OF THE APOSTLES AND PROPHETS, CHRIST JESUS HIMSELF BEING THE CORNERSTONE, IN WHOM THE WHOLE STRUCTURE, BEING JOINED TOGETHER, GROWS INTO A HOLY TEMPLE IN THE LORD. IN HIM YOU ALSO ARE BEING BUILT TOGETHER INTO A DWELLING PLACE FOR GOD BY THE SPIRIT." - EPHESIANS 2:19-22

This week, you'll continue your look at the big-picture story of the Bible by taking an in-depth look at Jesus' Sermon on the Mount. The teachings contained in the Sermon on the Mount would have completely blown away Jesus' audience. They had based their faith in a strict keeping of the Law. As such, their lives had become a lot about religious rule following, and not much about imitating the heart of God in their daily interactions. Jesus turned this understanding on its head by drawing people back to an authentic faith life.

This week, as you read Jesus' moral teachings, do so as a citizen of God's Kingdom. That's what Paul calls us in Ephesians 2. The Sermon on the Mount has been called a collection of the ethical standards of citizens of God's Kingdom. In other words, it's a guideline for how you're supposed to live if you're a Christ-follower.

As you go through your week, focus on Paul's words to the Ephesians. It's a lot to memorize, but let it sink in as much as you can. If you're a Christ-follower, you're knit together with other Christ-followers. You are the Church, the Body of Christ. Live as such this week.

WEEK 33, DAY 2

"YOU HAVE HEARD THAT IT WAS SAID TO THOSE OF OLD, 'YOU SHALL NOT MURDER; AND WHOEVER MURDERS WILL BE LIABLE TO JUDGMENT.' BUT I SAY TO YOU THAT EVERYONE WHO IS ANGRY WITH HIS BROTHER WILL BE LIABLE TO JUDGMENT; WHOEVER INSULTS HIS BROTHER WILL BE LIABLE TO THE COUNCIL; AND WHOEVER SAYS, 'YOU FOOL!' WILL BE LIABLE TO THE HELL OF FIRE." - MATTHEW 5:21-22

READ MATTHEW 5:21-26. Keep in mind that what Jesus is doing is comparing the traditional way of thinking about faith and godliness to what God actually wants from His people. He is essentially saying, "This is the way you've been doing it. You're blowin' it. You need to be doing it THIS way." Those that took the time to listen (other than His disciples, whom we HOPE were listening) would have been dialed in, hanging on to every word Jesus was saying.

Don't you just love to dig into the scriptures and find out the real meaning of a passage? At first glance, today's reading may be seen as a way to say anger is the same as murder in God's eyes. Let's go a little deeper and see a beautiful form of teaching used by Jesus. Jesus notes three forms of judgment in His day – the local authorities, the Jewish council, and God's judgment. The Jewish leaders had reduced God's highest law, the Ten Commandments, to the lowest form of judgment, the local authorities. Jesus takes the lowest form of murder, expressing anger in words, and says that should be handled by the highest form of judgment, which is God.

So what does this all mean? Jesus was pointing out that the Jewish leaders had turned the Law into something ridiculous. Jesus was preparing them for God's ultimate plan of salvation: through faith in Him, not strict obedience to the Law! Thank God today for your freedom from the Law through Jesus Christ!

SOMETHING TO THINK ABOUT . . .
· Why is it so easy to equate faith with rule following?
· What is so wrong with this? What impact does it have on how we see the Gospel?

WEEK 33, DAY 3

AND IF YOUR RIGHT HAND CAUSES YOU TO SIN, CUT IT OFF AND THROW IT AWAY. FOR IT IS BETTER THAT YOU LOSE ONE OF YOUR MEMBERS THAN THAT YOUR WHOLE BODY GO INTO HELL. - MATTHEW 5:30

A.J. Jacobs wrote a book called The Year of Living Biblically, which is about his experience of literally living out the Old Testament law for an entire year. Jacobs is not a Christian, so far as his public comments go. He was writing the book, which is highly entertaining, as a stunt of sorts. Jacobs' conclusion was that it is impossible to live under the burden of the Old Testament Law. This should come as no surprise to anyone who has actually read the Bible, as this is sort of Jesus' entire point. That is exactly what Jesus is doing in today's reading, pointing out the absurdity of trying to obtain salvation by obeying not only written law, but all the additions made by the Jewish leaders.

READ MATTHEW 5:27-30. There is no way we can be good enough to take care of the sin that separates us from God. Jesus death on the cross wouldn't abolish the Law, but would remove us from the judgment of the law. In its place, we are under the wonderful covering of grace.

Thank God today that you live under the grace and not under Law. The gift of grace through Christ is life! There is no restriction or condemnation anymore from the kind of legalism that dominated Jesus' culture. We're free in Christ to pursue godliness, knowing that Jesus has already made us holy in God's sight.

SOMETHING TO THINK ABOUT . . .

· How do you make sense of the tension that comes with being forgiven in Christ, and yet still being called to live a life free from sin?
· Do you feel like you have a good grasp on the concept of grace? If not, what are some steps you can take to better understand it?

THIS DEVOTION SPEAKS TO GOD'S FORGIVING NATURE. GO TO PAGE 4 FOR A DESCRIPTION OF THIS ATTRIBUTE.

WEEK 33, DAY 4

"FOR IF YOU LOVE THOSE WHO LOVE YOU, WHAT REWARD DO YOU HAVE? DO NOT EVEN THE TAX COLLECTORS DO THE SAME?" - MATTHEW 5:46

Think about someone you might call an "enemy." It's not a word we use very often. There are people who are mean to us, or people we simply don't get along with. We may even have people we'd call "bullies" in our lives. However, we rarely think about someone being an "enemy." (But you probably have someone in your life that, if you're honest, may fit the description.) Take a moment and reflect on those people in your life. Don't overthink it. Who are they? Who have they been?

Now reflect how you feel about them. Is your first inclination to pray for them? Or be nice to them? Or think about ways you can help them? Probably not.

READ MATTHEW 5:43-48. What does Jesus say here? He turns our normal inclination on its side, and instead pushes us to be more like Him. We know how to hate our enemies, but Jesus challenges us to actually LOVE them. As a matter of fact look at these two verses 46 and 47. In other words, even bad guys know how to be friends with people who are already like them. It takes a lot more to be kind to those who are unkind to us.

This is challenging, and we can't do it on our own. We need Jesus to help us love those who are unlovable. Without relying on the Lord we could never do something this crazy. This is not to say that we accept the way bullies treat us. But it might mean we pray for them. No one is beyond God's love. Not even your "enemies."

SOMETHING TO THINK ABOUT . . .
· Why is it a real struggle to love our enemies?
· What is one practical thing you can do this week to be kind to those unkind to you?
· Do you think it will change anything? Why or why not?

WEEK 33, DAY 5

"BUT WHEN YOU GIVE TO THE NEEDY, DO NOT LET YOUR LEFT HAND KNOW WHAT YOUR RIGHT HAND IS DOING." - MATTHEW 6:3

Has your youth group, church, or school ever done a service project of any kind? What about a mission trip? Have you ever volunteered with someone in need? Maybe it wasn't an event, but have you ever helped anyone in anyway? If you have done something like this, then it probably made you feel pretty good. It's easy to announce to the world when we serve, and how we are doing something amazing. We want people to see how we have helped.

READ MATTHEW 6:1-4 and see how Jesus wants us to serve those in need. This is probably not exactly what you were expecting. Does this mean you can't tell anyone that you are headed on a mission trip, or helping in a nursing home this Saturday? No. It is responding to the heart behind WHY we are giving. If it is about the way WE feel, or what WE do, then we have missed the point. This is about serving God, seeing a need and meeting that need. God wants us to serve and help the needy because we understand His love, and can't wait to give that away. God also wants to remind us that doing good things doesn't change how He feels about us. God loves us just because He loves us.

Helping those in need should be motivated by our knowledge of God's love. It should be so about that love that we aren't even really aware we are serving. We have to ask if we're looking for a program or event that makes us feel good? Or are we willing to make serving a lifestyle because we are in awe of an amazing God who takes care of our needs? There's a difference. What is your motivation?

SOMETHING TO THINK ABOUT...
· Have you ever thought about what it means to love and be loved by Christ?
· How does serving from that place of love change the way we approaching helping the needy?

**THIS DEVOTION SPEAKS TO GOD'S COMPASSION.
GO TO PAGE 4 FOR A DESCRIPTION OF THIS ATTRIBUTE.**

WEEK 34

"WHAT MAN OF YOU, HAVING A HUNDRED SHEEP, IF HE HAS LOST ONE OF THEM, DOES NOT LEAVE THE NINETY-NINE IN THE OPEN COUNTRY, AND GO AFTER THE ONE THAT IS LOST, UNTIL HE FINDS IT? AND WHEN HE HAS FOUND IT, HE LAYS IT ON HIS SHOULDERS, REJOICING. AND WHEN HE COMES HOME, HE CALLS TOGETHER HIS FRIENDS AND HIS NEIGHBORS, SAYING TO THEM, 'REJOICE WITH ME, FOR I HAVE FOUND MY SHEEP THAT WAS LOST.' JUST SO, I TELL YOU, THERE WILL BE MORE JOY IN HEAVEN OVER ONE SINNER WHO REPENTS THAN OVER NINETY-NINE RIGHTEOUS PERSONS WHO NEED NO REPENTANCE." - LUKE 15:4-7

You're going to spend another week picking through some of Jesus' words from the Sermon on the Mount. It's too rich not to spend another few days on it. Then, at the end of the week, you'll begin to move forward with the story of Jesus' days here on this earth.

It's interesting when you think about how detailed the Sermon on the Mount is. It's so much teaching. It's almost like Jesus just opened the floodgates and everything just poured out. But if you know Jesus, you know that He was deeply invested in individuals. He cared about the people who were listening. He wanted them to have a clear, complete picture of what it means to live as a Christ-follower.

The words from Jesus in Luke 15 speak to this kind of care for the individual. How many countless people over the centuries have come to faith in Christ? And yet, Jesus longs for one more, and celebrates when it happens. This week, as you meditate on these words, consider what it would be like to have Jesus' heart for others. What would it practically look like in your life if you saw everyone as valuable?

WEEK 34, DAY 2

Do you like to pray? Why or why not?

Many times people avoid praying because they don't really know what to do. Praying is really just talking and listening to God. Have you ever really thought about that? Other times we might avoid praying out loud because we are afraid we might get it "wrong." We listen to other people pray and think, "Wow they have it together. I could never pray like that." Last week, you looked at how God is concerned with the heart behind why we serve. Today, think about God looking at the heart behind why you pray. Are we focusing on the words or sounding great? Prayer is about connecting to the Lord, not about sounding eloquent.

READ MATTHEW 6:5-15. In Jesus' time there were people who tried to appear really spiritual by having the loudest prayers. Those people were missing the point. Jesus didn't pass this prayer on to us so we could just memorize the words. Instead, He wanted us to know, in every line, that we can recognize God, trust Him, listen to Him, ask Him to meet our deepest needs, ask him to forgive our sins, help us forgive those who hurt us, and remember our relationship with Him.

Praying is talking to God helps us ultimately forgive others and not carry bitterness and anger. It's about spending time with Him in honesty so we can draw close to Him that matters.

SOMETHING TO THINK ABOUT...
· Walk through each line of the Lords prayer, stopping to pray for something specific in each line. What is a way you can focus on God's awesome need? What specifically do you need today? Go through it and talk to Him. Then sit in silence for a few moments just to remember how much He loves you.

"THEREFORE DO NOT BE ANXIOUS ABOUT TOMORROW, FOR TOMORROW WILL BE ANXIOUS FOR ITSELF. SUFFICIENT FOR THE DAY IS ITS OWN TROUBLE."
- MATTHEW 6:34

Have you ever had one of those dreams where you were falling, or showed up to a test unprepared, or walked out of your house naked? They say these dreams speak to our biggest sources of panic. What makes you anxious? What is your biggest worry? We all have a fear. What is yours?

NOW READ MATTHEW 6:25-34. Sometimes it can feel like we have been left alone by God. This is a great passage that helps us not only know what God will do to take care of us, but how and why. Have you ever looked at grass before, or a flower? Like, really looked at them? God takes care of each blade and petal, and makes them beautiful. Yet, they will last for a season and be gone. A plant when all is said and done is insignificant; here today and gone tomorrow. In His nature, if God would do so much to take care of these little things, how much more will He take care of us?

The Lord wants us to trust Him. He asks us to seek Him, His Kingdom, and His righteousness. When you look hard enough for something you find it. When we look for God, we can trust who He is and the way He will take care of us. He will make sure all of our daily needs are met. Now, does this mean we sit around hoping that clothes and food will appear out of thin air? Could God take care of us this way? Sure. That's not what He means here. It also isn't a call to be lazy. Instead, this is about not trying to figure out things on our own. Instead, can we lean on God and rely on who He is. Then we can ask, "What do we do today?" as we remember He already has tomorrow taken care of.

SOMETHING TO THINK ABOUT...
· What do you think keeps you from trusting God to take care of you?
· What is one way today you can take your worries and put them on the Lord?

THIS DEVOTION SPEAKS TO GOD'S PERFECT KNOWLEDGE.
GO TO PAGE 4 FOR A DESCRIPTION OF THIS ATTRIBUTE.

WEEK 34, DAY 4

"JUDGE NOT, THAT YOU BE NOT JUDGED." - MATTHEW 7:1

Have you ever stood in line at the grocery store and paid attention to the magazines they sell there? They are usually celebrity magazines, telling you all of the latest gossip they think you need to know. "Such and such broke up with so and so." If you look hard enough there is usually at least one article telling you someone is too fat or skinny, has horrible style, and has ugly hair. There is something in finding flaws in a rich, beautiful person that makes us feel better about ourselves. So we think.

TAKE A LOOK AT MATTHEW 7:1-6. Those magazines are not how God asks us to respond. Picking on the flaws of someone else is like making fun of a piece of lint on their shirt while we have a huge ketchup stain on ours. In other words, to judge someone else is to ignore the huge issues we face. They have a tiny piece of sawdust in their eye, while we ignore the board coming out of our own eye.

We don't really need to point out everyone else's flaws. When we do, we become very aware that we mess up too, and need help. God replaces our desire to judge others with compassion for their circumstances. We might even look at those famous people a little differently. We should ask Him to help us see others, and ourselves, through His eyes.

SOMETHING TO THINK ABOUT...
· Do you sometimes judge others? Why?
· What can you do today to change the way you look at others?
· Is there a "plank" in your eye in which you need God's help with today?

> "WHEN JESUS HEARD THIS, HE MARVELED AND SAID
> TO THOSE WHO FOLLOWED HIM, 'TRULY, I TELL
> YOU, WITH NO ONE IN ISRAEL HAVE I FOUND SUCH
> FAITH.'" - MATTHEW 8:10

Have you ever had a strong belief about something, but felt like you were all alone in believing it? It can mess with your mind a little bit, can't it? You stop and think about whether or not you might be a little crazy. If everyone else is thinking one way, maybe they're all right about the issue. "Maybe I'm the one that has lost my mind."

READ MATTHEW 8:5-13. So, the centurion found himself in a place where he was pretty desperate. He sent for Jesus and asked Him to heal his servant that was sick. Jesus agreed to do it, but the centurion responded in a way that stood out to Jesus. The centurion showed a sharp awareness for who Jesus was. He refereed to Jesus as Lord, acknowledged who he was in relation to Jesus, and demonstrated great faith in Jesus' power. All of this stood out to Jesus; He was in awe of the centurion's faith.

And here is where we see just how great the centurion's faith really was. Jesus was so struck by his faith, He commented on just how strong it was. He went on to say while many would join Him in heaven, the "sons of the kingdom" would be thrown into darkness. The "sons of the kingdom" was a reference to Israel. You see, the centurion had a faith that stood out among the rest. So many Israelites were putting their faith in their good works and rituals that they were missing the Messiah right in front of them. But the centurion recognized Jesus for who He really was. He wasn't afraid to put it out there. He wasn't shy about Jesus, regardless of what everyone around him thought!

SOMETHING TO THINK ABOUT....
· Is your approach to Jesus similar to the centurion's? How so?
· Is your faith strong enough that you're willing to put it out there regardless of what people around you think? If no, why not? If yes, how so?

WEEK 35

WEEK 35, DAY 1

"JESUS SAID TO HIM, 'I AM THE WAY, AND THE TRUTH, AND THE LIFE. NO ONE COMES TO THE FATHER EXCEPT THROUGH ME.'" - JOHN 14:6

You're nearly three-quarters of the way done reading through the big-picture story of the Bible. This week you'll primarily be looking at some of Jesus' miraculous works. It's easy to get caught up in the wonder of Jesus' miracles. And it's not a bad idea. But there's something interesting about the purpose of Jesus' miracles.

Too many people will see the primary purpose of Jesus' miracles as the meeting of people's needs. It's true that Jesus' miracles did in fact dramatically meet the needs of the people on the other end. Healings. Feedings. Bringing people back to life. Those are real needs being met. BUT, the primary purpose behind Jesus' miracles is tied to His identity. Jesus' miracles show who Jesus really is: the Son of God. The Messiah. God Himself.

And so this week is mostly about Jesus' identity. Who He is. What He stood for. And if you look at John 14:6, you'll see that Jesus' identity is wrapped up in providing access to God. Jesus is the only way to God. Not one of many. The only way. There is no other way to gain access to God except through faith in Jesus. Memorize this verse today. It's short and sweet. Hold on to it. There is power in its message.

THIS DEVOTION SPEAKS TO GOD'S HOLINESS. GO TO PAGE 4 FOR A DESCRIPTION OF THIS ATTRIBUTE.

WEEK 35, DAY 2

"HE SAID TO THEM, 'WHY ARE YOU SO AFRAID? HAVE
YOU STILL NO FAITH?' AND THEY WERE FILLED WITH
GREAT FEAR AND SAID TO ONE ANOTHER, 'WHO THEN
IS THIS, THAT EVEN THE WIND AND THE SEA OBEY
HIM?'" - MARK 4:40-41

It's pretty amazing to think about the times we're living in. The technology we have access to today would have sounded nuts not too long ago. And the crazy thing is that most of it fits in our pocket. What would happen, though, if all of your devices stopped working at the same time? What if you had no online access? If you couldn't return that text, or get on Snapchat, or get that picture to upload to Instagram? But what if you had the person that made your phone or tablet or computer sitting right next to you? Would you have a little faith that they could fix your problem?

READ MARK 4:36-41. After teaching a pretty large crowd, Jesus and some of the disciples got in a boat to head to the other side. But this didn't turn out to be a leisurely boat ride. Instead a huge storm came. This seemed like the perfect time to be scared. Some anxiety and a minor panic attack don't seem that out of line in a situation like this. Or do they?

Think about it for a second. Were the disciples alone? Not exactly. Jesus was in the boat with them. So, why is that significant? Think back to your thoughts about all your devices going out at the same time, yet having the person that actually made them sitting next to you. You probably wouldn't freak out because she would know what to do to get you back online. Well, the disciples were sitting there with the one who made the rain and the wind and waves. He spoke them into existence and controls their every move. Why the panic, then?

SOMETHING TO THINK ABOUT...
· Are the situations you face in life that much different from the disciples?
· Is Jesus further from you than He was from the disciples? Why do you think that?
· What's your response to Jesus asking you, "Why are you so afraid?"

WEEK 35, DAY 3

"SO THEY SAT DOWN IN GROUPS, BY HUNDREDS AND BY FIFTIES. AND TAKING THE FIVE LOAVES AND THE TWO FISH HE LOOKED UP TO HEAVEN AND SAID A BLESSING AND BROKE THE LOAVES AND GAVE THEM TO THE DISCIPLES TO SET BEFORE THE PEOPLE. AND HE DIVIDED THE TWO FISH AMONG THEM ALL. AND THEY ALL ATE AND WERE SATISFIED." - MARK 6:40-42

Take a second and think about the best present you've ever received. Did it being the best have anything to do with the person who gave it to you? Sometimes we're really thankful for the person that gave us the gift. But most of the time, it seems we're just focused on whether or not the gift was cool or not. As much as we want to think about the heart of the person that gave it, we tend to focus more on the gift itself.

READ MARK 6:35-44. People were flocking to Jesus to hear His teaching and this time, things went late. The disciples mentioned that Jesus needed to send everyone on so they could get some food. But Jesus took things a different direction. He told the disciples to get everyone something to eat. The disciples were quick to remind Jesus that they didn't have that kind of cash on them. So, Jesus told them to go ahead and bring him what food they had on them. Well, that only turned out to be five loaves of bread and two fish. What exactly was Jesus doing?

Jesus was essentially asking them to trust Him. Regardless of what they thought was about to happen, Jesus came through and fed the whole crowd with leftovers to spare. But is this story just about a miracle? Is it just about Jesus giving everyone a super cool gift? Or is it about Him? Is this story, with an incredible miracle and gift at the center of it, more about the gift or the giver? The way we operate, we would probably focus more on the gift. But here Jesus is asking everyone to let the gift point to the gift-giver.

SOMETHING TO THINK ABOUT....
· Are you more concerned with the things God can do for you, or with knowing God?
· How can you learn to love the giver Himself more than His gifts?

WEEK 35, DAY 4

"HE SAID TO THEM, 'BUT WHO DO YOU SAY THAT I AM?'" - MATTHEW 16:15

If someone you didn't know walked up and asked who you were, what would you say? You'd probably tell them your name, but what else? Would you tell them how old you are? Where you go to school? What sports or activities you're involved in? Would you mention your family? Or where you go to church? Whatever you'd choose to say, those are things you identify with. They're things that make up part of your identity. But in reality, the source of our true identity is found in the identity of someone else.

READ MATTHEW 16:13-20. In this passage Jesus doesn't ask anyone "Who are you?" Instead, He turns the question on Himself. He starts by essentially asking His disciples who other people think He is. After they give a few answers, He gets even more direct. He asks, "Who do you say that I am?" Peter crushes the answer. He said, "You are the Christ, the Son of the living God."

What Jesus asked in this passage is the most important question a person can be asked. So many of us struggle with coming to grips with our identity. We worry about what seems cool, and what other people think about us. But the reality is that our identity is found in Christ's identity because we were created to be in relationship with God. So, how we answer Jesus when He asks, "Who do you say that I am?" is the most important question we'll ever answer.

SOMETHING TO THINK ABOUT....

· Where do you try and find your identity? Do you look for it in the approval of other people? Do you look for it in being true to yourself regardless of what other people think? Why are both of those routes to finding your identity flawed?
· What does it look like for you to find your identity in Jesus?

WEEK 35, DAY 5

"HE ANSWERED, 'WHETHER HE IS A SINNER I DO NOT KNOW. ONE THING I DO KNOW, THAT THOUGH I WAS BLIND, NOW I SEE.'" - JOHN 9:25

Let's face it: we all tend to overcomplicate things at times. A lot of times we don't take what people say at face value. We read into what was said (and how it was said, how the person looked when they said it, and on, and on, and on). And sometimes we go looking for the most complicated solution to a problem, when the simple, straightforward answer is right in front of us.

READ JOHN 9:1-38. Jesus and the disciples come across a man that has been blind since birth. The disciples want an explanation. Surely there's someone to blame for this man being blind. But Jesus responds with a simple truth. He basically tells them that God is in control, and sometimes people go through hardships so He can display His power. Then Jesus healed the man, and for the first time in his life, the man could see! You would think everyone would be pretty pumped, right?

Well, the Pharisees weren't having it. They kept asking the man about who healed him. They asked him what he thought about Jesus. They accused Jesus of not being from God. They just wouldn't let it go. They were looking for any explanation other than Jesus is from God and He healed the man. Finally the man that used to be blind essentially said to them, "Look, all I know is that I used to be blind and now I can see. What more do you want from me?" The Pharisees wanted to not believe. They complicated the whole thing by refusing to accept what was right in front of them. The man, however, took what happened at face value and trusted Jesus on the spot.

SOMETHING TO THINK ABOUT....

· Are you looking for answers all around you when Jesus is right in front of you? Why is that?

WEEK 36

WEEK 36, DAY 1

"MY LITTLE CHILDREN, I AM WRITING THESE THINGS TO
YOU SO THAT YOU MAY NOT SIN. BUT IF ANYONE DOES
SIN, WE HAVE AN ADVOCATE WITH THE FATHER, JESUS
CHRIST THE RIGHTEOUS. HE IS THE PROPITIATION FOR
OUR SINS, AND NOT FOR OURS ONLY BUT ALSO FOR THE
SINS OF THE WHOLE WORLD." - 1 JOHN 2:1-2

Jesus came to take away the sin of the world. Plain and simple.
As you trace the big-picture story of the Bible this week, you're
going to notice Jesus really beginning to prepare Himself for
the cross. It's getting closer and closer. His interactions seem to
have more urgency to them. He is more intentional. He knows
what is coming.

Jesus fully embraced His mission. He knew who He was and
what He was here for. Jesus' life was all about getting people
on board with His purpose of leading people to know and
love God, free from the burden their unforgiven sins weighed
them down with. In John's words, Jesus was the "propitiation"
for the sins of all people. That's just a fancy way of saying that
Jesus satisfied God's demands for payment for sin. He paid our
sin debt.

The beautiful thing about these verses, and about the Gospel
in general, is that we don't have to earn Jesus' favor. It's freely
given. Through faith in Jesus and His work on the cross, we can
be forgiven. Meditate on this truth this week.

THIS DEVOTION SPEAKS TO GOD'S RIGHTEOUSNESS.
GO TO PAGE 4 FOR A DESCRIPTION OF THIS ATTRIBUTE.

WEEK 36, DAY 2

"BUT MANY WHO ARE FIRST WILL BE LAST, AND THE LAST FIRST."
- MARK 10:31

Everyone wants to be the best. Many teenagers spend hours working on school, sports, music, and other activities to try to become the best they can be. You are also constantly challenged to rank yourself against others whether it's grades, starting positions on the team, or a chair placement in band. The fight for number one is a constant fight. But what does Jesus say about this fight to become the best?

READ MARK 10:29-37. In this passage, Jesus begins the passage by speaking of the cost of following Him. Many people will leave many worldly things behind to follow Jesus. Yet Jesus assures those who leave things behind for His sake that it will be worth it in the end. Then Jesus makes a statement that redefines the search for number one: "many who are first will be last, and the last first" (v. 31). Jesus then gives an example of living as last by going to the cross for our sins. The passage ends with James and John still fighting to be first like they totally missed the point of Jesus' teaching.

What if you lived like you were last? That would not mean being bad at everything and not trying. It would mean living in a way where you put others first. You loved others, served others, and encouraged others to succeed. When you live this way, you show the world Jesus, who went to the cross as the ultimate act of being last.

SOMETHING TO THINK ABOUT . . .
· What are some areas of your life where you are likely to compete to be number one?
· How are some ways that you can put others first today?
· Take a marker and draw a cross on your hand. Let this cross be a reminder for you today to imitate Jesus by being last.

WEEK 36, DAY 3

"WHOEVER DOES NOT BEAR HIS OWN CROSS AND COME AFTER ME CANNOT BE MY DISCIPLE." - LUKE 14:27

Do you know someone who leaves things unfinished? Half mowed lawns? Half consumed lattes? Puzzles missing pieces? Unfinished things are a waste, but most people who leave things unfinished do so because they did not understand the investment that the task required. They ran out of time, money, or simply got full. Wise people calculate the cost before they do something. What about when it comes to following Jesus? Is there a cost? Have you understood the cost?

READ LUKE 14:25-35. In this passage, Jesus is teaching a crowd of people. These people have not really considered that following Jesus might actually cost them something. To these people, Jesus says that those who follow Him must be willing to leave their families, their lives, pick up their cross, and give up everything to be His disciple. These are some hard statements that show us that following Jesus must be the first and foremost priority in your life. Those who don't have Jesus as their ultimate priority are not truly following Jesus; they are just another person in the crowd.

Jesus says that there is clearly a cost for following Him: everything. Throughout the passage, Jesus gives examples of people who were foolish and didn't count the cost. Have you counted the cost? Are you ready to give all to Jesus?

SOMETHING TO THINK ABOUT...
· Are you like the people in the crowds who just like to follow Jesus at a distance, or are you truly a disciple of Jesus? Why would you answer the way that you did?
· Which cost of following Jesus seems the hardest to you? Why?
· What would it look like today to give everything to Jesus to truly be His disciple?

WEEK 36, DAY 4

"JESUS SAID TO HER, 'I AM THE RESURRECTION AND THE LIFE. WHOEVER BELIEVES IN ME, THOUGH HE DIE, YET SHALL HE LIVE, AND EVERYONE WHO LIVES AND BELIEVES IN ME SHALL NEVER DIE. DO YOU BELIEVE THIS?'" - JOHN 11:25-26

Death is something that affects all of us. It's something that people try to avoid. People take medicine, wear seatbelts, eat healthy, exercise, and many other things to try to avoid death. The scariest thing about death is that it often comes when we least expect it. No one knows the day that they will meet death, and so death is something that many people fear.

What if there was someone who could conquer death? **READ JOHN 11:1-44.** Today's passage is a story of Jesus conquering death. Lazarus, Jesus' friend, had died. Though Jesus was late to visit and heal Lazarus from his sickness, He came to visit the family once Lazarus' illness had taken its final toll. Lazarus' sisters were upset that Jesus didn't heal their brother. Jesus then wept at the sisters' pain and the death of His friend. This is a powerful truth for all of us when we face death: Jesus is with us, and He hurts with us. Jesus is a God who comforts those who mourn. This is a truth that we can share with others when they face times of death.

But Jesus does not leave the women in their mourning. He does the unthinkable. He raises Lazarus to life. In Jesus, we have a God who conquered and controls death. When you face times of death, you can hold on to the truth that Jesus controls death, and will ultimately bring death itself to an end.

SOMETHING TO THINK ABOUT...

· How does the fact that Jesus controls and conquers death give you hope?
· Who are people in your life that you can comfort and encourage who may have lost someone they love? Spend some time praying for them today.

WEEK 36, DAY 5

"THE NEXT DAY THE LARGE CROWD THAT HAD COME TO THE FEAST HEARD THAT JESUS WAS COMING TO JERUSALEM. SO THEY TOOK BRANCHES OF PALM TREES AND WENT OUT TO MEET HIM, CRYING OUT, 'HOSANNA! BLESSED IS HE WHO COMES IN THE NAME OF THE LORD, EVEN THE KING OF ISRAEL!'"
- JOHN 12:12-13

Have you ever been to a homecoming parade? Imagine that your favorite professional sports team won the biggest game for their sport and returned home to your town. People would be going crazy! The excitement level is through the roof. In today's passage, Jesus is in a parade not unlike a homecoming parade. He has been performing miracles, teaching people, and talking about a kingdom. Now, He is coming into Jerusalem, and people are rejoicing because they think Jesus is going to overthrow the Roman rule.

READ JOHN 12:12-18. Jesus was being celebrated. People were claiming that Jesus was the king. They were praising God that their king had come into Jerusalem, their hometown. But they had misunderstood Jesus' teaching about the Kingdom. The Kingdom that Jesus was coming to bring was a spiritual kingdom, a transformation that would take place in the hearts and lives of His followers.

Many people in the crowd thought that Jesus was coming to bring His final Kingdom to the earth, and when Jesus didn't bring in that Kingdom, the cries of the crowds changed. The same people who rejoiced on this day at Jesus' coming would soon cry out "crucify Him" just a few days later. Jesus was coming to bring a Kingdom, but many people missed that Kingdom because they were looking for the wrong thing.

SOMETHING TO THINK ABOUT...
· What does the fact that the same people that praised Jesus in this passage, yet crucified Him in another passage say to you about the human heart and people's praise?
· What is it about Jesus that makes you want to celebrate?
· Today, spend some time praying that Jesus would come back to finalize His reign as the ultimate King in His second coming.

WEEK 37

WEEK 37, DAY 1

"BY OPPRESSION AND JUDGMENT HE WAS TAKEN AWAY; AND AS FOR HIS GENERATION, WHO CONSIDERED THAT HE WAS CUT OFF OUT OF THE LAND OF THE LIVING, STRICKEN FOR THE TRANSGRESSION OF MY PEOPLE? AND THEY MADE HIS GRAVE WITH THE WICKED AND WITH A RICH MAN IN HIS DEATH, ALTHOUGH HE HAD DONE NO VIOLENCE, AND THERE WAS NO DECEIT IN HIS MOUTH."
- ISAIAH 53:8-9

You're coming to arguably the main climax of the big-picture story of Scripture. Over the next two weeks, you'll be looking at Jesus' arrest, crucifixion, death, and resurrection. As we think about the story, the culmination of God's plan of redemption is about to be completed. Jesus is in the final moments with His disciples. He's agonizing over what is coming. And He is arrested even though He is innocent of any crime.

The coolest thing about Scripture? God spoke through Isaiah to predict all of this, hundreds of years before Jesus ever came on the scene. What you see at the top of the page is Isaiah predicting the final moments of Jesus' life. Keep this in mind as you read this week's accounts of Jesus' final moments with His disciples.

WEEK 37, DAY 2

"HE CAME TO SIMON PETER, WHO SAID TO HIM, 'LORD, DO YOU WASH MY FEET?' JESUS ANSWERED HIM, 'WHAT I AM DOING YOU DO NOT UNDERSTAND NOW, BUT AFTERWARD YOU WILL UNDERSTAND.'" - JOHN 13:6-7

When you think of a servant, who comes into your mind? Is it your mom, your teacher, your youth pastor, or someone else? What is this person like? A servant is someone who willingly puts themselves before others. A servant helps others in whatever ways they need to be helped, no matter how dirty or difficult that help may be. Today, you'll see that Jesus set us an example of serving that we should follow.

OPEN YOUR BIBLE AND READ JOHN 13:1-17. In this passage, Jesus did something that would have been completely shocking to His disciples. He washed their feet. This is a task that only the lowest of servants would do. In Jesus' day, people walked around either without shoes, or in sandals. As you can imagine, their feet were not very clean. In washing His disciples' feet, Jesus showed them how much He loved them by putting them first and serving them. Washing feet is a simple task, yet it was a great way for Jesus to show love and service.

As the passage ends, Jesus tells His disciples to wash each other's feet based on His example. As modern day followers of Jesus, we may not literally wash someone's feet. But we have opportunities to serve others in little ways every day. As we serve others by putting them first, we model Jesus' example of humility and service.

SOMETHING TO THINK ABOUT...
· Who has served you well? Spend a few minutes this morning calling or texting the person who has served you, and thank them for modeling Jesus for you.
· What are some small ways that you can serve people around you today?

WEEK 37, DAY 3

"NOW AS THEY WERE EATING, JESUS TOOK BREAD, AND AFTER BLESSING IT BROKE IT AND GAVE IT TO THE DISCIPLES, AND SAID, 'TAKE, EAT; THIS IS MY BODY.' AND HE TOOK A CUP, AND WHEN HE HAD GIVEN THANKS HE GAVE IT TO THEM, SAYING, 'DRINK OF IT, ALL OF YOU, FOR THIS IS MY BLOOD OF THE COVENANT, WHICH IS POURED OUT FOR MANY FOR THE FORGIVENESS OF SINS. I TELL YOU I WILL NOT DRINK AGAIN OF THIS FRUIT OF THE VINE UNTIL THAT DAY WHEN I DRINK IT NEW WITH YOU IN MY FATHER'S KINGDOM.'" - MATTHEW 26:26-29

READ MATTHEW 26:17-29.

Jesus was so good at taking old traditions and turning them into fresh, new, and exciting celebrations. Such was the case with the Old Testament ritual known as the Passover feast. The bread that was broken and given to the people by the priest symbolized the sufferings their ancestors went through while in slavery in Egypt, during the wandering in the wilderness, and in other difficult times. In other words, it was a time to think back on tough times they and their Jewish ancestors had been through, and to be thankful for God's deliverance.

Jesus took the elements from the Passover feast and instituted the Lord's Supper, a time to think about the sufferings He would go through for our sin. Instead of a vague remembrance of things in the past, the Lord's Supper would forever become a deeply personal time to be reminded that Christ died for each individual. The bread and the wine would forever be powerful pictures of Jesus' purpose on earth, which was to save us from our sin and provide a way to have an intimate relationship with God both now and forever.

SOMETHING TO THINK ABOUT . . .
· When you take the Lord's Supper remember what He did for you on the cross and celebrate the personal relationship you now have with your Heavenly Father.
· As you pray today, pause and reflect on Christ's crucifixion. Reflect on how His death and resurrection aren't just vague events, but extremely personal sacrifices that were made for you.

WEEK 37, DAY 4

"AND GOING A LITTLE FARTHER HE FELL ON HIS FACE AND PRAYED, SAYING, 'MY FATHER, IF IT BE POSSIBLE, LET THIS CUP PASS FROM ME; NEVERTHELESS, NOT AS I WILL, BUT AS YOU WILL.'" - MATTHEW 26:39

You may have been through some tough times in life. You may have been through times that felt so heavy you didn't think you could bear the weight. Maybe you are experiencing something like that right now. It could be a problem with your parents, financial struggles, or some health concerns in your family. Jesus knew what it felt like to be burdened.

READ MATTHEW 26:36-46. In today's Bible passage, Jesus asks God to take away the heavy burden of having to go to the cross and experience incredible pain and suffering. God's response was no. And you know what? Jesus was good with that. He knew all along His path to the cross couldn't waiver.

The heavy weight Jesus was bearing would eventually free mankind from the curse of sin, and forever open the gates of heaven for all those who would confess Jesus as Messiah. Your burden may not have such eternal consequences, but it still feels heavy to you. Keep praying and God may lift that issue from you. If He doesn't, then allow God to use the situation to strengthen your faith, and continue the process of perfecting you as a Christian.

SOMETHING TO THINK ABOUT . . .
· Pray today and give your cares and concerns completely to God and trust Him to do what is best in your life.

WEEK 37, DAY 5

THEN JESUS SAID TO HIM, 'PUT YOUR SWORD BACK INTO ITS
PLACE. FOR ALL WHO TAKE THE SWORD WILL PERISH BY THE
SWORD. DO YOU THINK THAT I CANNOT APPEAL TO MY FATHER,
AND HE WILL AT ONCE SEND ME MORE THAN TWELVE LEGIONS
OF ANGELS? BUT HOW THEN SHOULD THE SCRIPTURES BE FUL-
FILLED, THAT IT MUST BE SO?'" - MATTHEW 26:52-54

READ MATTHEW 26:47-68. It can be called an instinct or a flinch. Con-
sciously or subconsciously we sometimes react to a situation without giving
it much thought. That is what Peter did in today's passage. Jesus was threat-
ened and Peter drew his sword to defend Him.

Think about that for a moment. Peter was going to defend Jesus, who said
He could call down twelve legions of angels if He chose. That's an army
of 72,000 angels, a staggering amount. But it's still merely a fraction of the
full power that Jesus commands.

Whether Jesus had let Peter go for it with his one sword, or called down
72,000 swords didn't matter, because Jesus knew He had to go to the cross.
The power of God is great, but the plan of God is great as well.

God has a plan for your life, too. God wants to use you to make His name
known in this world. He wants to work in you and through you to accomplish much for the sake of His glory. How willing are you to be used by Him?

SOMETHING TO THINK ABOUT . . .
· Are you following God so closely that you could hear His Spirit if He were
leading you?
· How in tune are you to obeying God's leading in your life? What's keeping
you from being more obedient?

THIS DEVOTION SPEAKS TO GOD'S FORGIVING NATURE.
GO TO PAGE 4 FOR A DESCRIPTION OF THIS ATTRIBUTE.

WEEK 38

"THEREFORE, SINCE WE ARE SURROUNDED BY SO GREAT A CLOUD OF WITNESSES, LET US ALSO LAY ASIDE EVERY WEIGHT, AND SIN WHICH CLINGS SO CLOSELY, AND LET US RUN WITH ENDURANCE THE RACE THAT IS SET BEFORE US, LOOKING TO JESUS, THE FOUNDER AND PERFECTER OF OUR FAITH, WHO FOR THE JOY THAT WAS SET BEFORE HIM ENDURED THE CROSS, DESPISING THE SHAME, AND IS SEATED AT THE RIGHT HAND OF THE THRONE OF GOD." - HEBREWS 12:1-2

This week you'll have the chance to read about Jesus' crucifixion, death, burial, and ascension. It's a big deal. It's maybe the biggest deal in history. Don't rush through it, and don't miss it. As we mentioned last week, it's more or less the culmination of God's plan to rescue humanity from our sin.

The cross was brutal for Jesus. And not just the physical pain He went through. Consider that Jesus is perfectly holy, perfectly righteous. And on the cross, He took our sin on Himself. That in itself is probably the most brutal part of the cross. But look at the words of Hebrews 12:1-2. Can you spot anything that reveals Jesus' mindset about going to the cross?

The writer of Hebrews says here that Jesus endured the cross because of the JOY it brought Him. Amidst the terrifying pain of His death, and the punishing weight of all humanity's sin, Jesus could still rejoice in the outcome. He knew what His death was accomplishing. And He did it all for us. Hebrews 12:1-2 is a long couple of verses. Take the challenge to memorize them this week. And use these verses to motivate you to praise and thank Jesus for going to the cross on your behalf.

WEEK 38, DAY 2

THE GOVERNOR AGAIN SAID TO THEM, 'WHICH OF THE TWO DO YOU
WANT ME TO RELEASE FOR YOU?' AND THEY SAID, 'BARABBAS.'
PILATE SAID TO THEM, 'THEN WHAT SHALL I DO WITH JESUS WHO IS
CALLED CHRIST?' THEY ALL SAID, 'LET HIM BE CRUCIFIED!' AND HE
SAID, 'WHY, WHAT EVIL HAS HE DONE?' BUT THEY SHOUTED ALL THE
MORE, 'LET HIM BE CRUCIFIED!'" - MATTHEW 27:21-23

TAKE A FEW MINUTES AND READ MATTHEW 27:11-26.

The people in the courtyard that day had a choice as to who would
be freed. On one hand you have Barabbas, a habitual criminal. He
was a robber and most recently a murderer. On the other, you have
Jesus, a perfect man who spent His life giving back to others. He wasn't
done giving. Based on the response of the crowd, Jesus would soon
give His life as a ransom for all.

The people chose to let Barabbas go free instead of Jesus. We can get
mad at those people and call them cowards, but the simple fact is that
it was God's will for Barabbas to be freed. It was God's plan for Jesus
to go to the cross to free humankind from the chains of sin and death.

Maybe you have looked around your town, your country, or around the
world and noticed perceived injustices taking place each day. Have
you considered that God is allowing those things to happen so His
great plan can continue to be carried out on the earth? The Bible says
that God can't cause evil. But God allows bad things to happen. And
while this is a mystery to us, in some ways, we have to trust that God
has a plan, and that His plan is for our good and His glory.

SOMETHING TO THINK ABOUT . . .
· As you pray today, ask God to give you His eyes to see the things
around you in the lens of His plan and purpose.

**THIS DEVOTION SPEAKS TO GOD'S PERFECT UNDERSTANDING.
GO TO PAGE 4 FOR A DESCRIPTION OF THIS ATTRIBUTE.**

> "AND BEHOLD, THE CURTAIN OF THE TEMPLE WAS TORN IN TWO, FROM TOP TO BOTTOM. AND THE EARTH SHOOK, AND THE ROCKS WERE SPLIT. THE TOMBS ALSO WERE OPENED. AND MANY BODIES OF THE SAINTS WHO HAD FALLEN ASLEEP WERE RAISED, AND COMING OUT OF THE TOMBS AFTER HIS RESURRECTION THEY WENT INTO THE HOLY CITY AND APPEARED TO MANY. WHEN THE CENTURION AND THOSE WHO WERE WITH HIM, KEEPING WATCH OVER JESUS, SAW THE EARTHQUAKE AND WHAT TOOK PLACE, THEY WERE FILLED WITH AWE AND SAID, 'TRULY THIS WAS THE SON OF GOD!'"
> - MATTHEW 27:51-54

What's the most amazing, unbelievable, expectation-shattering thing you've ever seen? Was it a positive thing? Or was it a negative thing? How did it make you feel? Most of us will have an encounter of some sort where we will see something that blows away our expectations so thoroughly that we're left shaking our heads. But nothing we've ever seen, no matter how amazing, compares with what the people saw the day Jesus was crucified.

READ MATTHEW 27:32-66. What happened the day Jesus died would have definitely been the lead story on all the news channels if they had been around back then. The sky turning dark, the curtain in the temple ripping apart, and tombs opening up were all headlining news events. It was definitely a big show, so big that even some of the soldiers at the cross that day declared that Jesus was the Son of God.

You may have been to some big events like a concert, a retreat, or a Disciple Now weekend. You may have noticed the spiritual high soon fades away. What sustains you as a Christian is the Holy Spirit living in you, your daily time of reading the Bible and praying, and the time you spend with good Christian friends.

SOMETHING TO THINK ABOUT . . .
· Pray today that God will energize you through the mountain top experiences in your youth group, and grow you through the simple daily walk with Him.

"THEN GO QUICKLY AND TELL HIS DISCIPLES THAT HE HAS RISEN FROM THE DEAD, AND BEHOLD, HE IS GOING BEFORE YOU TO GALILEE; THERE YOU WILL SEE HIM. SEE, I HAVE TOLD YOU." - MATTHEW 28:7

Road trips are the greatest. What could be better than you and your closest friends out on the road looking for adventure? Of course, there is one thing that can destroy a road trip before you even get started: not having fuel. Your car needs fuel to go. Before you head out, you probably want to raid your piggy bank, or beg your parents for gas money.

READ MATTHEW 28. This chapter contains one of the most famous passages in all the Bible, the Great Commission. If we're not careful, we might skip right to what we need to do for Jesus. But the reason for the Great Commission is based on a truth from earlier in the chapter: Jesus is alive! We hear it so often, it can lose its power. Jesus was dead, and then three days later He rose from the dead.

In verse 6, the angel tells the women to be sure of the resurrection. Then, in verse 7, he says, "...go quickly and tell..." The order is crucial. We must be persuaded that Jesus is alive before we go and tell people about Him. Our tendency is to rush to what we must do. But first we must be convinced of what Jesus did for us. He died on the cross for our sins, and then three days later He arose, defeating sin and death.

Today, you are definitely called to "go and tell" your friends and family the story of Jesus, but before you can "go and tell," you must "come, see." Spend a few moments thinking about the resurrection. As you mediate on Jesus' death and resurrection, you'll find the fuel you need for the mission. Like you need gas for a road trip, the adventure God has for you runs on this truth: Jesus is alive!

SOMETHING TO THINK ABOUT...
· How does the resurrection change the lives of the disciples? How does it change your life?
· What does it mean to you that Jesus is alive? How does that truth shape how you understand your mission?

"BUT YOU WILL RECEIVE POWER WHEN THE HOLY
SPIRIT HAS COME UPON YOU, AND YOU WILL BE MY
WITNESSES IN JERUSALEM AND IN ALL JUDEA AND
SAMARIA, AND TO THE END OF THE EARTH."
- ACTS 1:8

Imagine you lived two thousand years ago in a country that was overtaken by another king and his country. Remember, you don't have a cell phone, Instagram, or a TV with nightly news. Now here is the question: how do people even know that they're the citizens of a new country with a new king?

READ ACTS 1:1-11. Notice in verse 8, Jesus says, "you will be my witnesses." When we hear the word "witness," we immediately think of someone giving a testimony in a courtroom. Jesus isn't talking about a courtroom witness; instead He is describing a herald. A herald is a person who would run from town to town and deliver news.

Back to our question: How do you find out news of a new king ? Well, the new king would send out heralds who would run from city to city and proclaim, "There is a new king." You'd know the news, because someone sent from the king would tell you. The heralds didn't make up the message; they delivered exactly what they'd been told. The heralds didn't decide their own route; they went wherever the king commanded. The heralds weren't responsible for people loving the new king; they just told the news of the new king.

Jesus commissions His disciples (you included) to be heralds. Our job is to deliver a simple message to all people in all places: There is a new king, and his name is Jesus. We don't make up the message. We don't decide where we feel like going. And we aren't responsible for how people respond. Our job is to go where Jesus commands, proclaiming His message as we go. People will know the good news when a herald sent from the King tells them.

SOMETHING TO THINK ABOUT...
· Where has God currently placed you? How can you be a herald there?
· Where do you think God might be directing you? How can you be a herald as you go to that destination?

WEEK 39

_____

WEEK 39, DAY 1

**"WE KNOW THAT OUR OLD SELF WAS CRUCI-
FIED WITH HIM IN ORDER THAT THE BODY OF
SIN MIGHT BE BROUGHT TO NOTHING, SO THAT
WE WOULD NO LONGER BE ENSLAVED TO SIN."
- ROMANS 6:6**

You're going to really be advancing the story this week. You're going to jump into some major narratives from the big-picture story of the Bible. You're going to learn about the Holy Spirit coming, the martyrdom of Stephen, and Paul's conversion. These are really important stories in the BIG story.

One of the things these stories represent is the newness of things. Jesus had changed everything. And so you see a new gift from God (the permanent indwelling of the Spirit in all Believers). We see a new threat to the church (the murder of Stephen). And we see a new, powerful voice of truth emerge out of spiritual darkness (the conversion of Paul). The old ways were passing. Jesus had made things new.

Jesus makes us new too. That's what Paul is saying here in Romans 6:6. When you came to a saving faith with Jesus, you became a new creation. Your old self died with Jesus. The power of sin and death has been broken. The question then is whether or not you're living out this new life, or are you still holding onto old, dead ways? Memorize Romans 6:6 this week to help encourage you to boldly live out your faith.

**THIS DEVOTION SPEAKS TO GOD'S RIGHTEOUSNESS.
GO TO PAGE 4 FOR A DESCRIPTION OF THIS ATTRIBUTE.**

WEEK 39, DAY 2

**"AND SUDDENLY THERE CAME FROM HEAVEN A SOUND
LIKE A MIGHTY RUSHING WIND, AND IT FILLED THE ENTIRE
HOUSE WHERE THEY WERE SITTING. AND DIVIDED TONGUES
AS OF FIRE APPEARED TO THEM AND RESTED ON EACH ONE
OF THEM. AND THEY WERE ALL FILLED WITH THE HOLY
SPIRIT AND BEGAN TO SPEAK IN OTHER TONGUES AS THE
SPIRIT GAVE THEM UTTERANCE." - ACTS 2:2-4**

Have you ever been confused? Maybe the first day of Pre-calculus left you scratching your head. Maybe you received mixed signals from a member of the opposite sex. Whatever the situation, we all know what it's like to be confused. Today's Bible reading can be confusing. But don't worry: there's a clear point.

READ ACTS 2:1-41. This story is crazy, right? Tongues of fire, rushing winds, and everyone miraculously speaking in different languages. How do we make sense of what is going on here? The best way to determine the point of this chapter is to closely examine Peter's message to the gathered crowd. Depending on how you count, Peter refers to Jesus at least 12 times. He says Jesus was crucified according to God's plan. Twice he says God raised Jesus from the dead. He says Jesus is the one about whom David prophesied. Death could not hold Jesus down. He was not abandoned, corrupted, or left for dead. Jesus is the one who sent the Holy Spirit, and He is the one whom God chose to be Lord. And, most crucial for the crowd, and for us, our sins are forgiven through trusting the name of Jesus.

This passage contains much that can be confusing. But don't get bogged down in the confusion. The point is "Jesus." The tongues and rushing wind are intended to exalt Jesus. The message is all about Jesus. The desired response is that people would trust Jesus. He is the center of this story. He is the point.

SOMETHING TO THINK ABOUT...

· How does understanding that Jesus is the point of this chapter help clarify its meaning for you?
· If Jesus is the point of this story, what does that say about His place in your life? Is it possible that Jesus is the point of your life? If true, how would that change the way you live?

WEEK 39, DAY 3

"AND HE SAID, 'BEHOLD, I SEE THE HEAVENS OPENED, AND THE SON OF MAN STANDING AT THE RIGHT HAND OF GOD.' BUT THEY CRIED OUT WITH A LOUD VOICE AND STOPPED THEIR EARS AND RUSHED TOGETHER AT HIM." - ACTS 7:56-57

Albert Einstein is credited with saying, "I have no special talents. I am only passionately curious." Whoa! If one of the most intelligent men credits his passion and not his mental ability as vital to his success, what does that mean for us? Let's look at an example of passion in the scriptures.

READ ACTS 6:8-7:60. Stephen was the first Christian to lose his life for the cause of Christ. Did you notice anything interesting about him? Stephen was not one of the twelve apostles. That's right, the first martyr of the church was not a pastor. If he wasn't an apostle or a pastor, then who was he?

In this passage we learn that Stephen was a deacon in the first church, called to help serve widows. His position was not to lead or to preach in front of thousands, but to serve food. He was described as being "full of grace and power." He did miraculous signs. He taught with wisdom so forceful even men trained to understand the Bible could not compete with him. When he was falsely accused and put on trail, he didn't back down, but preached an unbelievable sermon to his accusers.

All this from an ordinary guy . . . an ordinary guy with an extraordinary passion to know Jesus. God used Stephen to accomplish extraordinary things. Think about it. His story of faithfulness to Jesus is included in the Bible and has been told countless times over the past 2000 years. Wow! So here's the question, what is keeping you from passionately following Jesus like Stephen? Stephen was an ordinary guy with an extraordinary commitment to Jesus. How can you follow his example today? Passion is powerful, and a passion to know Jesus can be world changing.

SOMETHING TO THINK ABOUT...
· How does the story of Stephen encourage you? How does it challenge you?
· Stephen considered Jesus as more important than his own life. How do you view Jesus' worth? What are you most passionate about in your life right now?

WEEK 39, DAY 4

"BUT THE LORD SAID TO HIM, 'GO, FOR HE IS A CHOSEN INSTRUMENT OF MINE TO CARRY MY NAME BEFORE THE GENTILES AND KINGS AND THE CHILDREN OF ISRAEL.'"
- ACTS 9:15

A lot of people want to change something about their lives. People would love to change a physical characteristic, or a habit, or a family circumstance. Some people are looking for huge sweeping changes that completely redefine who they are. Other people just want to change their hairstyle.

READ ACTS 9:1-19. We meet two men in this story who experience radical transformations. The first is Saul. Saul was the chief persecutor of the church. Saul is not impressed with Jesus, His way, or His followers. Then, he meets Him. And meeting Jesus changes everything for Saul. It changes his life mission, his feelings toward Christians, and, most importantly, his belief about Jesus. Second, is Ananias. He loves Jesus and His church, but is skeptical of Saul. When God instructs him to go meet Saul, Ananias objects. He has heard the stories of how Saul's life mission is to imprison Christians. Then, Ananias hears from the Lord regarding Saul, changes his attitude, and goes to pray for Saul.

The point is that Jesus changes people. He changed Saul from a murderous zealot, who was an enemy of the church, into the greatest missionary and theologian in the history of the church. Jesus changed Ananias from being fearful and skeptical of Saul, to being able to embrace Saul as a brother in Christ.

The change Saul experienced was massive, changing the direction of his life. The change Ananias experienced was small - a simple change in attitude. But the catalyst for both was Jesus. Like these men, you need change in your life. Here's the good news: in both big ways and small ways, Jesus is still in the business of changing lives. Yours included.

SOMETHING TO THINK ABOUT...
· What areas of your life do you need to experience change? Pray that Jesus would bring change where it is needed.
· How has Jesus transformed your life? Write down both big ways and small ways.

WEEK 39, DAY 5

"AND THE HAND OF THE LORD WAS WITH THEM, AND A GREAT NUMBER WHO BELIEVED TURNED TO THE LORD." - ACTS 11:21

Have you ever seen something spread like crazy? How does that even happen? How does a small spark turn into a forest fire that spreads to the point where it gets out of control? And how does one ant going across your counter quickly turn into ants all over the place? What about something more positive? Like love, or hope, or redemption? How exactly do those things spread?

READ ACTS 11:19-30 and think about what you see spreading throughout those verses. It's really amazing to see, but it's also a lot less complicated than we usually make it.

This whole passage starts with people willing to share the good news of Jesus with people around them. And what happens? The Lord blessed their obedience, and people followed the Lord. That was so awesome that people heard about it, and Barnabas and Saul made their way to Antioch to spend time teaching the new believers.

The cool thing is, it didn't stop there. They didn't just sit and learn. When they learned that a famine was coming, their faith was put into action and they sacrificially gave to send relief to their brothers in Christ in Judea. So disciples (people following Jesus) made new disciples that were willing to put their faith to work and invest in the Body. That is how hope and re-demption are spread.

SOMETHING TO THINK ABOUT...
· Have you ever seen the Gospel spread like that? Why or why not?
· What does it mean to be a disciple that makes disciples?
· Do you believe that accurately describes your walk with Jesus? How so? If not, how can you become a disciple that makes disciples?

WEEK 40

> "AND JESUS CAME AND SAID TO THEM, 'ALL AUTHORITY
> IN HEAVEN AND ON EARTH HAS BEEN GIVEN TO ME. GO
> THEREFORE AND MAKE DISCIPLES OF ALL NATIONS,
> BAPTIZING THEM IN THE NAME OF THE FATHER AND OF
> THE SON AND OF THE HOLY SPIRIT, TEACHING THEM
> TO OBSERVE ALL THAT I HAVE COMMANDED YOU. AND
> BEHOLD, I AM WITH YOU ALWAYS, TO THE END OF THE
> AGE.'" - MATTHEW 28:18-20

As you continue in uncovering the big-picture story of Scripture, you're going to be looking at Paul's influence. This week, you'll see snippets from Paul's missionary journeys. Once he was converted, Paul became one of the most influential messengers of the Gospel in all of history. He went on at least three missionary journeys, planting churches and preaching the Gospel wherever he went.

Read Jesus' words in Matthew 28. These were the last words Matthew recorded Jesus saying to His disciples. They were super important. They contained Jesus' plan to spread the Gospel far outside of Jerusalem and Israel. When we think about Paul and his influence, all Paul was really doing was obeying Jesus' last commands. Paul is a direct connection to Jesus' command to share the Gospel. His impact was amazing. Ours can be too.

If you don't already have the Great Commission memorized, now would be a good time to do it.

WEEK 40, DAY 2

"AND SAID, 'YOU SON OF THE DEVIL, YOU ENEMY OF ALL RIGHTEOUSNESS, FULL OF ALL DECEIT AND VILLAINY, WILL YOU NOT STOP MAKING CROOK- ED THE STRAIGHT PATHS OF THE LORD? AND NOW, BEHOLD, THE HAND OF THE LORD IS UPON YOU, AND YOU WILL BE BLIND AND UNABLE TO SEE THE SUN FOR A TIME.' IMMEDIATELY MIST AND DARKNESS FELL UPON HIM, AND HE WENT ABOUT SEEKING PEOPLE TO LEAD HIM BY THE HAND."
- ACTS 13:10-11

Have you ever been around someone who loves nothing more than to put a damper on anything fun? They don't like puppies, or apple pie, or fluffy clouds. What makes them want to suck the life out every situation? Most of the time it seems like these folks just want some company in their misery. But maybe their motive in dragging people down isn't just to see people be miserable. Maybe it's actually a tactic for their gain.

READ ACTS 13:1-12 and pay special attention to the motives of Bar-Jesus. Think about his motives and why he did what he did. Barnabas and Saul are sent out to spread the Gospel, and eventually arrived in Salamis. While there, they come across a magician named Bar-Jesus who Luke referred to as a "false prophet." Now, the next sentence says that Bar-Jesus was with the proconsul. What's important to know is that the proconsul was a very high-ranking official in Rome. The proconsul called for Barnabas and Saul and wanted to hear about God, but Bar-Jesus tried to turn them away. He didn't want the proconsul to come to faith in the Lord!

The question is, why not? Why did he care so much? Well, you see, he was a false prophet that was in nice and cozy with a high-ranking official. He knew that if the proconsul came to faith, his gig was over! The Gospel forces us to confront our priorities. It forces us to think about how we do things and what we value. The truth is that many people don't want to give up any aspect of their lives. Some are even willing to drag others down in order to not change.

SOMETHING TO THINK ABOUT....
· Has the gospel ever forced you to come face-to-face with your priorities?
· How did that go? Did you put your priorities or the Gospel first? Are you willing to give up a comfortable set up if it conflicts with the Gospel?

THIS DEVOTION SPEAKS TO GOD'S SENSE OF JUSTICE. GO TO PAGE 4 FOR A DESCRIPTION OF THIS ATTRIBUTE.

WEEK 40, DAY 3

"THEN HE BROUGHT THEM OUT AND SAID, 'SIRS, WHAT MUST I DO TO BE SAVED?' AND THEY SAID, 'BELIEVE IN THE LORD JESUS, AND YOU WILL BE SAVED, YOU AND YOUR HOUSEHOLD.'" - ACTS 16:30-31

If you had to describe yourself, would you say that you're someone that likes to shakes things up a bit? Or are you someone that doesn't like to rock the boat? There's not a right or wrong answer. And one personality type isn't better than the other. Think about it.

IN THE MEANTIME, TAKE A LOOK AT ACTS 16:16-40 and think about those personality types. Who was shaking things up and who wanted things to keep going like normal? At the beginning of the passage Paul comes across a slave girl who is possessed by a spirit, and makes her owners money by telling people's fortunes. Paul eventually commanded the spirit to come out of her. But the owners were upset because their profit just went down the drain. The power of Jesus disrupted the status quo of the owner's nice, comfortable, money-making system.

They were so upset, the owners were successful in getting Paul and Silas beaten and thrown in jail. While in jail, they sang. Suddenly, there was an earthquake that shook the prison and opened the doors. The guard woke up and thought he had just let everyone escape. But Paul and Silas remained, and used the opportunity to share the Gospel with the guard. He put his faith in Jesus.

All through the story things are shaken up a little bit. Why is that? It's because the power of the Gospel moves in a new direction. It flips the old way and normal ways of doing things on their head. Sometimes it pushes us to uncomfortable places, and it causes us to act differently than previously acted.

SOMETHING TO THINK ABOUT....
· Would you rather have things stay "normal," or have the Gospel shake things up?
· What are areas of influence you have that need to be shaken up by the power of the Gospel? What can you do about it?

WEEK 40, DAY 4

"NOW WHEN THEY HEARD OF THE RESURRECTION OF THE DEAD, SOME MOCKED. BUT OTHERS SAID, 'WE WILL HEAR YOU AGAIN ABOUT THIS.' SO PAUL WENT OUT FROM THEIR MIDST." - ACTS 17:32-33

Do you know what it's like to feel completely outmanned on something? As in, you're up against someone or something and you don't have a chance? Maybe you're a younger sibling that's had to helplessly endure getting roughed up by an older brother or sister. These are pretty lonely feelings, right?

READ ACTS 17:16-43, and think a little bit about how Paul must have felt. Paul recognized the spiritual darkness of Athens we he saw how the city was full of idols. He could have kept quiet and moved on, but the Gospel compelled him to address the issue. He began talking about Jesus in the synagogues. Some people criticized him, and others asked him to explain what he was talking about a little more. Paul seized the opportunity and laid out a clear, respectful, and direct presentation of the Gospel.

Paul didn't let the fear of being outmanned intimidate him. He saw the depravity and darkness of Athens, and called it out. How much easier would it have been to just let it slide? And when he got put on the spot to go even deeper with what he was talking about, he didn't shy away from the opportunity. He took it and ran with it. Were some people critical? Of course. But others were intrigued and wanted to hear more about the Gospel, and that's what is most important.

SOMETHING TO THINK ABOUT....
· What would you have done if you were in Paul's shoes?
· What fears get in the way of you stepping up and talking about the Gospel in the midst of spiritual darkness?
· Do you feel prepared to talk about the Gospel if people are interested? Why or why not? If not, what can you do to get more comfortable?

WEEK 40, DAY 5

"SO THE CITY WAS FILLED WITH THE CONFUSION, AND THEY RUSHED TOGETHER INTO THE THEATER, DRAGGING WITH THEM GAIUS AND ARISTARCHUS, MACEDONIANS WHO WERE PAUL'S COMPANIONS IN TRAVEL. BUT WHEN PAUL WISHED TO GO IN AMONG THE CROWD, THE DISCIPLES WOULD NOT LET HIM."
- ACTS 19:29-30

There's nothing quite like getting really amped up about something only to be told that it's not that big of a deal. When we're done with our freak-out we feel a little relieved, and a little silly. We wonder what all the fuss was about.

READ ACTS 19:23-41, and look at who is getting riled up and worried. Do they have a legit concern or are they overreacting? This passage starts off letting us know that a disturbance was arising because of Jesus and His followers. See, there was this guy named Demetrius who was in the business of making silver shrines of Artemis. The Gospel was spreading and Demetrius wasn't down at all. Why? Because if people started following Jesus, they wouldn't have any use for his silver shrines. And that meant his cash flow was going to dry up. He wasn't having it.

So, he got his fellow craftsmen riled up with him. They were fired up, and they started going around the city yelling, "Great is Artemis of the Ephesians!" Maybe they believed it, but their main concern was convincing everyone else it was true. Things were getting crazy, so the town clerk worked to calm everyone down. His main point was, "What's the big deal?"

God is in control of all things. We can freak out if we want when life throws us a curve ball. But God is never caught off guard. We can trust in His provision.

SOMETHING TO THINK ABOUT....
· Is your faith strong enough to ever rock the boat?
· Or is it something that is so passive, no one notices?
· Or is it something that might have a little spark, but is dangerously close to fizzling out?

WEEK 41

WEEK 41, DAY 1

**"NEVERTHELESS, I TELL YOU THE TRUTH: IT IS TO YOUR ADVAN-
TAGE THAT I GO AWAY, FOR IF I DO NOT GO AWAY, THE HELPER
WILL NOT COME TO YOU. BUT IF I GO, I WILL SEND HIM TO YOU."
- JOHN 16:7**

This marks a departure of sorts from your look at the big-picture story of the Bible. Starting this week, you'll be looking at
the story of Scripture through a different lens. You'll be looking
at the story through letters written along the journey by various
key New Testament figures. It's a cool way for you to encounter
the rest of the richness of the New Testament while keeping
the story in mind.

For the next few days you'll be looking at Paul's letter to the
Romans. Paul most likely wrote Romans from Corinth, while on
his third missionary journey sometime in 57 AD. Romans is an
awesome letter that communicates the fullest picture of Paul's
theology in all of Scripture. It's a powerful book that guides,
encourages, and instruct all who read it. God can transform
lives through it, and has for centuries.

Part of this life transformation is achieved through the Holy
Spirit working in and through you. If you're a believer, the
Holy Spirit literally lives inside you. This is an amazing gift. So
much so, that Jesus Himself said it was actually GOOD that He
would be leaving this earth. He knew His leaving would usher
in the Spirit's permanent work in the lives of all Christ-followers.

Memorize this simple, but powerful verse this week. It's a great
reminder of God's everyday presence in your life.

WEEK 41, DAY 2

"THEREFORE GOD GAVE THEM UP IN THE LUSTS OF THEIR HEARTS TO IMPURITY, TO THE DISHONORING OF THEIR BODIES AMONG THEMSELVES, BECAUSE THEY EXCHANGED THE TRUTH ABOUT GOD FOR A LIE AND WORSHIPED AND SERVED THE CREATURE RATHER THAN THE CREATOR, WHO IS BLESSED FOREVER! AMEN."
- ROMANS 1:24-25

Have you ever seen one of those cartoons where a snowball starts rolling down a hill and keeps getting bigger and bigger and bigger? In the cartoons it's usually meant to be pretty funny, and no one really gets hurt. But it's an image of what happens in real life all too often. We tell a simple lie. Then we lie more to cover that lie. Eventually it crashes somewhere. This is the consistent pattern sin creates in our lives.

READ ROMANS 1:18-32. In the beginning of the passage, Paul lets us know that the issue at hand is that people had suppressed the truth about God, truth that was made plain to them from the beginning. Once people began to worship what God had created rather than worshipping the One who created it all, the snowball began to form.

One of the most devastating phrases we can read in all of Scripture is found in verse 24: "God gave them up . . . " This means that God let us have exactly what we wanted. He let us go after the things we craved. And it spiraled out of control very quickly. Maybe people think they can simply live peacefully without the Lord. But Scripture tells us that's not possible. Left on our own, once the snowball starts, it's all downhill from there.

SOMETHING TO THINK ABOUT...
· What are some ways you've seen sin spiral out of control in your own life? In the lives of people around you?
· Even if your sin doesn't seem as ugly and in-your-face as some people you know, why is it just as serious?
· Who or what can stop the snowball from ultimately crashing? How so?

WEEK 41, DAY 3

"FOR ALL HAVE SINNED AND FALL SHORT OF THE GLORY OF GOD, AND ARE JUSTIFIED BY HIS GRACE AS A GIFT, THROUGH THE REDEMPTION THAT IS IN CHRIST JESUS."
- ROMANS 3:23-24

We love to put people in categories. Sometimes it's fair. A lot of times it's not. We see them as rich or poor. We see them as cool or dorky. Smart or dumb. Athletic or clumsy. Attractive or not. The distinctions are endless. And these distinctions usually determine how we value people. We see certain categories as more worthy of our attention, and ignore others. Have you ever stopped and wondered what makes us value one over the other? Are these categories helpful? Or harmful? More importantly, are they the way the Lord sees things?

READ ROMANS 3:1-26. Prior to the coming of Jesus, God's righteousness was made known through the standard that was put forth in the Old Testament law. What Paul tells us is that God's righteousness was now being made known in a new way: through Jesus. This doesn't mean there was anything wrong with the Law; in fact, he tells us that the Law was always pointing to Christ.

When God's righteousness was being made known through the Law, it was super easy for people to throw others into categories and point fingers. "You are good at keeping the Law, so you're a good person that's worthy of attention and love. You're bad at keeping the Law, so you're not worthy." This isn't how God ever intended the Law to be used. But people's pride and sin got in the way. But now when Jesus came, those distinctions and categories disappeared. The truth is that everyone is a sinner. We're all just as messed up as the next person. We all need Jesus just as much. We might think we look, act, or perform better than someone else, but when it comes to what matters most, we all fit in the same category.

SOMETHING TO THINK ABOUT...

· In what ways does your pride cause you to point fingers and put people in different categories?
· What does Jesus do to our pride and to our categories?

WEEK 41, DAY 4

**"BUT GOD SHOWS HIS LOVE FOR US IN THAT WHILE WE
WERE STILL SINNERS, CHRIST DIED FOR US."
- ROMANS 5:8**

Any great TV show or movie has a conflict that must be resolved. Life is similar. There are things that need to be fixed. The awesome thing about TV shows and movies is that some sort of resolution takes place inside of a nice, tidy timeframe. We sit down to watch them and expect to get answers before we get up. This is where life is different. We don't always get to have the conflict wrapped up within the hour. However, even though it doesn't work like TV, we can rest assured that there is an answer to our greatest problem.

READ ROMANS 5:1-11. In the chapters leading up to this passage, Paul has laid the groundwork for what our greatest problem is. We have a sin problem that has lead to all sorts of chaos, strife, and darkness. In this passage, Paul reminds us that we were sinners, we were weak, and we were even enemies of God. But all throughout the passage, he highlights how things are different for those who have been made right with God through Christ. We now have peace with God!

The greatest conflict we have in life - our separation from God - has been put to rest in Jesus. The peace we have with God gives us a different outlook on the suffering we see and experience. We have salvation. We have access to God's grace. We have a reason to rejoice. Paul lets us know that Jesus is the "fix" to the world's greatest conflict. He's the one who will ultimately make all the "messed up" right. It might not be in one sitting on the couch with the TV on, but when we look at things with an eternal focus, we know that through Him, our conflict will be resolved.

SOMETHING TO THINK ABOUT...
· Have you experienced what it means to be at peace with God? What does that look like?
· Do you long for Jesus to simply fix your individual problems? Or are you satisfied in the truth that He has fixed your greatest problem? What's the difference between the two?

**THIS DEVOTION SPEAKS TO GOD'S LOVE. GO TO PAGE 4
FOR A DESCRIPTION OF THIS ATTRIBUTE.**

WEEK 41, DAY 5

"AND WE KNOW THAT FOR THOSE WHO LOVE GOD ALL THINGS WORK TOGETHER FOR GOOD, FOR THOSE WHO ARE CALLED ACCORDING TO HIS PURPOSE." - ROMANS 8:28

"It's gonna' be OK." That's a phrase we've probably said or heard a few hundred times. A lot of times it's said when we're trying to comfort someone, and we don't know what else to say. We're trying to let someone know that even though things seems rough right now, they'll eventually get better. It's a nice thought. And the heart behind saying it is kind. But the question is: is everything really going to end up being OK? How can we know?

READ ROMANS 8:28-39. Well, this passage gets right to the heart of the question we just asked. Verses 28-29 tells us that things do end up being OK for those that love God. In fact, things end up being more than OK. Paul tells us that everything actually works out for the good of those who love God, and have been called according to his purpose. This doesn't mean that nothing bad will happen to us. But it does mean that things will ultimately turn out for our good.

And how do we know it's true? We know that it's true because it isn't dependent on us. It's dependent on Jesus. It says that we'll ultimately be conformed to His image. Because of this, Paul says we are more than conquerors; not because we're strong, but because the One who loves us is perfectly strong. Paul never says life will always be easy. But in the midst of our tough times, we can take confidence that God is at work, and His purpose will ultimately prevail. That's how we know everything will end up being just fine.

SOMETHING TO THINK ABOUT....
· What give you confidence in life? What do you cling to when things are tough? What gives you hope that things will be ok?
· Are you able to think about ultimate victory in Jesus when you're going through tough times? Why or why not?

WEEK 42

"FOR THE WORD OF THE CROSS IS FOLLY TO THOSE WHO ARE PERISHING, BUT TO US WHO ARE BEING SAVED IT IS THE POWER OF GOD."
- 1 CORINTHIANS 1:18

This is another week you'll be spending looking at samples of Paul's letters. This week, you'll be mostly looking at Paul's letters to the Corinthians. Paul had a really interesting relationship with the church in Corinth. He had helped get the church going, but they had encountered a ton of internal strife. Paul wrote them letters to help correct what was going on in their church.

Sometimes we will have problems in our churches, and in our groups of Christian friends. It's all because of our sin nature. We're imperfect people. And when we fight, or act in other dysfunctional ways, outsiders can often have a little fun at our expense. We become easy targets for people who want to poke fun at the church and of Christ-followers. But Paul's words in 1 Corinthians 1:18 are helpful in helping us deal with this dynamic.

For those who have rejected Christ, our lifestyles, our faith, and ultimately, the Gospel just sounds foolish. They dismiss us because in their hearts they have dismissed God. Instead of being upset when people do this, we should be heartbroken because of what that means for them in terms of their standing with God.

Let Paul's words here be a reminder of those in your school who are separated from God. Let it pierce your heart and motivate you to reach out to them.

WEEK 42, DAY 2

"BECAUSE, IF YOU CONFESS WITH YOUR MOUTH THAT JESUS IS LORD AND BELIEVE IN YOUR HEART THAT GOD RAISED HIM FROM THE DEAD, YOU WILL BE SAVED." - ROMANS 10:9

Are you a curious person? Do you find yourself wondering about the "why," and "how" behind how things work? Or are you more of a "go with the flow" person? Are you more content to use whatever is in front of you, and not really care how it got there, or how it operates? Both approaches can be helpful in different situations. But what about when it comes to our salvation? Is that a "go-with-the-flow" subject, or would it be helpful to know how that works?

READ ROMANS 10:9-15. This is a great passage to turn to if you ever wonder, or are asked, "How exactly is someone saved?" The answer is straightforward in verse 9. Paul tells us that it involves confessing with our mouth, and believing in our heart. The mouth and heart are involved because trusting Jesus involves knowing who He is and what he's done, and truly believing in Him. It involves trusting the full story of the Gospel, that Jesus is truly Lord, and that after His crucifixion He defeated death by rising from the dead. This is how someone is saved.

One question that remains is: "How do people learn about this?" Someone has to tell them. How are they going to believe if they aren't told? So, this can't be a "go-with-the-flow" matter. We have to dig into it. We have to trust, and know it ourselves. And then, we have tell people. How else are they going to hear?

SOMETHING TO THINK ABOUT...

· In your life, do you see how your heart and mind both come together in trusting and following Jesus? How so?
· Are you confident in your ability to tell someone that hasn't heard about the good news of Jesus? Why or why not? If not, how do you get to that point?

"NO TEMPTATION HAS OVERTAKEN YOU THAT IS NOT COMMON TO MAN. GOD IS FAITHFUL, AND HE WILL NOT LET YOU BE TEMPTED BEYOND YOUR ABILITY, BUT WITH THE TEMPTATION HE WILL ALSO PROVIDE THE WAY OF ESCAPE, THAT YOU MAY BE ABLE TO ENDURE IT."
- 1 CORINTHIANS 10:13

Doing the right thing is hard, especially when no one will know whether you did the right thing or the wrong thing. Imagine you found an envelope with $1,000 in an empty parking lot. No one's around. There are no cameras. You know the right thing to do, but on the other hand, it's a lot of money. It's almost like you're being pulled in two different directions.

READ 1 CORINTHIANS 10:1-13. When you struggle with temptation and sin, it can feel like you are the only person in the world that wrestles with those things. And when you feel like you're the only one, you feel alone. Paul brings up some of the dark times in the history of the Israelites to make a point: This whole sin thing is nothing new. It's easy to feel alone when you struggle with temptation, but the reality is that it's something every other human being experiences.

You're not alone. God hasn't left you alone. Because of our sin, temptation is something we're all very familiar with. But God isn't distant when you are tempted. He is faithful. He loves you. He is for you. And He has provided a way out.

Of course, you'll still stumble and fall. You're not alone in that, either. But know that when right and wrong seem to pull you in two different directions, God is faithful. He loves you, and He is for you.

SOMETHING TO THINK ABOUT...
· What is one area in your life where you feel pulled between choosing what is right and what is wrong?
· How can today's passage change how you think about that temptation?

THIS DEVOTION SPEAKS TO GOD'S FAITHFULNESS.
GO TO PAGE 4 FOR A DESCRIPTION OF THIS ATTRIBUTE.

WEEK 42, DAY 4

"DO YOU NOT KNOW THAT IN A RACE ALL THE RUNNERS RUN, BUT ONLY ONE RECEIVES THE PRIZE? SO RUN THAT YOU MAY OBTAIN IT."
- 1 CORINTHIANS 9:24

When was the last time you did something awesome for someone (don't worry, this devotion's between you and God, so it's not really bragging) that you didn't have to do? What did it feel like to spend your own time, money, or energy on someone else rather than on yourself? Pretty good, right?

READ 1 CORINTHIANS 9:21-27. Paul's talking about how he did everything he could to convince people to follow Jesus. Rather than put his own desires first, he served others by stepping into their lives to share with them the most important news they would ever hear. In essence, Paul is saying, "Even if it meant putting aside what I would normally want to do, I did whatever it took to serve others and give them the opportunity of knowing Jesus."

Then, Paul brings up training for a race to drive home his point. Just like it takes lots of discipline and sacrifice to train for a marathon—eating right, getting up early for training runs, etc.—it takes discipline and sacrifice to live in such a way that helps others know Jesus. When your goal is to tell those around you about Jesus, you'll live differently. You'll put others first. And you'll serve others, even when it's hard to do.

Just like training for a marathon requires discipline, living a life that is constantly pointing others to Jesus is tough. But when you think about it, there's nothing better to do with your live than giving others the opportunity to know Jesus.

SOMETHING TO THINK ABOUT...
· Why is it so hard to put your desires aside to serve others?
· What is one person in your life who doesn't yet know Jesus that you can serve and show God's love to?

"SO NOW FAITH, HOPE, AND LOVE ABIDE, THESE THREE; BUT THE GREATEST OF THESE IS LOVE."
- 1 CORINTHIANS 13:13

Have you ever faked your way through a school assignment? Maybe it was that book report you wrote without actually reading the book. Or perhaps you somehow got an "A" on a research paper—without really doing much research. But there are some assignments you can't fake, right?

READ 1 CORINTHIANS CHAPTER 13. The main theme of this passage isn't hard to miss: love. But Paul doesn't talk about love the way we're used to hearing about it. It's easy to look really spiritual, or like we have this whole following Jesus thing down. But, Paul says, all of the super-spiritual things you do don't really matter if you're missing a key ingredient: love. And love is something that you just can't fake. When you say that Jesus is the center of your life, but you're a jerk at the same time, your faith comes across as empty.

Real love is hard. It's easy to sing songs on retreats, to go to youth group when all your friends are there, and to serve dinner at a homeless shelter when everyone else is going, too. But patience, kindness, and forgiveness? That's not easy at all. But if you want to live a faith that's more than just going through the motions, a faith that actually matters, maybe it's time to ask yourself: does my faith in Jesus cause me to really love others, or am I just a noisy gong?

SOMETHING TO THINK ABOUT...
· Gut check: when it comes to following Jesus, does your faith in Jesus cause you to really love others, or are you just going through the motions?
In verses 4-6, Paul lists a lot of things that love is, and a lot of things that love is not. Which of those things do you maybe need to work on the most?

THIS DEVOTION SPEAKS TO GOD'S LOVE. GO TO PAGE 4 FOR A DESCRIPTION OF THIS ATTRIBUTE.

WEEK 43

WEEK 43, DAY 1

**"I HAVE SAID THESE THINGS TO YOU, THAT IN
ME YOU MAY HAVE PEACE. IN THE WORLD YOU
WILL HAVE TRIBULATION. BUT TAKE HEART; I
HAVE OVERCOME THE WORLD." - JOHN 16:33**

You're going to continue to hang out in Paul's letters this week, and a little bit of next week. Paul wrote most of the New Testament, so giving his words a little more time than others is probably not a bad idea. You'll be looking at Paul's words in Corinthians, as well as parts of his letter to the Ephesians. Paul's letter to the Ephesians - as well as letters he wrote to the Philippians, Colossians, and Timothy - was written while Paul was in prison in Rome. He had been imprisoned because of his faith.

Paul suffered tremendously for the Gospel. He was chased out of most cities he visited. He was beaten, imprisoned, and almost murdered along the way. And he would ultimately be killed for his faith. But Paul understood this was part of the role he was playing. Jesus understood this too. Jesus' words in John 16:33 should come as a comforting reminder for us when we experience hardship. If we're living for Christ, life will be tough at times. But Jesus assures us that in the end He's already conquered.

If you get the chance, memorize this verse this week.

**THIS DEVOTION SPEAKS TO GOD'S POWER.
GO TO PAGE 4 FOR A DESCRIPTION OF THIS ATTRIBUTE.**

WEEK 43, DAY 2

"WE ARE AFFLICTED IN EVERY WAY, BUT NOT CRUSHED; PERPLEXED, BUT NOT DRIVEN TO DESPAIR; PERSECUTED, BUT NOT FORSAKEN; STRUCK DOWN, BUT NOT DESTROYED.
- 2 CORINTHIANS 4:8-9

Think about the last time a tech-company launched a major new device, whether it was a phone, a tablet, or some other incredible new product. What were the commercials like? How did the company promote the product on social media and online? Chances are, they pulled out all the stops, and did everything they could to convince you how amazing their product was. When a company wants to convince you to buy something, they do their best to make their product look perfect. But have you ever noticed that God doesn't work the same way?

READ 2 CORINTHIANS 4:7-12. Paul has endured a lot as he's travelled thousands of miles to tell everyone he can about Jesus. He's been beaten, ridiculed, and experienced natural disasters. By our standards, much of what he did was a failure because he didn't gain a lot of popularity. But as far as Paul was concerned, all that failure was a part of God's plan.

God didn't want to package the Gospel—the incredible good news that God gave His own son to die so that we could live—in slick packaging, and market it so that we were tricked into buying something we didn't want. Instead, God entrusted His message to real people who experience real difficulties. Paul calls us clay jars, which is the modern day equivalent to a cardboard box. Not the most precious container for such valuable truth!

God's entrusted His message to you. Yeah, you might be broken, dusty, and imperfect. Life has probably knocked you around a bit. But God wants to use you just as you are. That way it will clear that it's about God and not about you. But God's promise is that He won't abandon you, or let you be destroyed. And God always keeps His promises.

SOMETHING TO THINK ABOUT...
· What difficult circumstance in your life do you think God could use to help someone meet Jesus for the first time?

WEEK 43, DAY 3

Have you ever been put in charge of an important task? If you have a job, maybe your boss had to leave for a little while and you had to run the store for a few minutes. Or maybe your mom or dad left for the day and left you in charge. Sometimes we take those opportunities seriously, and sometimes we don't.

READ 2 CORINTHIANS 5:16-21. If the Gospel could be summed up in a few short sentences, this paragraph might be it. Paul makes some incredible statements: You're forgiven. We have a restored relationship with God, all because Jesus paid the debt of our sin by dying on the cross. To top it off, when God looks at us, He doesn't see our sin, but rather Jesus' righteousness. Incredible!

But this short passage contains something even more incredible than that. God has entrusted you with the most important task you've ever been given. You are Christ's ambassador, and God is making His appeal to the world through you. Sort of makes babysitting your little brother seem like small potatoes, doesn't it?

You are God's "Plan A" to share this incredible news with those around you. There is no Plan B. You're God's ambassador. Your job is to tell people that they can be reconciled to God because of what Jesus did for them on the cross. And because Jesus has already done it, you've got the easy part: spreading the word. The only question is, "Are you willing"?

SOMETHING TO THINK ABOUT...
· How does it make you feel to imagine yourself as God's ambassador? Excited? Nervous? Scared?
· Who is one person in your life God is leading you to tell about Jesus' love for him/her?

THIS DEVOTION SPEAKS TO GOD'S RIGHTEOUSNESS.
GO TO PAGE 4 FOR A DESCRIPTION OF THIS ATTRIBUTE.

WEEK 43, DAY 4

**"FOR BY GRACE YOU HAVE BEEN SAVED THROUGH FAITH.
AND THIS IS NOT YOUR OWN DOING; IT IS THE GIFT OF GOD,
NOT A RESULT OF WORKS, SO THAT NO ONE MAY BOAST.
FOR WE ARE HIS WORKMANSHIP, CREATED IN CHRIST JESUS
FOR GOOD WORKS, WHICH GOD PREPARED BEFOREHAND,
THAT WE SHOULD WALK IN THEM." - EPHESIANS 2:8-10**

We live in a culture that is used to the saying, "Nothing is for free." If someone wants to give us a gift for no reason at all we ask, "What's the occasion"? We are used to everything being a transaction. We put the ATM card in, and the money comes out. If I'm good to my friends, then my friends will be good to me. However, Jesus sort of broke the rules on this entire idea.

READ EPHESIANS 2:1-10. As you do, underline the word "grace" every time you see it, and circle the words "saved" or "salvation." The passage unfolds by talking about our sin. It uses words like "disobedience," and "dead." Yet, do you also see that it uses words like, "used to"? If you have a highlighter looking at the first three verses, highlight all of the times it says, "used to." Before Christ, we were stuck in our sin. All of us. When we have a relationship with Jesus, we are different now.

Finally, reread verses 8-10. It discusses grace. Grace is a gift we can't earn. We can't take credit for what God did. In other words, we can't put our prayers, good deeds, or anything before God, and get anything in return. He loves us just because He made us. He loves us just because. This might be the hardest concept for any of us to truly understand. Focus on verse 10. Grace is free, but when we accept it, then we are new. This changes everything. Grace motivates us. Grace compels us to want to live as children of God. It isn't a transaction at all. Our relationship with God is founded on and motivated by grace.

SOMETHING TO THINK ABOUT . . .
· What is grace according to this passage?
· Do you keep thinking you have to be "good enough" for God?

WEEK 43, DAY 5

**"THEREFORE BE IMITATORS OF GOD, AS BELOVED
CHILDREN. AND WALK IN LOVE, AS CHRIST LOVED
US AND GAVE HIMSELF UP FOR US, A FRAGRANT
OFFERING AND SACRIFICE TO GOD."
- EPHESIANS 5:1-2**

Have you ever heard anyone say, "You're a child of God?" Maybe. Maybe not. At church we like to tell kids we are ALL His children. This statement is "sort of" true. Yes, since we are all created in His image, technically we are all His kids. However, the Bible is clear that we are given the "right" to be called His children when we have a saving relationship with Him.

It's an interesting concept. **SEE WHAT EPHESIANS 5:1-7 HAS TO SAY** about being God's children. When we know we are His children and what this means, it also comes with some hard responsibility. Our Father wants us to live like Him. That means we can't do whatever we want. It's not meant to be a checklist of "do's and don'ts," or to feel like we can't have fun. Instead out of our love and respect for our Father, we want to live close to Him.

Does this mean if you make a mistake God will turn his back on you? No! This passage is about people who want to do their own thing and then say they love God. When you truly have a love for your parents, you don't WANT to hurt them. Others are always going to distract us, and tell us that life with Jesus is too much work. They are going to tell you their life is more enjoyable living the way they want. Yet, when you live as a true child of the Lord, you know that the rewards of love, peace, and hope far outweigh any good time that could be had.

SOMETHING TO THINK ABOUT...
· What do you think it truly means to "be in the light"?
· How can the world recognize you are a person filled with light?
· Do you ever struggle with wanting to do things that seem more "fun," but aren't what God wants? Why do you think that is?

WEEK 44

WEEK 44, DAY 1

"BUT GOD, BEING RICH IN MERCY, BECAUSE OF THE
GREAT LOVE WITH WHICH HE LOVED US, EVEN WHEN
WE WERE DEAD IN OUR TRESPASSES, MADE US ALIVE
TOGETHER WITH CHRIST—BY GRACE YOU HAVE BEEN
SAVED." - EPHESIANS 2:4-5

As you continue to work through Paul's letters, you'll notice how practical and application-oriented they are. Paul was often concerned with helping people young in their faith know how to live as Christ-followers. Keep in mind, this was a new religion, so to speak. The new Believers were surrounded by people who worshipped all manner of false gods. These Christ-followers needed to be shaped. They needed to be led. And we are not that much different.

By the grace of God, as Paul puts it in Ephesians 2:4-5, we have been saved from our old lives. Our old way of living won't work anymore. By God's grace, He has given us a new path, a new story, and a new motivation for our journey.

This week, memorize Ephesians 2:4-5. It's a super-powerful verse. It is, in a nutshell, the Gospel. Hide it in your heart so that you will always be reminded of God's love for you.

**THIS DEVOTION SPEAKS TO GOD'S LOVE. GO TO PAGE 4
FOR A DESCRIPTION OF THIS ATTRIBUTE.**

WEEK 44, DAY 2

"DO NOTHING FROM SELFISH AMBITION OR CONCEIT, BUT IN HUMILITY COUNT OTHERS MORE SIGNIFICANT THAN YOURSELVES. LET EACH OF YOU LOOK NOT ONLY TO HIS OWN INTERESTS, BUT ALSO TO THE INTERESTS OF OTHERS." - PHILIPPIANS 2:3-4

Imagine you are at an event where they are giving out free food. There are two choices, and you get only one. One thing is your favorite food in the whole world. The other is something you absolutely despise. You are standing in a very long line to get the food with your best friend. They feel the same way about the food choices that you do. Finally, after being in line for a seeming eternity, it's your turn. When you step up and they ask you what you want, you realize there is only one serving left of the best food. Your friend is standing behind you. There is a choice at hand. What do you do?

We all want to say we would choose to put our friend first. Yet, if we are honest, it's more of an internal wresting match than that. We might give up the food, but then be bitter we had to let it go. Let's face it: our nature is to be selfish. This is hard to hear. But it's true for all of us.

READ PHILIPPIANS 2:1-11. We are told to be like Jesus. We are told to be humble. When we think of others as better than ourselves, our desire is for them to have the best before we ever think about our own wants and desires. However, the Lord knows we can't feel this way on our own.   It's only through Christ that we can be selfless instead of selfish. When we reflect on Jesus, and live for Him, only then can we put self aside totally.

SOMETHING TO THINK ABOUT...
· What ways do you struggle with being selfish?
· Reflect on Philippians 2:7- 8. How does this change the way you look at your own selfishness?

WEEK 44, DAY 3

"CONTINUE IN THE FAITH, STABLE AND STEADFAST, NOT SHIFTING FROM THE HOPE OF THE GOSPEL THAT YOU HEARD, WHICH HAS BEEN PROCLAIMED IN ALL CREATION UNDER HEAVEN, AND OF WHICH I, PAUL, BECAME A MINISTER." - COLOSSIANS 1:23

Wherever you are right now, take an assessment of your surroundings. Put your hand on the wall in the room you are in and feel the texture. Get up and look out the window. What do you see? Take a deep breath and hold it for a moment, now let it out slowly.

NOW READ COLOSSIANS 1:15-23. Have you ever thought about how God made it all? Everything we see, and don't see, God put in place. And He keeps it in its place. He's the one that keeps our little planet from tipping off of its axis and spinning wildly into space. Through sin we became separated from understating this truth. Christ's death and resurrection restored our ability to have a relationship with Him. The word used in this passage is "reconciled." Once we were selfish and disobedient, like a toddler having a tantrum. What Jesus did for us meant we didn't have to be far away from Him anymore.

Yet, people can try to cause us to doubt Jesus and His role as Creator and Sustainer. This is where faith comes in. Faith is standing firm and choosing to believe that Jesus offers truth. It's remembering He is who He says He is, and that matters most. Good news means we aren't merely saved FROM our sin, but we are saved TO a new life with Christ, in peace and assurance.

SOMETHING TO THINK ABOUT...
· Do you ever feel like you are "drifting away" from knowing Christ is who He says He is? Why?
· What is one way today you can put your hope and assurance in the Lord?

WEEK 44, DAY 4

"IF THEN YOU HAVE BEEN RAISED WITH CHRIST, SEEK THE THINGS THAT ARE ABOVE, WHERE CHRIST IS, SEATED AT THE RIGHT HAND OF GOD. SET YOUR MINDS ON THINGS THAT ARE ABOVE, NOT ON THINGS THAT ARE ON EARTH. FOR YOU HAVE DIED, AND YOUR LIFE IS HIDDEN WITH CHRIST IN GOD."
- COLOSSIANS 3:1-3

We all know people who claim to be Christians, but whose lives don't seem to match their claims. Maybe if we are honest, this is even who we are sometimes. We treat following Jesus like a list of actions we should and shouldn't do. This isn't the way Jesus wants it though.

READ COLOSSIANS 3:1-17 TO SEE WHAT I MEAN. This passage gives us line-by-line what it means to live in Christ. Notice something interesting. This isn't just a list of "don'ts." It's also a list of "do's." See, Jesus wants us to put on forgiveness, love, and kindness like the clothes we wear everyday. We can get overwhelmed and worried we are doing it wrong. What if we mess up what it means to live for Jesus? What if sometimes we aren't kind, or are selfish, or lie?

We have to be willing to give God our entire selves. Our hearts and souls. And when we do, we're made new. With a new heart we now WANT to be close to Jesus. Then we desire to do all of the things in this passage, and whatever else it takes to live close to the Lord. It's always about where our heart is. Is your heart with Him or not?

SOMETHING TO THINK ABOUT...
· What's the hardest part for you in this passage?
· Go through this whole passage and underline anything that stands out to you in what Christ is asking of you today.

 THIS DEVOTION SPEAKS TO GOD'S HOLINESS. GO TO PAGE 4 FOR A DESCRIPTION OF THIS ATTRIBUTE.

WEEK 44, DAY 5

"FOR GOD HAS NOT CALLED US FOR IMPURITY, BUT IN HOLINESS." - 1 THESSALONIANS 4:7

There are times in our lives when someone calls us out. This can be a good thing, or a bad thing. Think about a teacher who calls out your name in class. They may say that you scored the highest grade in the class on a test. Or you could get called out for not paying attention to the teacher. Sometimes it's a good thing. And sometimes it's anything but good.

READ 1 THESSALONIANS 4:3-8.

Here, Paul is calling out the Thessalonians. Paul reminds the Christians in Thessalonica that living a life of impurity is not what God called them out for in life. Impurity here means to live contrary to the Bible, to live selfishly, and to have the aim or goal of living like a non-Christian. It had to sting a bit for Paul to get on them like he did. But, here's a truth in life: When someone you know and respect calls you out, it's almost always because they want something better for you. They care enough about you to want more for you. And though it may sting, in the long run, it's a good thing.

The beautiful part of the verse is that God called us to live in holiness. Simply put, we're called to live a life that resembles that of Jesus more and more every day. You are holy because God who lives in you is holy. And you are called to live a life that reflects God more and more each day.

SOMETHING TO THINK ABOUT . . .
· What does holiness mean to you?
· Think of some practical ways you live a holy life in your world each day? What are some examples?

WEEK 45

WEEK 45, DAY 1

"SO EVERYONE WHO ACKNOWLEDGES ME BEFORE MEN, I ALSO WILL ACKNOWLEDGE BEFORE MY FATHER WHO IS IN HEAVEN, BUT WHOEVER DENIES ME BEFORE MEN, I ALSO WILL DENY BEFORE MY FATHER WHO IS IN HEAVEN." - MATTHEW 10:32-33

This week, you're continuing your journey through Paul's letters. This week focuses entirely on Paul's letters to the Thessalonian church. Paul most likely wrote 1 and 2 Thessalonians while in Corinth on his second missionary journey, sometime around 49-51 AD. Paul deals with quite a few themes in the letters. But the most prominent is the theme of Jesus' second coming. Apparently there was some confusion about what would happen when Jesus returned. Paul was helping the Thessalonian Christ-followers have a better grasp of how things would go down when Jesus returned.

Jesus will one day return. We can know that for sure. And regardless of exactly when and how it happens, we know this: those who have been saved through faith in Christ will spend eternity with Him. Those who have not will spend eternity separated from Him. This is what Jesus alludes to in Matthew 10.

When you come to saving faith in Jesus, you are made new. There is a transformation that takes place. Part of this transformation is a new identity in Christ. Our call is to publicly identify as Christ-followers, boldly standing strong in our convictions. On what levels do you acknowledge Jesus before others? As you memorize these verses this week, think about the message behind them. What do you need to learn from them?

WEEK 45, DAY 2

"NOW CONCERNING BROTHERLY LOVE YOU HAVE NO NEED FOR ANYONE TO WRITE TO YOU, FOR YOU YOURSELVES HAVE BEEN TAUGHT BY GOD TO LOVE ONE ANOTHER." - 1 THESSALONIANS 4:9

Reminders come in all kinds of forms these days. Your parents may leave you notes on your door to remind you to take out the trash, or clean up your room. The alarm on your phone reminds you what time to get up each morning. You may even put reminders in the calendar on your phone or tablet to remind you about a birthday, or some other special occasion.

READ 1 THESSALONIANS 4:9-13. Paul told the Thessalonians that they had a great record of showing love to others. They did not need any written reminders to love people because they had something new: They had the Spirit of God living in them. God could teach them, and remind them to love others as a way of showing His love to the world.

If you have come to a saving faith in Jesus, you have the Spirit living inside of you to serve as your reminder. Daily, the Holy Spirit works behind the scenes to encourage you, remind you of God's truth, convict you of sin, and empower you to be messengers of the Gospel. The Holy Spirit is your constant companion, a full-time reminder to pursue God and His ways.

Today, when the Holy Spirit prompts you to show and display His love, don't hit the snooze button. Act on His reminders.

SOMETHING TO THINK ABOUT . . .

· Are you able to tell when the Holy Spirit is leading or nudging you? What does your answer say about your connectivity to God?
· Pray today that you will always be sensitive to the voice of God reminding you to love others in His name.

WEEK 45, DAY 3

"BUT WE DO NOT WANT YOU TO BE UNINFORMED,
BROTHERS, ABOUT THOSE WHO ARE ASLEEP, THAT YOU
MAY NOT GRIEVE AS OTHERS DO WHO HAVE NO HOPE."
- 1 THESSALONIANS 4:13

The English language is a difficult one for people of other cultures to learn because so many of our words have multiple meanings. For example, you could say, "The youth pastor had a good point tonight," or, "That pencil sure has a sharp point." Another example would be to say, "I love the time of year when the leaves change color," versus, "My sister leaves for college this weekend."

READ 1 THESSALONIANS 4:13-18. The word "asleep" in today's passage is one that had a dual meaning in Jesus' day. "Asleep" could mean a person had gone to bed for the night, or it could refer to someone who had died. The problem Paul was addressing was that Christians were afraid those who had died would not be around to experience all the wonderful things that were to happen when Jesus returned. They were sure that Jesus' return was not far off. Paul reminded them that people who die without a relationship with God through Christ have no hope. But Christians have hope galore.

Will we be here when Jesus returns? The Bible says no one knows when that will happen but what we do know is that we believers have the sure hope and promise of life in Christ forever.

SOMETHING TO THINK ABOUT . . .

· Do you have questions about death and dying? Make it a point to search out a parent, youth pastor, or other adult to discuss some of your questions with.

THIS DEVOTION SPEAKS TO GOD'S SOVEREIGNTY. GO TO PAGE 4 FOR A DESCRIPTION OF THIS ATTRIBUTE.

WEEK 45, DAY 4

"SO THEN, BROTHERS, STAND FIRM AND HOLD TO THE
TRADITIONS THAT YOU WERE TAUGHT BY US, EITHER BY
OUR SPOKEN WORD OR BY OUR LETTER."
- 2 THESSALONIANS 2:15

A very strange thing is happening in our culture. Students like you are part of a generation known as Generation Z, or the Homelander Generation. (Actually, there is an interesting debate over what to call you. Funny, isn't it? Time will tell what everyone eventually settles on.) The generation right above you is called the Millennial Generation. And while they are not attending church in large numbers, many of the ones who DO go to church still opt for "old school" churches. While there are a lot of church plants, or even home churches, most churches in the US are still more traditional in nature.

READ 2 THESSALONIANS 2:13-17. While churches today have different looks, music, and preaching styles than churches in the past, one thing that should never change is our teaching and practicing God's Word. A church should be observing the Lord's Supper, baptizing people, meeting together for fellowship, and ministering to the needs of others.

SOMETHING TO THINK ABOUT . . .
· As you pray today, thank God for the teachings from His Word that were passed on to you by your family and your church.
· Ask God to help you to stand firm and hold on to these teachings as you live your life for Him.

WEEK 45, DAY 5

**"MAY THE LORD DIRECT YOUR HEARTS TO THE LOVE OF GOD AND
TO THE STEADFASTNESS OF CHRIST." - 2 THESSALONIANS 3:5**

Years ago there was an episode of the television series The Twilight Zone which featured an older man who had a suitcase of things he was selling. He somehow knew just what certain people needed from his box of goods to help them, or protect them in the future.

READ 2 THESSALONIANS 3:1-5. Today's passage includes some things that the apostle Paul believed were just what the Christians in Thessalonica would need, both in the present and the future.

They needed a pure understanding of God's love.

They needed patient endurance like the kind Jesus demonstrated while He lived on earth.

Why did they need these things? The Thessalonians were being persecuted for their faith. Paul knew that what they needed to get through the tough times was an understanding of God's love, along with the patience of Jesus. God knows just what you need, too. He will always provide just what you need just when you need it in order to live your life for Him.

As you think about God's calling on your life, what will you need to get where God wants you to be? Some of those things God has already given you. Others will be provided at just the right time. Thank God today for His provision in your life and for His perfect timing by providing you what you need.

SOMETHING TO THINK ABOUT . . .
· What do you find you most need from God to live your life as a Christ-follower?

WEEK 46

WEEK 46, DAY 1

"BLESSED BE THE GOD AND FATHER OF OUR LORD
JESUS CHRIST, WHO HAS BLESSED US IN CHRIST
WITH EVERY SPIRITUAL BLESSING IN THE HEAVENLY
PLACES, EVEN AS HE CHOSE US IN HIM BEFORE THE
FOUNDATION OF THE WORLD, THAT WE SHOULD BE
HOLY AND BLAMELESS BEFORE HIM."
- EPHESIANS 1:3-4

This week you'll be reading through some of Paul's words to his young disciple, Timothy. Timothy was a young man who was asked to accompany Paul on a missionary journey. He quickly became indispensible to Paul, and rapidly rose to one of the more influential leaders in the early church. Paul's two letters to Timothy represent an elderly leader passing on words of advice and encouragement to his protégé.

Timothy had no idea how accompanying Paul on a simple mission trip would change his life. But God did. Look back at Ephesians 1:3-4. Before God even created the world, He knew the plan He had for your life. God knows exactly how He will use your life to impact the world for His sake. Like Timothy, we have to be willing to embrace the journey, stay faithful in the tasks God puts before us, and grow in our faith as we continue to walk with God.

Meditate on Ephesians 1:3-4 this week. Think about how amazing it is that God not only wants to use you, but knows how He will do it.

THIS DEVOTION SPEAKS TO GOD'S PERFECT KNOWLEDGE.
GO TO PAGE 4 FOR A DESCRIPTION OF THIS ATTRIBUTE.

WEEK 46, DAY 2

"LET NO ONE DESPISE YOU FOR YOUR YOUTH, BUT SET THE BELIEV-
ERS AN EXAMPLE IN SPEECH, IN CONDUCT, IN LOVE, IN FAITH, IN
PURITY." - 1 TIMOTHY 4:12

Did you know that it's often more expensive to get auto insurance for a teenager than it is for an adult? Insurance companies often follow the statistical, and popular, belief that younger people are less responsible drivers than adults. Taking driver's education and showing good grades are ways to lower your costs, because these measures prove that you are more disciplined and knowledgeable than the average teen. While this may frustrate you a little, this way of thinking is not entirely new!

READ 1 TIMOTHY 4:11-16. The apostle Paul had mentored Timothy since Timothy's teen years. Greek culture in Timothy's time placed great value on age and experience, and Timothy didn't have much of either. While there is no quick fix to gain respect, here Paul gives Timothy a great set of guidelines to make up for what he lacked in years. Paul emphasizes the importance of being grounded in Scripture, and striving to live a life that represents the power of the Gospel over sin. That doesn't leave much room for gray areas, but requires that every deed be evaluated according to the teaching of God's Word. The entire tone of this passage shows that this has to be a consistent choice.

Earning the respect of others isn't always easy, especially when you're young. To do this effectively, we have to move beyond belief and practice a lifestyle that honors Christ at all times!

SOMETHING TO THINK ABOUT . . .
· Look at the list of categories in verse 12. How does your life set a godly example in each of these areas?
· What do you think it means in verse 15 when it says to "practice these things . . . so that all may see your progress"?
· How does being a godly example help in pointing others toward the power of the Gospel?

"FIGHT THE GOOD FIGHT OF THE FAITH. TAKE HOLD OF THE ETERNAL
LIFE TO WHICH YOU WERE CALLED AND ABOUT WHICH YOU MADE THE
GOOD CONFESSION IN THE PRESENCE OF MANY WITNESSES."
- 1 TIMOTHY 6:12

Every major battle in history began with a cause. Some people are willing to fight for no reason, but a true movement hinges on the deeper motivation of those moved to action. Christianity is that kind of movement. It has always faced opposition, seen and unseen, but there have always been those willing to fight for the cause of the Gospel.

READ 1 TIMOTHY 6:11-16. The Greek word for "fight" is where we get our word for "agonize." The fight to be a godly influence in an ungodly world is not easy, and may even be agonizing at times. This passage teaches that a child of God is known by what he or she avoids, as well as what he or she pursues. The spiritual battles of the Christian life are not just won by standing strong in the face of external persecution. We have to fight with ourselves, as well, when we face our inward sin nature, and choose to pursue righteousness at all costs. When Paul tells Timothy to 'take hold' of the life in Christ that he has confessed, he is telling him to chase after it with everything in him!

When you think of an agonizing fight in war, athletics, or even homework, it all comes down to one question: is it worth it? Those who truly believe that eternal dominion belongs to the King of Kings - and trust that He is coming back for His people - have a pretty strong motivation to fight for His cause.

SOMETHING TO THINK ABOUT . . .
· In what areas of your life do you feel you have to fight to live out your faith?
· Is your struggle mostly from outward circumstances or inward desires?
· What does it look like when you are fighting the good fight?

WEEK 46, DAY 4

"BUT I AM NOT ASHAMED, FOR I KNOW WHOM I HAVE BELIEVED, AND I AM CONVINCED THAT HE IS ABLE TO GUARD UNTIL THAT DAY WHAT HAS BEEN ENTRUSTED TO ME." - 2 TIMOTHY 1:12

The scariest thing about taking any risk is that our minds always fear the worst-case scenario. When we ponder the unknowns, we are not ever afraid of something good happening. We are afraid that we might fail or come to some kind of harm. The good news is that when we follow Christ, we do not need to fear because the results are in His perfect hands!

READ 2 TIMOTHY 1:8-12 and pay close attention to the reasons Paul gives for his confidence. Paul knew better than anyone that the Christian life carried risk. In fact, he wrote this letter to Timothy from prison, facing his own imminent death. Even when Paul stood to risk it all, he recognized that following Christ was much bigger than just what happens here on earth. Paul knew that it was God's grace that saved him from his sin, and it would be God's grace that would see him through this trial.

Look back at verses 9 and 10. Paul points out that Christ's purpose was established before the ages began, and that it extends beyond death. Sometimes, when we feel small, the best thing we can do is remember how big God is. When we face fear, shame, or uncertainty in life as we seek to follow Christ, we can have confidence that we have a secure and eternal calling that is guaranteed by God Himself! Because of that, we can handle whatever life dishes out!

SOMETHING TO THINK ABOUT . . .
· How has following Christ ever made you feel ashamed or uncertain?
· How does knowing that you have a holy calling that is secure for all eternity give you confidence in tough times?

**THIS DEVOTION SPEAKS TO GOD'S POWER.
GO TO PAGE 4 FOR A DESCRIPTION OF THIS ATTRIBUTE.**

"DO YOUR BEST TO PRESENT YOURSELF TO GOD AS ONE APPROVED, A WORKER WHO HAS NO NEED TO BE ASHAMED, RIGHTLY HANDLING THE WORD OF TRUTH." - 2 TIMOTHY 2:15

Everyone wants to be liked. There are so many things that we do in life to seek the approval of others that we don't often stop to think about it. But, do we ever stop to think about God's approval?

READ 2 TIMOTHY 2:15-16 A COUPLE OF TIMES and ask God to help you evaluate how you are doing in His sight. It is very important here to make sure that we understand Paul's words. He is not saying that we have to earn God's approval to be saved. We know this because Paul himself said so in his previous letter to the Ephesians. In Ephesians 2:8, Paul wrote, "For by grace you have been saved through faith. And this is not your own doing; it is the gift of God." There is nothing we can do to earn salvation; that is why Jesus had to come and die on our behalf. But that's not the same as living with the blessing of God's approval.

Life has a pretty consistent way of distracting us from our purpose. We are called to walk in righteousness and share the truth of the Gospel with the world, and yet we spend so much of our lives doing anything but that. Paul is reminding Timothy here that the "irreverent babble" of the world does nothing to point others to Christ. As much as we may want to fit in and be liked by others, we must remember that we will face God one day, and His approval of our life lived on earth will be the only thing that matters.

SOMETHING TO THINK ABOUT . . .
· How does knowing that God gave you the free gift of salvation lead you to want to please Him?
· In what areas do you feel you have God's approval right now?
· Are there things going on in your life in which you know God does not approve? What are you willing to do to address them?

WEEK 47

_____

WEEK 47, DAY 1

"IN THE SAME WAY, LET YOUR LIGHT SHINE BEFORE OTHERS, SO THAT THEY MAY SEE YOUR GOOD WORKS AND GIVE GLORY TO YOUR FATHER WHO IS IN HEAVEN." - MATTHEW 5:16

Paul's letters to Timothy held a lot of Christ-centered advice on how to conduct ourselves as Christ-followers. Hebrews is a similar letter. But here's the deal: even though his name has been linked to the book often over the centuries, Paul is not believed to be the writer of this letter. In fact, no one has ever definitively determined who the author of Hebrews is. But that doesn't change the power of the letter. Hebrews is a power-packed letter full of valuable wisdom and insight. And it puts a tremendous focus on Christ as the center of our faith.

If you look at Jesus' words from Matthew 5:16, it becomes clear that Jesus and the writer of Hebrews understood the same thing: God has the power to change lives. They grasped another thing too. Both the writer of Hebrews and Jesus knew that a life with Jesus at the center is so powerful that it brings people into a relationship with God. When we focus on living for God, we differentiate ourselves from the world. In essence, we say, "Look at me. I'm different. And that difference in me is Christ." Not a bad way to live, right?

Memorize this verse this week. It's a powerful reminder of the impact your life can have on those around you.

WEEK 47, DAY 2

"ALL SCRIPTURE IS BREATHED OUT BY GOD AND PROFIT-ABLE FOR TEACHING, FOR REPROOF, FOR CORRECTION, AND FOR TRAINING IN RIGHTEOUSNESS, THAT THE MAN OF GOD MAY BE COMPLETE, EQUIPPED FOR EVERY GOOD WORK."

- 2 TIMOTHY 3:16-17

Have you ever stopped to think about how much you have been taught? There are very few things in life that we learn on our own. You may be able to think of certain people – like parents, or teachers – who have shaped who you are. But did you know that every time you read the Bible God is teaching you?

READ 2 TIMOTHY 3:14-17. Remember that Paul is speaking to Timothy, who is serving as a pastor in the early church. Paul acknowledged in his earlier letter that Timothy had been taught to live according to God's Word by, among others, his mother and grandmother. Here, he is calling Timothy to cling to those life-lessons and not take them for granted. Being raised in a Christian home may seem commonplace to some of us. But this is a valuable gift. Paul explains in verse 14-15 that being familiar with the Bible as children is what makes us wise to salvation, and equips us to follow Christ.

Perhaps the best part of this passage is that whether you were taught the Scriptures in your childhood or not, you can still gain the same benefits. Scripture isn't like other lessons you may learn in life. The truth of God's Word never changes; it is not influenced by opinion or time. When you read the Word of God, you are receiving His instruction and being raised into the man or woman that God desires you to be.

SOMETHING TO THINK ABOUT . . .

· Can you recall any spiritual truths that you learned about God when you were young?
· How does verse 16 shape your view of studying God's Word?

WEEK 47, DAY 3

"TAKE CARE, BROTHERS, LEST THERE BE IN ANY OF YOU AN EVIL, UNBELIEVING HEART, LEADING YOU TO FALL AWAY FROM THE LIVING GOD." - HEBREWS 3:12

LaDarius was the number one prospect at running back in his state coming out of high school. Even though he was raised in church, he let the teaching go in one ear and out the other. This was evident in his reckless behavior at parties, which included drinking and then driving himself home. One night his rebellion caught up with him.

When he woke up, his father, a police officer, and several people wearing scrubs were standing around him in a brightly lit room. He was in the hospital waking up from surgery on his right leg. The news was not good. LaDarius would walk again—even run—but not in a full contact sport capacity. The car accident not only totaled his Mustang. It also totaled his football future. LaDarius now had a long and difficult road ahead, in more ways than one.

TAKE OUT YOUR BIBLE AND READ HEBREWS 3:12-14.

Sooner or later bad decisions lead to disaster. Much like the accident changed the course of LaDarius' life, sin can really make your life a mess. That's why you need to examine your actions daily to make sure they align with Jesus' actions. And, that's why you need a church group where you can find friends who will help you stay out of sin, and encourage you to live for Jesus.

Fast-forward a couple of years later. LaDarius ended up on the dean's list, was involved weekly in his church's college ministry, and focused on being faithful to God in all that he did. LaDarius' story was redeemed. How will your story be written? Will you carefully protect your heart from evil? Will you find friends to share accountability with? Will you be faithful to God until the end? Ask God to help you choose wisely every day.

SOMETHING TO THINK ABOUT . . .
· Is there anything risky you are doing with your life right now that you know you need to stop doing?
· Do you have at least one friend that will warn you about bad decisions before you make them?
· If you are in a youth group, how regularly do you attend?

WEEK 47, DAY 4

"FOR THE WORD OF GOD IS LIVING AND ACTIVE, SHARPER
THAN ANY TWO-EDGED SWORD, PIERCING TO THE DIVISION
OF SOUL AND OF SPIRIT, OF JOINTS AND OF MARROW,
AND DISCERNING THE THOUGHTS AND INTENTIONS OF THE
HEART." - HEBREWS 4:12

Have you ever seen those late night commercials on TV for one of those knives that can cut through anything in the house? Frozen meat, cans, shoes . . . you name it, it can cut through it. For $19.95 you can get not one, but two of these amazing knives. What a deal! (But wait, why would you ever need to cut a shoe in half?)

You can download Fruit Ninja on your portable device and slice anything the game throws at your with a quick swipe of your finger. There's such power in being a Fruit Ninja! Go ahead. Play one game—one quick game if you have it.

Now that you're thinking about slicing and dicing, **GRAB YOUR BIBLE AND READ HEBREWS 4:12-13.** Read the passage once more. Then think about this: What are three facts you can pull from these two verses? There is an emphasis on the liveliness and unsurpassed power of the Bible. God's power reaches into even your deepest dreams and desires! Nobody else goes there without you letting them in.

SOMETHING TO THINK ABOUT . . .
· Pause for a few moments right now and try to clear your mind of all distractions. Be totally honest before God. You don't even have to say anything out loud. He hears even your thoughts! Take time to apologize for sins you haven't already apologized for. And, tell God some of your life dreams and your life concerns. As He slices through your core being with far greater efficiency than the highest scoring Fruit Ninja ever, you will begin to experience the peace that comes with knowing the God of the universe personally.

WEEK 47, DAY 5

**"FOR WE DO NOT HAVE A HIGH PRIEST WHO IS UNABLE TO SYMPA-
THIZE WITH OUR WEAKNESSES, BUT ONE WHO IN EVERY RESPECT HAS
BEEN TEMPTED AS WE ARE, YET WITHOUT SIN." - HEBREWS 4:15**

For years Mike Rowe hosted a television show called Dirty Jobs. He traveled all over the country taking on jobs that were considered some of the grossest, smelliest, filthiest, and most undesirable anywhere. From mud, to poop, to grease, Rowe stepped into the shoes of the actual people who did the jobs and worked alongside them. He learned every dirty detail of the dirtiest jobs in America. Google "Mike Rowe and Dirty Jobs" for an idea of what he got himself into each week back when the show was airing on Discovery Channel.

THEN, TAKE OUT YOUR BIBLE AND LOOK UP HEBREWS 4:14-16. REREAD VERSE 15.
Clearly Jesus has experienced every temptation you will every experience in life. Yet, He did not give into a single one of them! What is impossible for you, and any other human, is only possible for Jesus Christ. He took on the dirtiest job of them all when He came to earth to defeat every sin, and take them all to the cross with Him.

Imagine sin as being like the filth that got all over Mike Rowe on one of the Dirty Jobs sites. Then imagine the only way to know how to survive as Mike Rowe was to learn how to overcome the grossness on a job site from the worker who did it every day. Finally, realize that just like Mike Rowe probably ran to the shower after each episode was filmed, you can run to the throne of God, through prayer, to get clean from your sin every day!

Grace is a free gift. But Jesus had to conquer every temptation - and even defeat death - to give it to you. He paid the ultimate price.

SOMETHING TO THINK ABOUT . . .
· Living in this world is a dirty job in itself. Spend a few moments today before the throne of God in prayer. Get clean from the dirtiness of this world and ask for guidance throughout this day.

**THIS DEVOTION SPEAKS TO GOD'S FORGIVENESS. GO TO
PAGE 4 FOR A DESCRIPTION OF THIS ATTRIBUTE.**

WEEK 48

WEEK 48, DAY 1

**"MAY THE GOD OF ENDURANCE AND ENCOURAGEMENT
GRANT YOU TO LIVE IN SUCH HARMONY WITH ONE
ANOTHER, IN ACCORD WITH CHRIST JESUS, THAT TO-
GETHER YOU MAY WITH ONE VOICE GLORIFY THE GOD
AND FATHER OF OUR LORD JESUS CHRIST." - ROMANS
15:5-6**

As you continue looking at the big-picture story of the Bible, you're going to continue to look at some of the teaching from Hebrews this week. But, you'll also begin your look at the Book of James. James is a super-interesting book, as it was written by Jesus' earthly brother (in other words, Jesus' sibling born from the union of Joseph and Mary). There was a time when James was apparently skeptical of Jesus' identity and ministry. But, at some point, he came to faith in Christ, and became the leader of the church in Jerusalem.

James is a book known for its practicality. And the excerpts you'll be looking at this week from both Hebrews and James have a sort of practical bent to them. That's the thing about the Bible. There are so many different aspects of it. There is poetry, history, wisdom literature, and a ton of relevant teaching on how to live life as a Christ-follower. That's kind of the category that this week's memory verses fall in.

As you meditate on this week's verses, think about their message. When we are unified, we make a powerful statement to the world. We tell the world that Jesus makes a difference. Jesus transforms a group of different people into one cohesive body. That's a powerful truth for a world in desperate need of a Savior. If you have a chance, memorize these verses.

WEEK 48, DAY 2

"AND LET US CONSIDER HOW TO STIR UP ONE ANOTHER TO LOVE AND GOOD WORKS, NOT NEGLECTING TO MEET TOGETHER, AS IS THE HABIT OF SOME, BUT ENCOURAGING ONE ANOTHER, AND ALL THE MORE AS YOU SEE THE DAY DRAWING NEAR."
- HEBREWS 10:24-25

Encouragement is an interesting concept. Most people can do without it. Seriously. If no one ever encouraged you, you would most likely continue to accomplish your task, or errand, or assignment just fine. But, think for a moment the boost that encouragement provides. It can be a real game-changer when a coach, teacher, friend, or parent gives you a little bit of encouragement to keep up the great work. This is especially true if the task is difficult, or one you're relatively new to.

READ HEBREWS 10:24-25. This passage is about encouraging one another. The author of Hebrews is writing to a group of people who would have begun to experience persecution at the hands of the Roman government. These weren't people who had an easy life because of their faith in Jesus. Their faith made them a target. And so encouragement from their Christian brothers and sisters was a big deal.

The wording the author of Hebrews uses is awesome. He says that encouragement is like stirring each other up to do good work. This is such a great word-picture. We all need a little stirring up every now and then. Life can beat us up and bring us down. We can become complacent in our faith, just going through the motions at times. But encouragement from a friend can be the thing that lights a spark in us.

Be the voice of encouragement your friends need today. Stir them up to be all they can be for Christ.

SOMETHING TO THINK ABOUT . . .
· When is the last time you encouraged someone else in the faith?
· How faithfully do you attend youth group/church?
· Spend a few moments today reflecting on how faithful or unfaithful you have been to church attendance. Also, take a few moments to think about ways you can encourage others to stay true to the teachings of the Bible.

WEEK 48, DAY 3

"CONSIDER HIM WHO ENDURED FROM SINNERS SUCH HOSTILITY AGAINST HIMSELF, SO THAT YOU MAY NOT GROW WEARY OR FAINTHEARTED." - HEBREWS 12:3

Nate was on his first deployment to the Middle East. His unit was providing security for a town which had been riddled by gunfire and explosions for years. Nate experienced a weird mix of adrenaline and emotion as he went from manning the turret on his armored vehicle, to video chatting with his family during downtime. Fighting terrorism was something he had dreamed of since hearing his mother and father recall the World Trade Center and Pentagon attacks from when he was just a kindergartner. It was now a reality for Nate, complete with the threat of rocket-propelled grenades, roadside bombs, and small arms fire every day. Nate's mission required endurance on a level he had never required it before.

GRAB YOUR BIBLE AND LOOK UP HEBREWS 12:1-3. Picture a scene for each of these elements of this passage: huge crowd of witnesses; a weight that slows you down; sin that trips you up; running the race with endurance; keeping your eyes on Jesus. Now picture something for each of these snapshots of Jesus: enduring the cross; hostile treatment from sinful people; champion of your faith; honorably seated beside God's throne.

Jesus had to endure temptation and pain, just like any human, in order to fulfill His mission of salvation for all. His drive came from His obedience to His Father, and the opportunity to save people from the consequences of sin. Nate gained strength from reading about the countless soldiers who had left a legacy of bravery and honorable service before him. He was now part of that legacy. It was both humbling and invigorating! Even more than that, Nate knew Jesus personally. He wanted to finish His mission even if it cost him his life, just like Jesus.

SOMETHING TO THINK ABOUT . . .
· Remember today that you are a part of a long legacy of Christ followers.
· Let that fact keep your endurance level high as you strive to be on mission for Jesus in all you do today.

WEEK 48, DAY 4

**"LET NO ONE SAY WHEN HE IS TEMPTED, 'I AM BEING TEMPT-
ED BY GOD,' FOR GOD CANNOT BE TEMPTED WITH EVIL, AND
HE HIMSELF TEMPTS NO ONE." - JAMES 1:13**

Think about your temptations. I mean really think about the things that tempt you regularly. How does each temptation feel? Do you hate it, or secretly enjoy it?

As you imagine the temptations in your life, try to categorize them. It's likely that the various temptations in your life have their own emotion attached to them in your mind. If you're honest, there are probably sins in your life that you truly hate. When you're tempted with them, it's easy to say no. Or, if you give in, you're so disgusted with yourself it's easy not to do it again. But there are some sins we secretly enjoy. And so being tempted in that way is something that, if we were honest, doesn't cause us as much pain as it should.

Notice, however, as you **READ JAMES 1:12-15,** that the each temptation is not different. All temptations are dragging us to death. Whether we hate them or enjoy them, sin leads to death. Think again about the temptations in your life. Take an honest look at the path they lead you toward and through. Is that really where you want to go?

John 10:10 tells us that God's goal for our lives is just the opposite. He wants us to have a full life! Now try to think about the path that your walk with Jesus takes. Not only does the end of that path have a spectacular view, but God has planned that path so that it is full of amazing things!

SOMETHING TO THINK ABOUT
· Next time you are tempted, and it feels a little fun, remind yourself that this temptation has a goal: your death!
· List some of the things on God's full life path that you might miss if you allow yourself to be dragged around by temptation.

 **THIS DEVOTION SPEAKS TO GOD'S RIGHTEOUSNESS.
GO TO PAGE 4 FOR A DESCRIPTION OF THIS ATTRIBUTE.**

WEEK 48, DAY 5

"BUT BE DOERS OF THE WORD, AND NOT HEARERS ONLY, DECEIVING YOURSELVES." - JAMES 1:22

Did you ever dream that you went to school naked? Don't freak out; almost everyone dreams this dream at some point. But you sort of do freak out, right? You wake up with your heart pounding and your mind racing. What's really weird is that nobody ever seems to notice. What's that about?

Regardless of what dreams you have, what do you usually look like when you wake up? Drool on the pillow? Eye makeup down your cheek? What would happen if you just got up and went to school exactly as you were the moment you awoke? What if you just grabbed the first clothes that touched your fingers and off you went? I hate to imagine what everyone's breath would be like!

READ JAMES 1:22-25. As ridiculous as it sounds, James is describing this very situation. When we read God's Word, nod approvingly, and then continue living according to worldly standards, it's just like going to school naked. Except this time everyone will notice. The world is keenly aware of how Christians are hypocrites. And we are. There's no way around it. We believe things that we simply don't do. That's why we need God's grace. But there's no excuse for abusing God's grace.

SOMETHING TO THINK ABOUT

· Look into the mirror of God's Word. What in your life needs a little clean up? Make it happen. No excuses!
· If you're brave enough, challenge your Christian friends with this verse. Ask them not to let you "come to school as-is." God gave us a community of believers to help us fight hypocrisy. Remember however, to "speak the truth in love" as you challenge one another.

WEEK 49

WEEK 49, DAY 1

"BY THIS WE KNOW LOVE, THAT HE LAID DOWN HIS LIFE FOR US, AND WE OUGHT TO LAY DOWN OUR LIVES FOR THE BROTHERS."
- 1 JOHN 3:16

These words are a fitting introduction to where we find ourselves in the story. This week, you're going to continue to read a few selections from the Book of James. You'll also begin a look at Peter's letters. As you'll recall from last week, James, Jesus' brother, was the leader of the church in Jerusalem. Peter, just as he did when he was a disciple, held a place of prominence as a leader in the wider emerging Christian church. Both of these men, however, faced a harsh truth: they were leading a church under fierce opposition.

By this point in the big-picture story of the Bible, the Christian church had become a target for the Roman government. The Romans made everyone they ruled worship the emperor as if he were a god. Obviously, Christ-followers wouldn't do this. And so they were arrested, tortured, and murdered for their faith. James and Peter were two of the many church leaders who led a church under fierce persecution.

In this climate, John could write the words he wrote in 1 John 3:16. Love for each other was expressed through sacrifice. Everyone knew that following Christ was difficult. Everyone had to pitch in together to look after one another. In this climate, the love of Christ was shown through what you did for a brother or sister in Christ who was experiencing hard times. Can you think about how you might show the love of Christ to others? Memorize this verse this week as a reminder.

WEEK 49, DAY 2

"AND THE TONGUE IS A FIRE, A WORLD OF UNRIGHTEOUSNESS. THE TONGUE IS SET AMONG OUR MEMBERS, STAINING THE WHOLE BODY, SETTING ON FIRE THE ENTIRE COURSE OF LIFE, AND SET ON FIRE BY HELL." - JAMES 3:6

READ JAMES 3:1-12. Notice verse 6. Wow! That's some pretty strong language. Your tongue is fire by hell? Whoa. Read it again, but slower, and let it impact your heart.

> Your tongue stains the whole body . . . [it is] set on fire by hell.

What a harsh description of our tongues! James could have talked about the love words our tongues say. Or the kind words to a stranger. Or the powerful speeches world leaders have given that have changed the course of history. The tongue isn't all bad, is it? Let's face it: without your tongue you couldn't eat ice cream. And ice cream is awesome!

But seriously, James is right, isn't he? Our mouths are fountains of contradictions. Everyday, we pray and praise God. Everyday we say kind things to people we love. But somehow, we also manage to share a juicy bit of gossip. That same mouth finds the resources to speak contempt about the people who may have hurt us.

Fortunately, our big problem is that we're human. God knows this. He made us. And He loves us. He, and only He, has provided a way out of this mess. Look back at James 3:12. The key is not what comes out from the tongue, but where the words originate. The source of our words is our hearts. If we belong to God, our hearts are daily being transformed by the presence of God's Holy Spirit into hearts that look more and more like the heart of Jesus (2 Corinthians 3:18). That should be our goal.

SOMETHING TO THINK ABOUT . . .

· Next time a friend shares how someone has hurt him/her, don't immediately speak. Don't do it. Let your friend know he/she has been heard, but don't spew negative talk aimed at the person who hurt your friend. When you do speak, only speak refreshing words that lift them up.
· Actively seek God's transformation in your heart. Ask Him for it. Look for ways to encourage the Holy Spirit's work within you.

WEEK 49, DAY 3

"SUBMIT YOURSELVES THEREFORE TO GOD. RESIST THE DEVIL, AND HE WILL FLEE FROM YOU." - JAMES 4:7

READ JAMES 4:7-10. Focus on verse 7. Every time you see "therefore," there's something interesting to explore. You need to understand the full story.

Therefore (see what I did there?), read the verse in context. What is the whole chapter about? Why was this book of the Bible written? How does this verse fit with the Bible as a whole?

James was written to people that believed in Jesus, but were tempted to live like everyone else. We sometimes do that. But some of these people were apparently proud of their hypocrisy! Check out verse James 4:4. Or verse James 4:6. James is laying it down pretty heavy to a group of people who apparently deserved it.

But the coolest thing from James 4:7-10 are the two promises. The first promise is all about keeping the devil away. And the second promise is all about keeping God near. Look back and re-read the two promises. What is our role in both of them, respectively? In other words, what do we have to do to "trigger" the promise? First, we have to resist the devil. If we do, the Bible says he'll leave us alone (for a while at least). Second, we have to draw near to God. If we do, He'll draw near to us. As far as promises go, those two are big time, top notch, world class promises.

SOMETHING TO THINK ABOUT . . .
· How can you keep up your end of these promises today? Do you believe God will keep His end of the bargain?
· Do something today that helps you get near to God. Sing, pray, read your Bible, get out in the wild. You'll be amazed how God will join you there!

WEEK 49, DAY 4

"IS ANYONE AMONG YOU SUFFERING? LET HIM PRAY."
- JAMES 5:13

James 5:13-16 sounds a little redundant. Check it out. Are you in trouble? Then, pray. Are you happy? Then, pray. Are you sick? Then, pray. In other words, pray. But the Bible doesn't stop there. Don't believe it? **READ EPHESIANS 6:18.** (It reminds you to pray on all occasions.) Don't stop there. **READ 1 THESSALONIANS 5:17.** (It says to pray continually.) In other words, pray.

Have you ever prayed about something and didn't feel like God answered you? Maybe you aren't easily dissuaded, so you pray more. Still, God doesn't answer you like you want Him to. Not to worry, you know God is big and His timing is perfect. You pray even more . . . Eventually, many people would just give up. It sounds really sad, but many do. They give up on God and stop praying.

Here's the funny thing. The Bible is clear: God answers our prayers. God doesn't NOT answer them. But God only answers them according to His perfect plan as sovereign King. We may not be able to see His answer. We may see it and not understand it. Or, He may answer it exactly as he hoped He would. Either way, God hears all of our prayers. And He knows our needs.

God cares. He wants to hear your cares and concerns. He wants to listen. Your job? Simple. Pray.

SOMETHING TO THINK ABOUT . . .
· Pray. Pray like you're talking to your best friend. Just share yourself with Him.
· The next time you have a request of God, just put it in His hands. Release your expectations and hopes. Challenge yourself to trust God no matter what happens. Trust who He is not what you think He should do.

THIS DEVOTION SPEAKS TO GOD'S COMPASSION.
GO TO PAGE 4 FOR A DESCRIPTION OF THIS ATTRIBUTE.

WEEK 49, DAY 5

**"BLESSED BE THE GOD AND FATHER OF OUR LORD JESUS CHRIST!
ACCORDING TO HIS GREAT MERCY, HE HAS CAUSED US TO BE
BORN AGAIN TO A LIVING HOPE THROUGH THE RESURRECTION OF
JESUS CHRIST FROM THE DEAD." - 1 PETER 1:3**

Are you a "glass half empty," or "glass half full" kind of person? Oftentimes, people who tend to focus on the negative struggle with only seeing what's right in front of them. If you are shortsighted, it's easy to get bummed out when things aren't how you want them to be. Our faith can be the same way. When we focus just on the tangible struggles in life, we lose sight of the joyous truth that we have an eternal inheritance!

READ 1 PETER 1:3-9 and make note of what Christ's resurrection offers us. This letter from Peter is addressed to the Christians struggling to live out their faith in the Roman Empire. It's likely that their suffering at this point was rooted in intense ridicule and discrimination, rather than the physical suffering that would soon befall them under Emperor Nero. In either case, it was becoming increasingly difficult to enjoy being a Christian.

Peter had witnessed the miraculous events of Christ's crucifixion, resurrection, and ascension. He had experienced, first-hand, the power that Christ has over this world, and desperately wanted these oppressed believers to remember the power of their salvation! Peter reminds us that we can be filled with joy when we remember that Christ's victory on the cross means that we have victory in life. Our inheritance is the promise that we will be raised with Christ, and nothing in this world can take that from someone who has been born again!

SOMETHING TO THINK ABOUT . . .
· What kind of trials in life might be stealing the joy of your salvation right now?
· What are some truths about Christ that you see in this passage that are encouraging to you?
· What are some of the promises of God that you cling to?

WEEK 50

WEEK 50, DAY 1

"A NEW COMMANDMENT I GIVE TO YOU, THAT YOU LOVE ONE ANOTHER: JUST AS I HAVE LOVED YOU, YOU ALSO ARE TO LOVE ONE ANOTHER. BY THIS ALL PEOPLE WILL KNOW THAT YOU ARE MY DISCIPLES, IF YOU HAVE LOVE FOR ONE ANOTHER." - JOHN 13:34-35

As you work your way through the last few weeks of the big-picture story of the Bible, try to keep in mind that roughly 30 or more years have passed since Jesus died, arose, and ascended into Heaven. The young, Christian church is into its second generation. It has seen great growth, and is realizing pretty harsh persecution. It is learning how to conduct itself in the world.

Throughout all of the readings you've been doing the last few weeks, one of the coolest things to see is how the church stayed true to their identity in Christ. Sure, various churches had some bumps along the way. But all in all, the church conducted itself as Christ would have wanted. It was as if they were living out Jesus' words from John 13. Wait . . . . that's exactly what they were doing!

The church had grown. And they were known for many things, chief among them, for building communities of rich fellowship and service. In other words, living out Christ's command to love each other and the world.

How can you take Jesus' words to heart? Memorize these verses this week so that you can constantly be reminded to let the world see Christ's love flowing in and through you.

THIS DEVOTION SPEAKS TO GOD'S LOVE. GO TO PAGE 4 FOR A DESCRIPTION OF THIS ATTRIBUTE.

WEEK 50, DAY 2

"BUT AS HE WHO CALLED YOU IS HOLY, YOU ALSO BE HOLY IN ALL YOUR CONDUCT." - 1 PETER 1:15

When you first accepted Christ, you had to acknowledge two important truths. First, God is holy. Second, you are not. This is the grace of Christ. When we place our trust in Him, we get to live in the shadow of His holiness. We no longer belong to this world, but have a permanent reservation to live with Him as He reigns for eternity!

READ 1 PETER 1:13-16, paying close attention to the instructions given to believers.

Accepting the Gospel is easy, but living it out is hard. Peter reminds believers in difficult times to remember what it means to be identified with Christ. "Preparing your minds for action, and being sober-minded" means that we have to think about sin the way God does, not the way the world does. Being holy doesn't just mean avoiding sin and living by new rules; it means that we are to allow God's Word and Spirit to change our minds so that we can begin to desire what God desires.

To become holy is to live our lives in pursuit of the nature of Christ. This process of sanctification is how we show a lost and dying world that we belong to a God who offers hope. If we spend our lives desiring sin, looking just like the rest of the world, then we are concealing the power of the Gospel. Instead, as we faithfully obey God's commands, we have the privilege of giving the world a glimpse of the victory we will one day claim when Christ returns, and sin is forever defeated!

SOMETHING TO THINK ABOUT . . .

· Being holy is more than just an idea; it is an action! How can you prepare your mind for action before you face the temptations of the day?
· What accountability do you have in your life to keep you sober-minded so that your decisions consistently honor God?

"BUT YOU ARE A CHOSEN RACE, A ROYAL PRIESTHOOD, A HOLY NATION, A PEOPLE FOR HIS OWN POSSESSION, THAT YOU MAY PROCLAIM THE EXCELLENCIES OF HIM WHO CALLED YOU OUT OF DARKNESS INTO HIS MARVELOUS LIGHT." - 1 PETER 2:9

For many kids in America, there is the misconception that they have always been a Christian just because they can't remember a time when they didn't know about God. Consider this: you can know about your neighbors and live near them for your whole life, but that does not make you part of their family! The same is true for Christianity. It may be popular to say that we are all God's children, but Scripture is clear that this title is reserved only for those who have been set apart through a saving relationship in Christ.

READ 1 PETER 2:9-12. Think about the "before and after" description in verses 9-10.

The wording Peter uses here is not random, but is an echo of a singular promise made by God from the first pages of Scripture. God promised Abraham that his decedents would be a royal nation. Through Moses, God ensured the Israelites that they would be His treasured possession. Throughout the Old Testament, we see God preserving the remnant of believers to make good on that promise until Christ is born from the line of David and God reveals the rest of His plan. God has set apart a people for Himself so that the world, swallowed up by darkness, can see that He is the light!

There is no such thing as always having been a Christian. By definition, being in Christ means that you were brought out of death and into life, in order to proclaim the excellent nature of a God who saves!

SOMETHING TO THINK ABOUT . . .
· Can you recall a time in your life when you realized that you were separated from God and in need of a relationship with Him?
· If so, how does knowing that you were chosen by God to reflect His nature shape your conduct around those who may not know Him?

WEEK 50, DAY 4

"FOR IF THESE QUALITIES ARE YOURS AND ARE INCREASING, THEY KEEP YOU FROM BEING INEFFECTIVE OR UNFRUITFUL IN THE KNOWLEDGE OF OUR LORD JESUS CHRIST." - 2 PETER 1:8

You know that feeling you get when you walk into a room and forget why you are there? Or maybe you get someone's attention and forget what you were going to say. Those moments don't just make us feel silly; they are a huge waste of time! If we aren't careful, distracted moments like these can also characterize our spiritual lives.

READ 2 PETER 1:5-9. Pause for a moment at each of the traits listed in verses 5-7 and think about what they mean. Earlier this week you read 1 Peter 1:15 where God calls believers to be holy as He is holy. Peter wrote this second letter just a couple years later at a time when Christians were now fully suffering the brutal persecution of Emperor Nero. Peter himself was most likely writing from prison, facing his execution, and chose this instruction to leave to the church as part of his final words. Realizing that life is short and the mission is great, Peter warns believers not to let their faith be a waste by failing to become what God intended.

Peter gives practical advice, showing how holiness not only prepares the believer for the trials of life, but equips him to counter the deception of modern culture. In verses 5-7, Peter describes what spiritually maturing looks like. We begin with the simple faith that Jesus saves, but we must act on that faith in obedient, disciplined living. As we grow in our understanding of God, our love for Him and others naturally increases. Not seeking this kind of Christ-centered life is like forgetting why we were saved in the first place!

SOMETHING TO THINK ABOUT . . .
· Which of the traits listed inverses 5-7 do you need to focus on this week?
· How can the development of that trait in your life help you to be more effective in pointing others toward Christ?

> "THE LORD IS NOT SLOW TO FULFILL HIS PROMISE AS SOME COUNT SLOWNESS, BUT IS PATIENT TOWARD YOU, NOT WISHING THAT ANY SHOULD PERISH, BUT THAT ALL SHOULD REACH REPENTANCE."
> - 2 PETER 3:9

It is impossible to count how many predictions have been made as to how and when the world will end. Even among believers, there have been (very incorrect) public declarations that Jesus is coming back within a certain time frame. From the moment Jesus ascended into heaven and said that He'd be back, speculation and sin have seemed to run wild here on earth. So what is God waiting for?

READ 2 PETER 3:9-10. These two verses sum up some of the deepest theology in the entire Bible. First, we see that time is not the same to God as it is to us. God is eternal. It is easy for us to look at our physical lives as the most important part of who we are, but salvation is about an eternal relationship. Second, God is infinitely compassionate. Not only did He give Himself on our behalf, but He waits to declare His victory, allowing the Gospel time to reach the ends of the earth. Finally, this passage reminds us that God is trustworthy. His promises will be kept! He will return, and when He does everything of this world will be made final.

We should eagerly await the return of Christ. It is going mark the revelation of a glory that we cannot even begin to imagine. But, we must remember that our job is to share Him here and now. There are still those who have not heard! The more you anticipate heaven, the more you should want to share it with the world!

SOMETHING TO THINK ABOUT . . .

· What are you doing now to share Christ with a world that will one day face His judgment?
· How does the Gospel message reveal that God is a compassionate judge?

WEEK 51

WEEK 51, DAY 1

"THEREFORE, IF ANYONE IS IN CHRIST, HE IS A NEW CREATION. THE OLD HAS PASSED AWAY; BEHOLD, THE NEW HAS COME."
- 2 CORINTHIANS 5:17

This week and next week you'll be wrapping up your journey through the big-picture story of the Bible by looking at some of the writings of John the Apostle. John is such an interesting biblical character. He was believed to be the youngest of Jesus' disciples, thought by some to be as young as 13 when Jesus first called John to follow Him. Church history holds that John was the only disciple (besides Judas) not to be murdered for his faith. John supposedly lived to be an old man, which means his life saw Christianity start, grow, and flourish. What an amazing story!

Paul's words in 2 Corinthians 5:17 describe John's life perfectly. What if John had never come to faith in Christ? Who knows what his life would have been like? More than likely, he would have been a fisherman, like his father and brother. But look at the difference Christ made! John was truly a new creation in Christ. Jesus gave John a new life with a new purpose. God had a plan that involved using John to shape countless lives throughout history through his writings.

God has a plan for you too. And it began when you came to faith in Christ. You are a new creation in Jesus. The "old you" is no more. The "new you" is life full of powerful potential for God to use. Embrace this new life today. Memorize this verse as a way of reminding yourself that God has done and is doing amazing things in your life. And He's just getting started.

WEEK 51, DAY 2

"THIS IS THE MESSAGE WE HAVE HEARD FROM HIM AND PROCLAIM TO YOU, THAT GOD IS LIGHT, AND IN HIM IS NO DARKNESS AT ALL." - 1 JOHN 1:5

Have you ever been in complete darkness? Maybe it was a trip to a cave where you found yourself deep below the surface of the earth. Maybe it was a dark night in the woods where even the stars seemed to be absent. Many people are scared of the darkness. One of the reasons people fear darkness is that you can't see anything that's hidden. Something could sneak up on you. In today's devotion, you're going to see why as Christians it's important that we live in the light. Like all sorts of other creepy crawly things, our sins and struggles also like to hide in the darkness!

READ 1 JOHN 1:5-10. John begins this passage by reminding his readers that God is defined by light, and as followers of Jesus, they should be defined by light as well. Those who claim to be in light, but live in darkness, are liars because their words and actions don't line up. John then goes on to speak about living an authentic life in the Gospel. This is a life relying on the grace that you have already received in Jesus. Since you don't have to prove yourself to others, you are free to confess your sins to others so that you can fight together to faithfully follow Jesus. As followers of Jesus seek to live in the light, they need others to help them live lives of authenticity.

Do you have a group of friends that you can journey with as you follow Jesus together? The idea of confessing your struggles to one another may seem awkward at first, but as your friends begin to grow together, you can become allies for each other as you fight to live a life in the light, defined by the grace that Jesus showed you on the cross. Living in the light is a daily battle, but it's one you were not meant to fight alone.

SOMETHING TO THINK ABOUT . . .
· What are some sins and struggles in your life that like to hide in the dark?
· Is there someone today you could call to bring these struggles into the light so you can fight to follow Jesus together?
· Who are some friends that could join you in fighting to follow Jesus together?

WEEK 51, DAY 3

"AND BY THIS WE KNOW THAT WE HAVE COME TO KNOW HIM, IF WE KEEP HIS COMMANDMENTS." - 1 JOHN 2:3

Think about the cliques in your school. Everyone looks the same, acts the same, and talks the same. Cliques tend to not like people who don't follow the ways that are deemed socially acceptable for the clique. There is a level of exclusivity to a clique, yet people in a clique can be easily identified. Even though they may not be with other members, they will act, look, and talk in a way that makes it clear to others where their allegiance lies.

OPEN YOUR BIBLE AND READ 1 JOHN 2:3-6. In this passage, John encourages his readers that those who claim to follow Jesus must live the life Jesus would want them to live. Christians are supposed to not be hypocrites by saying they follow Jesus, and yet living like the world. They are supposed to keep God's commandments and live lives of love before a watching world. Christ-followers are supposed to function the opposite of how a clique does. And yet, similar to a clique, they are supposed to imitate Him in a way that shows the world who they follow. This call to follow Jesus is a daily struggle to remind yourself whom you follow, even though those around you may not be following Jesus.

If you were the only Christian your friends knew, what would your friends think of Jesus? Would they think Jesus' life was defined by love? Would Jesus be someone who lived in a way that was totally different than the world? Would the Jesus your friend saw be the Jesus who lives in you? The world is watching. You are living a story. What story does your life portray?

SOMETHING TO THINK ABOUT...
· What kind of Jesus are you showing your friends by your actions? Be honest.
· What areas of your life are you struggling to bring into conformity with Jesus' standards?
·What are some ways today that you can live like Jesus by showing love and keeping His commands?

WEEK 51, DAY 4

"DO NOT LOVE THE WORLD OR THE THINGS IN THE WORLD. IF ANYONE LOVES THE WORLD, THE LOVE OF THE FATHER IS NOT IN HIM." - 1 JOHN 2:15

Have you ever had to swim against the tide? Maybe you were swimming at the beach and didn't notice that you had drifted into an ocean current. Next thing you knew, you were far out from shore, in danger of being pulled out further. Even if you have never been in an ocean current, this metaphor applies to your life every day as you seek to follow Jesus.

READ 1 JOHN 2:15-17. The love for the world stands completely contrary to a love for God. The priorities are so different that they can't go together. As Christ-followers, we are swimming against the current of the world. The world is trying to tell us who we are supposed to be, how we are supposed to act, and what is supposed to matter to. In today's passage, John challenges us to swim against the tide. A Christ-follower can't live for both the world and for God.

Swimming against the current is a daily challenge. You must decide each day if you're going to fight to follow Jesus, or simply float in the current following the world and its ways. The fight is a difficult challenge, but John reminds us that the challenge is worth the reward.

SOMETHING TO THINK ABOUT...
· What are some areas where you're tempted to let the ocean current of the world carry you to places you shouldn't go?
· What are some things you can do to prepare yourself spiritually to swim against the current?
· Who is caught in the current around you? Who needs you to share the hope and freedom found in a relationship with Jesus?

THIS DEVOTION SPEAKS TO GOD'S RIGHTEOUSNESS. GO TO PAGE 4 FOR A DESCRIPTION OF THIS ATTRIBUTE.

WEEK 51, DAY 5

"ANYONE WHO DOES NOT LOVE DOES NOT KNOW GOD, BECAUSE GOD IS LOVE." - 1 JOHN 4:8

Love. It's a word we use for everything. You love Jesus, your mom, your bae, pizza, and the color blue. The word "love" is something that has lost its meaning for many people. Yet the clearest definition of the word love is seen in the story of the Gospel. If you want to see the truest definition of love, look no further than the cross. In today's devotion, John is going to invite us to look at true love, and then ask ourselves how we can live as people who have been truly loved.

OPEN YOUR BIBLE AND READ 1 JOHN 4:7-12. John defines true love as coming from God. This true love was displayed in Jesus, who became a human being, lived a life of love, and died on the cross for our sins as the ultimate act of love. As those who have been greatly loved by God through Jesus, we are called to let the love of God overflow in us. As we do this, John says that the love of God is made perfect.

So, how do we display this perfect love of God to others? At the cross, we see that love forgives, love is costly, and love extends to those who don't deserve it. As you go through your day today, how can you show love by forgiving others, loving others by putting them before yourself in a way that is costly, and loving those who don't deserve it? As we love, we reflect Jesus, and we see true love in action.

SOMETHING TO THINK ABOUT...
· What element of love (forgiveness, costliness, or love to those who don't deserve it) displayed at the cross is the hardest for you to show to others?
· What is a way that you can show love to someone today in a way that is costly?
·Who doesn't deserve love that needs your love today?

WEEK 52

WEEK 52, DAY 1

THUS SAYS THE LORD, THE KING OF ISRAEL AND HIS REDEEMER, THE LORD OF HOSTS: "I AM THE FIRST AND I AM THE LAST; BESIDES ME THERE IS NO GOD."
- ISAIAH 44:6

The words of God through the prophet Isaiah ring true throughout history. They serve as bookends, in a way, of our big-picture look at the Bible. While Isaiah wasn't the beginning of our story, God was. And Isaiah communicates this perfectly. God was first. "In the beginning, God . . ." These words start the Bible, and show in a profound way that before anything else was, God was. As you look at a few selections from Revelation this week, you'll see that God is indeed last. He was there at the beginning, and He will be there at the end. There is no one like God. Hopefully you've grasped this from your journey through the big-picture story of the Bible.

Revelation is just an amazing piece of literature. If you know it as that weird book at the end of the Bible, that's OK. It kind of is. Revelation is full of the kind of symbolism and imagery that blows our minds, confuses us in a wonderful way, and reminds us how far away God's ways are from ours. Revelation is difficult to understand in parts. And the reason is simple: John, a mortal, first-century man, was shown a glimpse of heaven. And he was tasked with writing it down using his language, experiences, and worldview as a basis. Of course, John was inspired by the Holy Spirit. But he was still the author. He still had to come up with words to describe what he saw. Can you imagine how difficult and awe-inspiring a task that would be?

As you read your devotions this week, take some time to venture outside of the suggested passages. Interact with some of the wonderful and amazing imagery of Revelation. And thank God that He is so incredible that language can barely describe the wonders of Heaven.

WEEK 52, DAY 2

"WHEN I SAW HIM, I FELL AT HIS FEET AS THOUGH DEAD. BUT
HE LAID HIS RIGHT HAND ON ME, SAYING, 'FEAR NOT, I AM
THE FIRST AND THE LAST, AND THE LIVING ONE. I DIED, AND
BEHOLD I AM ALIVE FOREVERMORE, AND I HAVE THE KEYS OF
DEATH AND HADES.'" - REVELATION 1:17-18

John the Apostle had walked the earth ministering with Jesus back in his younger days. John was so influential with his faith that the Roman government exiled him to a prison island called Patmos. Despite attempted execution and imprisonment with vile criminals, John outlived all of the other original disciples, and continued winning many people over to faith in Christ.

It was one Sabbath day while John was worshipping on Patmos that Jesus came to him with a message. Let's check this story out. **GRAB YOUR BIBLE AND READ REVELATION 1:9-20.** Revelation is full of symbolism that holds urgent warnings and beautiful promises all who read it. Think about the confidence God placed in John to be His messenger! John was about to pen bold encouragement and warnings to every organized church in existence. John didn't let his age stop him. He didn't let the threat of people attempting to kill him stop him. He didn't even let being exiled on a prison island destroy His trust in Christ. John trusted that God would use him, as imperfect a messenger as he was. And God did.

You have two paths to choose in your life: obedience to God's perfect plan regardless of circumstance, or letting the excuses of life get in the way of being obedient to God. Which will you choose?

SOMETHING TO THINK ABOUT . . .
· How would you react if Jesus showed up with a mission for you like the one He had for John?
· What are a few significant truths about Jesus that you can pull out of verses 17-18?

WEEK 52, DAY 3

**"BUT I HAVE THIS AGAINST YOU, THAT YOU HAVE
ABANDONED THE LOVE YOU HAD AT FIRST."
- REVELATION 2:4**

Matthew West wrote a song a few years ago called "The Motions." He wrote it because he was schedule to have throat surgery that might cost him his singing career. Thankfully, he fully recovered and is still making great music today. The experience made him realize he was taking his talent and platform for Christ for granted.

GRAB YOUR BIBLE AND READ REVELATION 2: 1-7. One of the early churches had started going through the motions. When Jesus gave John a message for the church at Ephesus, He wanted them to consider a similar scenario as Matthew West went through. You may find yourself in a similar spot. It's too easy to make going to youth group and church into a ritual. You can lose your passion for hearing and discussing God's Word, praising God through music, and even being in community with other Christ-followers. The thing is that you know best where your passion-level sits. You know if your commitment to Christ has gotten stale. If this describes you, listen to Jesus' warning to the Ephesian church.

The church at Ephesus had forgotten why they were even a church. They had forgotten the power of Christ on the cross. They were going through the motions. Ask Jesus today to help you learn from the warning to the church at Ephesus. In what areas of your life as a Christ follower do you need to stop going through the motions?

SOMETHING TO THINK ABOUT . . .
· What were some good things the church at Ephesus was doing?
· What are some things you are good at doing for Jesus?
· Where was the church at Ephesus missing the mark?
· Would you consider your passion for doing Jesus' work to be high, medium, or low?

WEEK 52, DAY 4

"THEREFORE THEY ARE BEFORE THE THRONE OF GOD, AND SERVE HIM
DAY AND NIGHT IN HIS TEMPLE; AND HE WHO SITS ON THE THRONE
WILL SHELTER THEM WITH HIS PRESENCE. THEY SHALL HUNGER NO
MORE, NEITHER THIRST ANYMORE; THE SUN SHALL NOT STRIKE THEM,
NOR ANY SCORCHING HEAT. FOR THE LAMB IN THE MIDST OF THE
THRONE WILL BE THEIR SHEPHERD, AND HE WILL GUIDE THEM TO
SPRINGS OF LIVING WATER, AND GOD WILL WIPE AWAY EVERY TEAR
FROM THEIR EYES." - REVELATION 7:15-17

When the world had gotten so full of sin that God had to destroy it with a great flood, He gave the people many years of warnings to turn to Him first. Unfortunately it only ended up being one man, Noah, and his family on the Ark. Thousands of years later, God once again made a dramatic interjection into the world on account of human sinfulness. God sent Jesus to offer forgiveness and eternal life to sinful humanity. Jesus took the sins of all people to the cross. Yet many chose, and still choose to this day, to reject Christ.

The next time God brings judgment upon the earth for sin will be the last time He does. The book of Revelation serves as a final warning not only to the church—meaning all followers Christ—but also all who have not yet trusted Him. This book also paints a beautiful picture of final redemption for all who gave their lives to Christ, even unto death.

TAKE OUT YOUR BIBLE AND READ REVELATION 7:9-17. The passage begins with John's vision of a huge crowd of people in white robes praising God for His salvation. In verse 14 these people are identified as representing the countless number of Christ-followers who died standing up for their faith in Jesus. While biblical scholars differ on their interpretation of exactly when this crisis happens, the point is that faithfulness in Christ will lead many to their deaths. But God redeems their death in the most amazing way.

SOMETHING TO THINK ABOUT . . .
· What are the many heavenly blessings listed in this passage for those who are persecuted in this world because of their faith?
· Spend a few moments in prayer today thanking God for how He provides for your physical and spiritual needs in this life and in eternity.

WEEK 52, DAY 5

"AND I HEARD A LOUD VOICE FROM THE THRONE SAYING, 'BEHOLD, THE DWELL-
ING PLACE OF GOD IS WITH MAN. HE WILL DWELL WITH THEM, AND THEY WILL
BE HIS PEOPLE, AND GOD HIMSELF WILL BE WITH THEM AS THEIR GOD.'"
- REVELATION 21:3

Smart phones are awesome. They've changed our lives and our world (for better or worse). But they can be a pain the tail, at times. Sometimes smart phones run out of storage. If you've ever had this happen, you know the drill: you have to delete any apps, photos, or videos you're not using. Other times, smart phones get their screens cracked. Only a repair can fix that.

Your life is kind of like smart phone. You can be overloaded with information and have to pull back and refresh your mind. And, you are breakable too. Furthermore, the world contains an entire of people like you. Every person has sin. Every person is breakable. Imagine a day when sin is abolished permanently and your body can't even get slightly broken.

It's not too hard to imagine. **TAKE OUT YOUR BIBLE AND READ REVELATION 21:1-4.** Sin is literally the reason for all of the world's problems. Today's passage is about God erasing all of the sin problems, replacing them with a new and perfect Kingdom, and setting up His throne among His people. The human mind cannot fathom what living forever will really be like. With the absence of death, sorrow, sin, and suffering in this new Kingdom of God, you can easily see that it will be quite terrific, regardless of our inability truly grasp its wonder now.

Spend a few moments throughout the day thinking about how great it will be to be in God's presence with the absence of everything that makes this world a fallen place. Your smart phone will be gone and not needed. Your body won't ever break. No one will steal, kill, or destroy. You won't have to struggle with temptation and sin. There will only be the perfect peace found in God's presence!

SOMETHING TO THINK ABOUT . . .
· What are some of the troubles that will be missing from the new earth?
· Which of these gives you the most joy? Why so?

**THIS DEVOTION SPEAKS TO GOD'S POWER. GO TO
PAGE 4 FOR A DESCRIPTION OF THIS ATTRIBUTE.**

CLOSING

If you've made it this far, you may very well be able to say something that many people never will: you understand the big-picture story of the Bible.

This is no small thing. There are quite a few Christ-followers who never fully grasp the story of the Bible. They see it as valuable, sure. And believe it's God's Word. But there is always a bit of a barrier to their understanding the Bible. They simply don't get how it all works.

Not you. You know the story. You know how God worked through history to create all things, call a people to Himself, and bless the world through those people. You know all about God's dramatic, miraculous, awesome rescue mission to save humankind from their sins. And, hopefully, your faith has grown as a result.

NOW, WHAT DO YOU DO WITH THIS KNOWLEDGE? GREAT QUESTION.

FIRST, as you no doubt know if you really did work through all or most of this book, there's a lot of the Bible this book didn't cover. So one challenge would be to go back through, find some spots that interested you, and dig in a little deeper. Grab a study Bible, or download a study Bible app. Go deep into the story, asking God to show you new and awesome things about His Word and Himself.

SECOND, the journey you've been on has made your faith stronger. You know more about God and about yourself. Put this knowledge to work. Make it a point to share your passion about the Bible with others. Show people through your words and actions what a vibrant faith looks like. As Jesus said in Matthew 5:16, when you live like this, people will notice a difference and will be drawn to God as a result.

More than anything, be encouraged that knowing God better is reward in itself. Your faith will be much stronger. And your life will make more of in impact as a result.

ACKNOWLEDGMENTS

This book is the result of the combined efforts of many people. The authors who worked on this project brought their own personality and experience to the work. They did an excellent job of communicating their own slice of the big-picture story of the Bible.

AUTHORS
Ben Birdsong
Andy Blanks
Kathleen Bryan
Heather Campbell
Leneita Fix
Eric Gargus
Mark Jenkins
Benjer McVeigh
Brandon Nichols
Richard Parker
Bob Rinella

PUBLISHER
Andy Blanks

GRAPHIC DESIGN
Laurel-Dawn Berryhill
Upper Air Creative

COPY EDITOR
Paige Townley

YM360 SUPPORT TEAM
Les Bradford
Lee Moore
Angela Terry

WHAT KEEPS YOU FROM BEING ALL THAT GOD HAS CALLED YOU TO BE?

Whatever it is, you need to know this: there is a better way. God wants you to face your fears and lean-in to who He desires you to be. If you're ready, Facing Your Fears is a great place to start.

Facing Your Fears, a 40-day, Scripture-driven devotional by Bethany Barr Phillips, helps reveal where fear has taken hold of your life and equips you to put an end to these strongholds.

TO VIEW SAMPLES OF FACING YOUR FEARS & TO ORDER, GO TO YM360.COM/FEARS

A 3-PART DEVOTIONAL EXPERIENCE
DESIGNED TO HELP YOU BECOME A DISCIPLE OF CHRIST.
IN A WORD, TO KNOW GOD AND MAKE HIM KNOWN.

The *New/Next/Now* Discipleship Bundle provides three powerful devotional experiences to help you grow from a new believer to an authentic disciple of Christ.

NEW: FIRST STEPS FOR NEW CHRIST-FOLLOWERS

One of the most used new believer resources in youth ministry, this powerful 4-week devotional experience will help new believers get off to a strong start on their new journey with Christ.

NEXT: GROWING A FAITH THAT LASTS

4-week devotional will help you take ownership of your faith. NEXT will teach: Why it's important to own your faith, What life's purpose has to do with God's mission, How to build spiritual habits that last a lifetime, and How to use the influence you already have for Christ.

NOW: IMPACTING YOUR WORLD FOR CHRIST (RIGHT NOW!)

You have the amazing potential to impact your world for Christ, not just some time in the future ... but right NOW! Today. Your world is rich with opportunities to share the hopeful message of the Gospel, and to show people the amazing difference Christ can make in their lives. Now will help you make the most of these opportunities!

TO VIEW SAMPLES OF *NEW, NEXT & NOW* AND TO ORDER, GO TO YM360.COM/DEVOBUNDLE